Useful Introductio
Information on 18
19 books Chapters 15 — 17

Chapters 12, 13 and 17
useful summary of the
techniques of bibliographical
description

BIBLIOGRAPHICAL METHOD

BIBLIOGRAPHICAL METHOD

AN INTRODUCTORY SURVEY

BY

E. W. PADWICK

JAMES CLARKE & CO. LTD.
Cambridge & London

First published 1969

© E. W. PADWICK

Published by James Clarke & Co. Ltd.,
7, All Saints Passage, Cambridge, England,
& distributed by Book Centre Ltd.,
110, North Circular Road, Neasden,
London, N.W.10

PRINTED IN GREAT BRITAIN BY HEADLEY BROTHERS LTD
109 KINGSWAY LONDON WC2 AND ASHFORD KENT

To my Wife and Family
who suffered as
a consequence

PREFACE

This book attempts to survey the methods used in analytical and descriptive bibliography and is intended primarily for students of librarianship. It makes no claims to originality for it is essentially the kind of book that depends on the work of others. For years the two aspects of bibliography under discussion have been dominated respectively by R. B. McKerrow's *An Introduction to Bibliography for Literary Students* and Professor Fredson Bowers' *Principles of Bibliographical Description*. My own debt to them is obvious. Recently, however, advances have been made in analytical techniques, particularly with regard to modern publications, and the more significant are recorded here. I have also sought to digest for students the principles of description formulated by Greg and Bowers.

The sources of my information are given by means of footnotes and I hope that I have not been unjust through any omissions. I am particularly grateful to the Guildhall Librarian for permission to reproduce the title-page to be found on page 161; to the Trustees of the British Museum and the Council of the British National Bibliography for the descriptive entries on pages 16 and 15 respectively; to Constable and Co. Ltd., for the extract on page 239 from Michael Sadleir's *Trollope: a bibliography*; and to Kaye and Ward Ltd., for the extract from *A Bibliography of the Works of Robert Graves* by F. H. Higginson published by Nicholas Vane (Publishers) Ltd., which appears on page 241.

Mr. John Bromley, Deputy Librarian of Guildhall Library, Mr. James Mosley, Librarian of St. Bride Printing Library and Mr. Gilbert Turner, Borough Librarian of Richmond, kindly read the manuscript and gave much helpful advice. I owe my thanks to them: any errors that remain are, of course, my own responsibility.

Contents

Part I

Introduction

Part II

Fifteenth Century Books

PART III

Sixteenth to Eighteenth Centuries

PART IV

Nineteenth and Twentieth Centuries

Evidence (You all know) is the life of Truth, and Method the life of Discourse: the former being requisite to convince the Understanding; the latter, to facilitate the searches of it.

Walter Charleton,
The Mysterie of Vintners, 1669.

Part I

INTRODUCTION

CHAPTER I

An Historical Survey

The beginnings of bibliographical study may be seen in the compilation of catalogues of the books contained in the great collections of classical times. At the famous library of Alexandria, which housed the most extensive collection of Greek literature in the ancient world, at least two catalogues were prepared by order of Ptolemy Philadelphus, one listing tragedies, the other comedies. The Greek poet Callimachus was librarian there for a time and his *Pinakes* formed a critical catalogue of the more important books which he arranged in 120 classes. On a much smaller scale another famous Greek, Galen, physician of the 2nd century A.D., compiled a list of his own books entitled *De libris propriis liber*. That he found it necessary to produce such a catalogue is not surprising for he was a very prolific author, reputed to have written 130 books on medicine alone as well as a further 125 on philosophy, law, mathematics and grammar. Galen grouped his books in 17 sections under such headings as commentaries, moral philosophy, grammar, etc.

This need, felt even in early times, to record the books contained in any large collection is further illustrated by the catalogues that are known to us of various mediaeval libraries. There were, also, isolated examples during this period which recorded the existence of books on a much wider scale. The Bodleian Library contains the *Registrum librorum Angliciae*, a catalogue of manuscripts in no less than 186 English monasteries, which was compiled by Franciscan monks in the xiv century. Almost contemporary with this joint production was the single-handed attempt of John Boston, a Benedictine monk of Bury, who, about the year 1400, catalogued the collections of 193 religious houses in England and Scotland. In this work he listed under their names the writings of about 700 authors and also entered their names under

I

the various books of the Bible about which they had written. The actual locations of the books are shown by numbers used to identify the holding libraries—a method not despised over 500 years later.

The examples mentioned above were catalogues rather than bibliographies. The books contained in a bibliography are not necessarily restricted to a single collection, library, or group of libraries. A bibliographer may confine himself to one subject, a particular period of book production, the works of an individual author, and so on, but the material he lists and describes may well be dispersed throughout libraries in many countries. The first true bibliographies were those produced by Johann Tritheim, abbot of Sponheim, towards the end of the xv century. He compiled an extensive bibliography of ecclesiastical writers, the *Liber de scriptoribus ecclesiasticis*, published 1494 in Basle by Johann Amerbach. This work enters about 7,000 books under their authors arranged in chronological order from Alexander, bishop of Cappodocia, onwards. A year later his second bibliography, *Catalogus illustrium virorum Germaniae*, was published in Mainz, recording the writings of the most eminent German authors. Over 2,000 works are listed by more than 300 authors also arranged chronologically. Both books were equipped with an alphabetical index of authors and were, as Besterman has pointed out, practical works of reference.[1]

After the invention of printing in the middle of the xv century the need to record literary output obviously increased, but for many years no major attempt was made. Eventually in 1545, Conrad Gesner, the Swiss-German writer and naturalist, published his *Bibliotheca universalis* containing in 1,264 folio pages some 12,000 books written or printed in Latin, Greek and Hebrew. The entries, which are arranged in alphabetical order of authors (complete with biographical details), include title, date and place of publication and name of publisher. Frequently an indication of a book's contents is given or else quoted extracts are supplied. For his sources of information Gesner ranged far and wide visiting libraries in Venice, Florence, Rome and Bologna, acquiring printers' and booksellers' catalogues from Germany, Italy and France and making use of previously published works such as

[1] T. Besterman. The Beginnings of systematic bibliography. O.U.P., (1935), p. 9.

Tritheim.[2] In 1548 appeared the second part of his bibliography—the *Pandectae* in 1,748 folio pages—which groups the titles listed in the *Bibliotheca universalis* under twenty-one subject headings. In fact the twentieth section, on medicine, never appeared in print and the list on Christian theology, which occupied over 350 folio pages, was published as a separate volume in 1549. Gesner continued to collect new material which was published as an *Appendix* to his main work in 1555. This added a further 3,000 books making a total compilation of some 15,000 titles by about 3,000 authors.

This was by far the greatest bibliography of the time and yet, notwithstanding his self-imposed limitation to record only those books in the classical languages, Gesner by no means exhausted the field. His 15,000 books probably only represent a quarter of the whole without taking into account books written in the vernacular languages. Nevertheless, considering the few means at his disposal for discovering the existence of books compared with the wealth of documentary sources available to the modern bibliographer, his work is truly remarkable. Although its title is a misnomer, Gesner is regarded as the first universal bibliographer and yet he was probably the last who had any chance of achieving universality.[3] By his day the tremendous increase in book production following the invention of printing had become almost too great for any one person to record. It is not surprising, therefore, that after Gesner bibliographies were confined to the more manageable fields of books published in separate countries, in individual languages, on specific subjects, etc.

An early example of this limitation was Andrew Maunsell's *Catalogue of English books* published in 1595, which introduced new methods of compilation. The entries were arranged under authors' surnames, whereas the general practice from mediaeval times had been to list authors by their Christian names. But what is perhaps of greater significance, by giving the names of the author together with a reasonably full title, the name of the translator where applicable, the printer or bookseller, date of publication and format, the descriptions were

[2] H. Fischer. "Conrad Gesner (1516–65) as bibliographer and encyclopedist". The Library. 5th series. Vol. xxi, (1966), p. 272.

[3] Besterman. *Ibid*, p. 19.

sufficiently detailed to make each book easily identifiable. The result was a two volume work of some 2,800 entries covering theology and the "Sciences Mathematicall." A third volume was also planned to include literature, logic, law and history, but it was never published owing to Maunsell's death in 1595.

From the xvii century bibliographies became more numerous and gradually won acceptance as recognised research tools. In England national coverage was the aim and a long line of bibliographies listing contemporary publications stretches from William London's *A Catalogue of the most vendible books in England* (1657), down to the *British National Bibliography* of the present day. But it was on the continent, particularly in France, that the first important development in bibliography appeared. To satisfy the requirements of an increasing number of book-collectors amongst the nobility of Europe, bibliographers provided their readers with book descriptions much more detailed than hitherto, distinguishing carefully between the various editions of a work. At the same time they catered for the growing interest in the works of the older, more important, authors; the products of the early years of printing especially receiving most careful attention.

One of the first bibliographers to list early printed books was Michel Maittaire who between 1719 and 1741 published at the Hague *Annales typographici*, a work in five volumes which included books published from the invention of printing to the year 1664. Maittaire was the first to arrange presses in chronological order of their appearance grouping them in decades or half-decades with a brief notice of the printers who had begun work in each period. Short titles were provided in the modern style and books of the same kind, e.g. Bibles, Works of the Church Fathers, etc., were collected together. Maittaire attempted to cover the whole field of European printing and the second edition of his first volume, dealing with incunabula and published in 1733, contained nearly 5,600 works. More than 4,000 of these were described by Maittaire himself or by trustworthy authorities[4] and he added two useful indexes of towns and printers. When judged by this work Dr.

[4] Konrad Haebler. The study of incunabula. N.Y., Grolier Club, (1933); repr. (1967), p. 9.

Johnson's opinion that Maittaire was "puzzle-headed" is hard to understand.

His method and even the title of his bibliography was subsequently borrowed by Georg Wolfgang Panzer for his *Annales typographici...ad annum* 1536 published in eleven volumes, 1793–1803 at Nuremburg. In the first part of this work are listed books printed to 1500, and in the second, those printed 1501–35. Panzer's book has been called the first important "modern" bibliography. His entries, which include detailed references to his sources, are fuller and more technical than Maittaire's and his annalistic arrangement shows a more scientific approach. Instead of trying to cover the whole of European printing year by year, he first divided his field into the main printing centres and listed the books produced annually at each under their respective printers whom he arranged in order of seniority. Moreover, when dealing with Strassburg printing he was able, by a careful examination of the types used, to assign certain books published without their printer's name to known printers of the city and grouped together others which he considered to be printed in the same types. This is an early example of how a detailed study of evidence afforded by printed books can add considerably to the knowledge of printing history.

The major object of both Maittaire and Panzer was to chart the course of early printing. In covering such a wide field the actual entries, even in Panzer, were still comparatively short. The xviii century brought more detailed descriptions and these are first seen in G. F. de Bure's *Bibliographie instructive: ou traité de la connaissance des livres rares et singuliers*, published 1763–8 in seven volumes. De Bure's bibliography was designed primarily to satisfy the requirements of the increasing number of wealthy bibliophiles, the books he listed being rare and unusual works likely to be prized as collectors' items. It was largely superseded in the early xix century by J. C. Brunet's *Manuel du libraire et de l'amateur de livres*, initially published in 1810, but frequently enlarged to culminate in a 5th edition in 6 volumes, 1860–65, with 3 supplementary volumes, 1870–80. Brunet arranged his entries by authors and added an index of subjects. For each work he provided a reasonably detailed description which included technical information on the pagination, the number of lines to the page, the signing of gatherings, etc., as well as notes on editions and sale prices.

However, the work that was to have the most lasting value was Ludwig Hain's *Repertorium bibliographicum*, published 2 volumes in 4, at Stuttgart, 1826–38. Hain listed in author order over 16,000 xv century books and, although the latter part of the alphabet is incomplete (he died before the work was finished), the *Repertorium* soon established itself as a standard work on the period. Its importance lies in the treatment given to each entry. In earlier bibliographies, incunabula, the majority of which were printed without title-pages, were supplied with titles based on their contents, but Hain recorded faithfully line by line and letter by letter the incipit and explicit of each book. In addition he supplied a technical description of sufficient accuracy which made it possible for the first time for books to be identified beyond question and checked for completeness. Of particular authority are the entries marked with an asterisk for these were compiled following a personal examination by Hain of copies under his charge in the Hof und Staatsbibliothek in Munich. The work is frequently consulted today and often provides the first source of reference for the identification of incunabula.

Between the publication of "Hain" and its modern counterpart, the unfinished *Gesamtkatalog der Wiegendrucke*, the study of incunabula was pursued by a more scientific application of Panzer's method. The origin of this development must be ascribed to Henry Bradshaw (1831–86), for many years Librarian of Cambridge University Library. The alphabetical listing by Hain, admirable as it is for identification purposes, was not designed to add much to what was already known of xv century printing. Bradshaw's method of grouping printed books by origin enabled comparisons to be made one with the other which, when fully developed later in the century by Robert Proctor, resulted in many previously unsigned books being attributed to their respective printers. Bradshaw explained his theory in a somewhat obscure publication: *Memorandum II: a classified index of the fifteenth century books in the collection of M. J. de Meyer, (1870)*:

The method of arranging these early books under their countries, towns and presses at which they were produced is the only one which can really advance our knowledge of the subject. This is comparatively easy with dated books, though there is no safeguard against the misleading nature of an erroneous date. But the study is of little use unless the bibliographer will be content to make such an accurate and methodical study of the types used and the habits of printing observable at different presses, as to enable him to observe and be guided by these characteristics in settling the date of a book which bears no date on the surface. We do not want the *opinion* or *dictum* of any bibliographer, however experienced: we desire that the types and habits of each printer should be made a special subject of study, and those points brought forward which show changes or advance from year to year or, where practicable, from month to month. When this is done, we have to say of any dateless or falsely dated book, that it contains such and such characteristics; and we therefore place it at such a point of time, the time we name being merely another expression for the characteristics we notice in the book. In fact, each press must be looked on as a *genus*, and each book as a *species*, and our business is to trace the more or less connection of the different members of the family according to the characteristics which they present to our observation.

Although Bradshaw's own bibliographical output was small consisting of a few thin pamphlets his theories were put to the test in the bibliographical work of two of his contemporaries, William Blades and J. W. Holtrop. Later they inspired Robert Proctor who in the 'nineties was engaged in cataloguing incunabula in the Bodleian Library. Proctor was also influenced by the publication in 1891 of Konrad Burger's *Index of printers contained in Hain*. Burger extracted all the printers mentioned in Hain and listed them in one alphabetical sequence. Under each printer his dated books were arranged in order of publication followed by the undated books in alphabetical order. For the first time it was possible to see at a glance the output of each press of the xv century. Many books, however, remained unassigned and it was due to the brilliant application of Bradshaw's "natural history method" that Proctor was able to make his great contribution to the study of early printing.

It has been said that Proctor found the history of early printing guesswork and left it a science.[5] Examining incunabula not only in the Bodleian Library but also in the British Museum, he grouped them in chronological order of publication under country, town and printer. By comparing the types used in signed and dated books against those in books without date, name of printer or even place of printing, he was able to assign the vast majority with such success that of the 3,000 or 4,000 unsigned books less than 200 could be allotted only to their

[5] V. Scholderer. "Early printed books". *In* The Bibliographical Society 1892–1942: Studies in retrospect, (1942), p. 34.

incunabula / book produced before 1501
manuscript

country of origin and less than 250 only to a town. Pollard has written of Proctor's skill at identifying types almost always on sight.[6] Naturally in handling such a mass of material he occasionally made mistakes but these are of trifling significance when set against his great achievement of bringing order to 10,000 examples of early printing. The result of his work was published in his *Index to the early printed books in the British Museum . . . with notes of those in the Bodleian. 2 vols. (1898–9)*, which has formed the basis of arrangement for the still incomplete British Museum *Catalogue of books printed in the fifteenth century.*

At the turn of the present century came the second great change in bibliographical study. This Greg has attributed in part to the detailed examination of incunabula which has been outlined above.[7] Although bibliography had been concerned with enumerating and describing books, in the latter years of the xix century this work had involved a very careful and detailed examination of the books themselves and particularly of the types used for their printing. Gradually the bibliographer was being forced to undertake a study of all the processes involved in the making of books and eventually he came to realize that the core of his work was, as Greg said, "to reconstruct for each particular book the history of its life". This, in turn, led to the belief that the bibliographer could, by such investigation, throw light on certain literary problems concerned with the transmission of texts from the author's manuscript to the finished printed book.

This change was also stimulated by the pride and interest shown in our national literature. Even the attempts of certain moralising editors of the Victorian era had not diminished the continuing demand for Shakespeare and other earlier writers. But there were many differences between the text of one edition and that of another. Editors of Shakespeare, for example, until well into the xix century studied the previous editions, listed the variations between one text and another, and chose the particular version which fitted their own conception of what Shakespeare had written. Thus Pope and Hanmer "threw to the bottom

---

[6] A. W. Pollard. *Introduction* to vol. I of British Museum Catalogue of books printed in the fifteenth century, (1908), p. xi.

[7] W. W. Greg. "Bibliography—a retrospect". *In* The Bibliographical Society 1892–1942: Studies in retrospect, (1942).

of the page" any passage which they could not accept and depended on their own judgement for their choice of text.

This practice, as McKerrow has shown,[8] was based on principles of textual criticism as applied to ancient classical works where each of many manuscripts of a particular text may represent the end of one line of descent. Each manuscript, therefore, no matter how inaccurate in general, may preserve some passages of the archetype not found in manuscripts of other lines of descent. Editors collected and listed all the variants in extant manuscripts and considered them on their intrinsic merits without attempting to discover their *relative* authority.

This practice eventually gave way in the latter part of the xix century to the "genealogical method" of textual criticism. The relationship of one manuscript to another was studied so that a family tree could be constructed to reveal their relative authority. By this means it was felt that a line of descent could be established which would lead ultimately to a reconstruction of the text of the original. An obvious extension for this method was into the field of printed books. It was known that during the period of hand-printing each new edition, unless revised, was normally copied from its immediate predecessor, so all that was necessary to establish the author's text was to work back to the first edition. In this field there was no question, as in the case of manuscript texts, of reconstructing an archetype, because the first printed editions, or the vast majority of them, were still available. This principle had, in fact, been understood by Samuel Johnson in the previous century. He was of the opinion that the second, third and fourth folio editions of Shakespeare's *Collected plays* only deviated from the First Folio because of their printers' negligence. He also warned of the dangers of accepting the texts of well-meaning but misguided editors:

> It has been my settled principle, that the reading of the ancient books is probably true, and therefore is not to be disturbed for the sake of elegance, perspicuity, or mere improvement of the sense. For though much credit is not due to the fidelity, nor any to the judgement of the first publishers, yet they who had the copy before their eyes were more likely to read it right, than we who read it only by imagination.[9]

[8] R. B. McKerrow. The Treatment of Shakespeare's text by his earlier editors. British Academy lecture, (1933), pp. 20–1.

[9] In the Preface to his edition of The Plays of William Shakespeare, (1765). 8 vols.

Eventually, however, it was realized that the actual transformation of the author's original manuscript into even the first printed version was fraught with possible dangers. Apart from their occasional negligence and carelessness, printers used methods which permitted the introduction of textual alterations at many stages of production. In addition, and this has been a comparatively recent study, the nature of the author's manuscript itself—its punctuation, the style of writing, the method of setting out speeches in play form—have an obvious bearing upon the problems of transmission. The interpretation of the author's manuscript was not the least problem facing the printer in setting up type for the first edition.

It was not until the beginning of this century that the assistance available from bibliographical study began to be appreciated by editors of English classics and then only by a very limited circle of scholars. The leaders of the movement were A. W. Pollard, W. W. Greg and R. B. McKerrow. Greg has recorded[10] that the real pioneer was A. W. Pollard whose monograph *Shakespeare Folios and Quartos*, (1909), was the first major publication to pursue a basic literary problem by means of a revolutionary bibliographical technique. His book created much opposition from the older generation of textual and literary critics who, not being versed in the new study, were unable to accept Pollard's findings.

The new method was based on a careful examination of the physical make-up of the book. By considering the book as a "material object" composed of paper, type, ink, printed decorations and illustrations, bibliographers sought to show how the evidence afforded by these materials and the printing methods practised in the period of hand printing could establish each particular copy of a book in its exact relationship to the whole life-history of the work in question. Factual evidence uncovered by an examination in detail of the book itself offered to both the textual and literary student a more sure and exact foundation on which to base their work than had hitherto been available. Bibliography could now offer objective assistance to literary studies which until then had been largely subjective, resting for the most part on the critic's or editor's own judgement in the acceptance or otherwise of disputed texts.

[10] *Op. cit.*

Recognition of the possibilities of this new aspect of bibliography came slowly and not without engendering considerable opposition. The watershed was reached following an investigation into the early quarto editions of nine individual plays of Shakespeare. This particular batch, which at one time had apparently been bound together, bore dates on their title-pages ranging from 1600 to 1619. Because of certain typographical similarities Pollard suspected that, although the imprints would lead one to believe that they had been separately published and bound together at some later date, the plays may have all been printed at the same time and issued together. The investigation was taken up by Greg who compared the watermarks found in the paper of the nine plays. He was able to show that as many as five of the watermarks found in *The Merchant of Venice* and *Midsummer Night's Dream* both dated 1600 were also present in the *Lear* dated 1608 and in the *Pericles* of 1619. It is inconceivable that unused batches of paper from an initial printing in 1600 would be passed from one publisher to another eventually to be used up in printing four more plays in 1619. Some of the plays had been accepted by scholars as first editions, or at least had been regarded as possible rivals to other editions bearing the same date, and so the bombshell thrown by Greg in 1908 suggesting that the dates were false and that the plays were all printed in 1619 caused considerable consternation in the field of literary studies.[11] Pollard returned to the attack a year later and by a skilful examination of the types used was convinced that Greg was correct in his assumption. The matter was finally resolved in 1910 by careful photographic measurements of the various title-pages made by William J. Neidig in an American laboratory. These proved beyond question that they had been printed from the same skeleton setting of the type and therefore most probably within a few weeks of each other.

So with its new approach based upon a scientific analysis of the make-up of printed books, bibliography was shown to be of immense

[11] Forty-two years later Dr. Allan H. Stevenson when re-examining the quartos now in the Huntington Library discovered two dated watermarks that had escaped the notice of Greg. Both are pot watermarks with dates woven in their designs. The wires forming the dates are broken but sufficient remains to determine that the one found in *Sir John Oldcastle* (1600) represents 1608, and the second in *Henry V* (1608) is either 1617 or 1619. *See* Stevenson's account in Studies in Bibliography. Vol. IV, (1951–2), pp. 159–64.

value to those concerned with literary texts. For the first time concrete evidence for the dating and ordering of editions was now being made available. Indeed the reasons for many of the variations of text that existed in different copies of the same edition could now be explained by bibliographers, thus enabling the authors' original words to be verified. The rules for this new discipline were first formulated by R. B. McKerrow in *Notes on bibliographical evidence* (1913), which he later expanded into his *An Introduction to bibliography for literary students* (1927). This manual has remained the only general attempt to examine the use of printing materials and methods of Elizabethan times and to relate them both to the transmission of text from the author's manuscript to the printed copy and to the subsequent changes appearing in later editions. It immediately became the essential textbook for any student of bibliography and a seminal work for all literary editors and textual critics working on Elizabethan and later texts. It is of less value for the analysis of incunabula and a "McKerrow" dealing with xv century printed material is earnestly desired. Moreover, much has been added to our understanding of hand-printing methods since 1927 yet it is a tribute to McKerrow's scholarship that his work has retained its authority for all the fundamental bibliographical techniques.

Further development of the "new bibliography" has been restricted almost entirely to scholars working in Britain and America. There is no doubt that this is largely due to the joint heritage of the riches of English literature but the removal in large numbers of early printed English texts to American libraries and private collections is also responsible. Analytical or critical bibliography is practically unknown on the Continent where books have been examined for the evidence they offer to the study of printing history and not to the same degree for their textual significance. In Britain and America the range of publications now being studied has widened from the earlier concentration on the xv to xvii centuries to include the xviii century with some brave excursions into xix and xx century material. Bibliographical scholarship continues to grow in stature and contemporary leading exponents such as Professor Fredson Bowers wish to see it accepted as an independent discipline no longer to be regarded solely as a handmaid of literature.

CHAPTER 2

Aspects of Bibliography

We are now in a position to consider in more detail the two major aspects of bibliography:

(1) enumerative or systematic

(2) analytical or critical

and to note their relationship with "descriptive" and "historical" bibliography.

The terms "enumerative" and "systematic" refer both to the technique used by the bibliographer and to the published results of his study. Thus Gesner's *Bibliotheca universalis*, the outcome of a painstaking recording and enumeration of titles, is an "enumerative" bibliography. This, as we have seen, was the earliest form of bibliographical activity and it remains the starting point of all bibliographical study for unless a book is known to exist it cannot be analysed or described. The word suggests a straightforward listing in alphabetical or chronological order but in many cases entries are arranged systematically to serve a particular purpose, e.g. books are grouped by their subject matter to form a subject bibliography. The enumerative or systematic bibliography normally requires only brief entries sufficient enough for identification purposes and to enable the reader to assess the significance in their field of the books listed.

"Analytical" or "critical" bibliography refers to a different kind of technique and sometimes to the published results of such study, although, because of the more intensive descriptive treatment required, these are more frequently called "descriptive" bibliographies. A prime example is Sir Walter Greg's *A Bibliography of the English printed drama to the Restoration*, the outcome of a lifetime's close analysis of early plays considered as products of the printing press. All bibliographies describe books to a greater or lesser degree but a true descriptive bibliography demands an exacting technique which, by means of commonly accepted formulae, enables a book to be fully yet economically described in a way that is intelligible to all who have acquired a basic knowledge of this aspect of bibliography. It endeavours to provide as full a picture as possible of each book examined based on an analysis of its manufacture, and consequently it would be quite wrong to bestow the term "descriptive" on a purely enumerative bibliography.

The ability to analyse a book successfully demands a detailed knowledge of the book production methods in use at the time of its publication. This study is termed "historical bibliography". Although sometimes considered as an independent discipline, its account here is strictly subordinated to its application in bibliographical analysis and its significance in this field was well explained by A. W. Pollard in a speech to the Bibliographical Society in October, 1913:[1]

> Between us and the author of any old book stand scribes or printers, publishers, and even binders, and until we have eliminated the errors due to these we cannot reach the true text in which the author has expressed his thought. Now and again we may eliminate these errors by study only of the book itself with which we are concerned, but more often than not it needs a general knowledge of the ways of the scribes or printers, or publishers or binders of the day to enable us to see what has been done wrongly, and the accumulation of knowledge as to these ways is an important branch of Bibliography.

Enumerative or systematic bibliography

The main purpose of enumerative or systematic bibliography is to record and list rather than to describe in any great detail. The amount of description tends to vary according to the scope of the work, but normally the author's name, the title, edition, publisher, date of publication, together with some details of the collation, e.g. pagination, illustrations, etc., are regarded as adequate. The use of a minimum entry, yet one sufficient for identification may be seen in Pollard and Redgrave's *Short-title catalogue of books printed in England, Scotland, and Ireland and of English books printed abroad, 1475–1640*, (1926), from which the following entry is taken:

Erasmus Desiderius

10455—A mery dialogue, declaringe the propertyes of shrowde shrewes, and honest wyues. *Tr.* in to Englysche. 8°. *A. Kytson*, 1557. L.

[1] Transactions of the Bibliographical Society. Vol. xiii, (1916), p.25

A rather more detailed description, conforming to standard cataloguing practice is typified by the entries in the *British National Bibliography* which records, with certain exceptions, all works currently published in this country. In addition to its role as a central cataloguing agency, its arrangement in Dewey classification order makes it an invaluable tool for library book selection. In fact many librarians place orders for books solely on the strength of the information provided by the descriptive entries:

BIBLIOGRAPHIES OF SUBJECTS

016.611—Anatomy
016.611 cq 25/27—*1525–1800*
RUSSELL, Kenneth Fitzpatrick
British anatomy, 1525–1800: a bibliography. Melbourne, Melbourne U.P.; London, Cambridge U.P., £15/15/–. 1963. *xvii, 254 p. front. 52 plates, bibliog. 26½ cm.*
Includes works by British authors published abroad and by Continental authors published in Britain.
In slip-case. Limited ed. of 750 numbered and signed copies.

(B64–2383)

The amount of information provided by a *B.N.B.* entry is normally adequate for most enumerative bibliographies, indeed in certain respects it may be considered too detailed. But one additional feature of particular value to any systematic arrangement would be the inclusion of annotations designed to evaluate the comparative importance of each entry within its subject field.

Some enumerative bibliographies or bibliographical catalogues, however, provide far more description of their material than is contained in a standard catalogue entry. For instance, the entries in the *Catalogue of Books printed in the XVth century now in the British Museum*, (1908-), offer a full and scholarly treatment as may be seen from the example given overleaf which is to be found listed under the works printed at Memmingen by Albrecht Kunne.

A description of this nature is not compiled without a painstakingly accurate study of the book itself combined with a knowledge of xv century printing methods and materials. Although the place of printing is given: "Impressus Memmingen", the book is unsigned and undated, but by identifying the types used, it has been possible for it to be assigned to its printer Albrecht Kunne. A detailed analysis of the

ES TU SCHOLARIS?   Undated.

1ᵃ. TITLE : ❡ Compendiosa materia pro juuenū informatione ‖ satis magistraliter composita Cuius titulus. ‖ ☞ Es tu scholaris. 14ᵃ. l. 24 : ❡ Scripsisti ne me etiam : Scripsi te : Nā Iohannes vidēs ‖ te cauillantem : vel in plateis currentem mihi ad scribendum ‖ tradidit. Ach mi custos ne corrigar me delebis. matrē me⸗‖am vt dat tibi magnum panem certe exorabo. ‖ ❡ Tace ergo te delebo. Laus deo carissime socie. Qui est be‖nedictus in secula seculoꝛ. Impressus Memmingen. 14ᵇ. ❡ Regule de modo ꝑstruendi ‖ pro pueris collecte. 15ᵇ. END : Finito libro sit laus ⁊ glʾia xp̄o.

Quarto. a bᵍ. 16 leaves, the last blank. 2ᵃ : 33 lines, 144 × 91 mm. Type : 87ᵃ, text ; 87ᵇ, glosses. Capital space, with guide-letter, on 2ᵃ. Hain *6680.

196 × 137 mm.

Bought in April, 1873.   IA. 11160.

evidence offered by the book is thus implicit in the description, but this analysis is of a different nature from that needed to provide a textual critic with the kind of information he requires to help him solve certain problems concerning the purity of the text. As we shall see in a later chapter, the bibliographical study of incunabula has been largely concerned with their identification and recording, and little attention has, as yet, been given to textual matters. Nevertheless, the compilation of any detailed description, for whatever purpose, involves to some extent the second aspect of bibliography—analytical or critical bibliography.

Analytical or critical bibliography

These terms are used to denote the technique of examining a book to discover three things:

1. What book it is, the name of its author and printer or publisher, the date and place of publication.

2. How the copy in hand stands in relation to all other copies of the same work. This, in turn, involves assigning the copy to a particular edition, perhaps to a particular issue of an edition, and discovering whether it differs in any way from other copies of the same edition or issue. The picture is not complete until the relationship of one edition to others of the same work is resolved and until the order of issues within each edition is satisfactorily established.

3. The completeness of the copy: whether all its leaves are present, intact, and in the correct order.

Analytical bibliography is thus concerned with minute classification by isolating and recording the characteristics which distinguish one particular copy from all others of the same work. The evidence for this comes from the volume itself both from the materials of which the book was made—the paper, type, initials, ornaments, illustrations—and the way these materials were used to construct the finished product—how the sheets of paper were folded and gathered together for sewing and how the type was composed and printed. The book is considered not as a work of literature but as a manufactured article, the product of a number of processes each of which, at least during the period of hand printing, could leave clues which might help to identify the book and offer explanations for the causes of variations between copies.

The isolating of unique features by bibliographical analysis is, however, only part of the process, for the characteristics of an edition or an issue can only be built up by finding common qualities in a number of similar copies. If the bibliographer's work is to be distinguished from that of the cataloguer, it is revealed in his concern not for a single copy but for all copies of a book.

As mentioned above, the publication of the results of analytical or critical bibliography incurs a further process: bibliographical description. There is often no distinct borderline between analysis and description since both are interdependent. As analysis proceeds so the bibliographer builds up his notes which form the basis of his description and in the formulation of his description new evidence is frequently suggested which must subsequently be verified by further analysis. In addition to providing a record of analysis, the aim of bibliographical description should be to establish a standard of reference against which all other copies of the book may be compared. Professor Fredson Bowers in the foreword to his *Principles of Bibliographical Description*, (1949), says that its methods

> seem to have evolved a triple purpose: (1) to furnish a detailed analytical record of the physical characteristics of a book which would simultaneously serve as a trustworthy source of identification and as a medium to bring an absent book before a reader's eyes; (2) to provide an analytical investigation and an ordered arrangement of these physical facts which would serve as the prerequisite for textual criticism of the book described; (3) to approach both literary and printing or publishing history through the investigation and recording of appropriate details in a related series of books.

Descriptions compiled with these aims in view are obviously more far-reaching than those exhibited in any catalogue or even in many so-called bibliographies. Even the example entry from the *British Museum's Catalogue of XVth century books* on page 16 does not fulfil the standards set by Bowers. It was, of course, compiled for a different purpose, that of enumeration, and so although it meets the requirements of the first aim stated above, and partly the third, no attempt is made to provide information of value to the textual critic. The entries do give information applicable to all copies of an edition in the collation paragraph, and this is something which is normally outside the scope of a cataloguer who as a rule only describes the particular copy in his library. But the bibliographer is not so easily satisfied: his concern is to discover the common characteristics of the whole edition of a work and to show where variations exist between copies. The common characteristics describe the "ideal copy" and thus establish the standard against which other copies of the same edition may be compared for completeness and variation. Ideal copy has been defined by Bowers[2] as "a book which is complete in all its leaves as it ultimately left the printer's shop in perfect condition and in the complete state that he considered to represent the final and most perfect state of the book".

The entries contained in a work which pretends to the name of a "descriptive" bibliography should, therefore, be as definitive as possible.

[2] *Principles of Bibliographical Description*, (1949), p. 113.

Each should set out to an accepted formula a full physical description of the book as exhibited by an ideal copy of an edition, distinguish between different issues and variant states, throw light on the reasons for these so as to be of value to the textual or literary critic and, finally, place the edition in its correct relationship with all other editions of the same work.

There is, however, a considerable difference of opinion amongst bibliographers on how much information needs to be provided by a descriptive entry in a bibliography. The more traditional view which accepts a varied treatment according to "the difference of the period treated or of the importance of the work to be described" originated in Falconer Madan's principle of "Degressive Bibliography." Having regard to these two factors Madan suggested the following categories of bibliographical description:

> Form (A) a *full description*, such as might be used for incunabula or products of a press which for special reasons has to be minutely described; (B) a *description*, adapted for books (for instance) of the seventeenth century, which require a certain amount of fulness and detail; (C) a *short description*, such as befits modern literature; (D) a *minimum description*, showing the briefest form which can be fairly employed, for a mere list of works.[3]

At the time Madan was writing, bibliographical study was still centred on early printed books and the products of later centuries, particularly those of the machine age, were given scant attention. Since then, however, interest has moved forwards and now increasing attention is being paid to xix and xx century material as a proper subject for investigation for which Madan's formula for a short description (see page 197) is no longer acceptable. But there are many who believe his basic principle to be realistic and sound. Mr John Carter, writing in characteristic vein in his *ABC for book collectors*, vigorously supports it: "Newtonian in its simplicity, Einsteinian in its weight, it has yet to penetrate the consciousness of our more pachydermatous bibliographers."

It is in this country that the degressive principle has been sustained, not necessarily by according a briefer treatment to more recently published books but by selecting the kind of information to be included in the descriptive entry. This has no doubt been influenced

[3] Transactions of the Bibliographical Society, Vol. ix, (1906–8), pp. 53–65.

2

by the close relationship in Britain between bibliographical investigation and the purity of literary texts with the result that descriptive bibliographies produced here tend to be slanted towards the student of literature and are of less value to other possible users: those interested in printing and publishing history, students of bibliographical technique, etc.

But in America a development stimulated by the writings of Professor Bowers seeks to elevate bibliography to "pure scholarship", releasing it from a dependence on literature and establishing it as an independent study. Although Bowers has admitted that "the subject and purpose of the bibliography may have some effect on the choice of detail", he considers that bibliographical description should not be weighted in favour of any particular user. The bibliographer who aims primarily at the needs, say, of the textual critic, may well be forced to omit elements of description of importance to a student of printing, illustration methods, etc. Any limitation of use resulting from deliberate omission Bowers finds hard to accept for he believes that in its highest form a bibliography should seek to provide descriptive entries that may be regarded as definitive. He sees bibliography as an end in itself and not just a means to an end.[4]

The nature of hand printing methods before the xix century resulted in many textual differences between one edition of a work and another, and even between copies of the same edition. As these differences largely disappeared following the introduction of machine printing with its greater uniformity, it may seem reasonable to describe the books of the last two centuries in less detail than those of earlier times. But new factors, such as the many variant bindings found on xix century books, need to be described when investigating modern books although they have no place in earlier studies. Thus although the nature of description is subject to variation, the overall amount required for a full entry is not greatly affected by the mass production of books of modern times.

Those who see bibliography as a means to serve the more important field of literature consider that Bower's aim to elevate it to an

---

[4] *See* Fredson Bowers. "Purposes of descriptive bibliography, with some remarks on methods". The Library. 5th series. Vol. viii, no. 1., March 1953.

independent study is to exaggerate its importance. They point out that there are many worthwhile tasks that need to be undertaken in bibliography which do not necessarily call for the very high standards of description propounded by Bowers. The trend, however, would seem to be moving towards the more detached, scientific, approach of the independent professional bibliographer, and perhaps the days are numbered for the amateur who felt a need to turn to bibliography to further his love and understanding of literature. His end, however, is likely to be far off. Analytical and descriptive bibliography is a new science and many books remain to be studied and described for an increasing number of purposes and at many levels of investigation.

Edition—impression—issue—state

Whatever feelings the analytical bibliographer may have regarding the amount of detail required in his descriptions, he cannot fail to be concerned with the classification of his material into edition, issue and state. These terms vary little in their meaning whether applied to hand printed or machine printed books, although the complexities of modern publishing require some modifications. "Edition" has to be defined more specifically and the term "impression" assumes a bibliographical significance and must be accounted for separately. These developments are discussed in the last part of this book but since edition, issue and state are common to all forms of descriptive bibliography, it is important that their general application should be understood at the outset.

An "edition" is the whole number of copies of a book printed from one setting of the type. It is the largest grouping used by a bibliographer and represents his first step in classifying the whole body of printed copies of an individual work. It thus includes all issues and states, as well as all impressions.

An "impression" is defined by Bowers as "all copies . . . of a book printed by any one run of the presses from one setting of the type or its equivalent. . . ". The "first" impression relates to the batch of copies first printed from a setting of type, but a "new", or second and subsequent impressions may be printed in one of many different ways. It may result from a reprinting from the original type which has been kept standing for the purpose; from a Monotype spool containing the original setting; from stereotype or electrotype plates of the original formes, the type from which has been distributed; or from a photographic copy of the original setting printed by the lithographic process. An edition may run into a number of impressions and its production extend over many years but until the text is substantially changed the printed copies from all these impressions make up the single edition.

In the days of hand printing the terms "impression" and "edition" were synonymous since the printer normally distributed his type immediately after printing and in order to print a subsequent batch of copies he was compelled to set up the type afresh, thus establishing a new edition.

An "issue" is part of an edition and refers to "the whole number of copies of a form of an edition put on sale at any time or times as a consciously planned printed unit" (Bowers). The "first" issue refers to those copies which formed the book's first appearance on sale to the public. A "new", "later", or "re-issue" is in most cases "some special form of the original issue put on the market at some later time in which for the most part the original printed sheets are substantially present but with a different title-leaf" (Bowers). In a few cases "re-issue" also refers to a group of copies in which the type-pages have undergone some re-imposition, and it will be found that the border-line between a new issue and a new edition is often confused, but for an examination of the finer points of these definitions, Bowers should be consulted.[5]

It should, however, be clear that a re-issue must be created at a later time and in a different form from the first issue. Each must form a "consciously planned printed unit" and one criterion for establishing that this was the intention of the publisher is that such a unit would be provided with its own title-leaf. A re-issue, therefore, must exhibit a new title-leaf from the one originally printed even though the only clue to its identification is a change of date or alteration to the imprint. A re-issue was, in fact, frequently caused when only part of the first edition was stitched-up and put on sale, the printer or publisher being unsure of the likely demand. The remaining copies would be left in sheet form in his warehouse until, perhaps after two or three years,

5 Principles of bibliographical description. Chapters 2 and 11.

their issue was necessitated by a continuing public interest when an astute printer might well up-date the title-leaves of these copies to give them the appearance of newly printed books. Alterations other than those to the date or imprint are, of course, found in re-issues. They may involve changes to the preliminaries or to the subsidiaries but not to the printed sheets of the main text which should remain substantially unaltered. Copies exhibiting minor changes from the printed state of the first issue which have not warranted the production of a new title-leaf are not regarded as belonging to a re-issue but are considered an attempt on the part of the printer to produce a more desirable state of the original issue.

It should be apparent that alterations constituting a re-issue must take place after the first printing of the book. Alterations made during printing result in "variant states" which may be present in either issue or edition copies. "State" is really synonymous with "variant" and according to Bowers "can be applied to any part of a book exhibiting variation in type-setting, including the addition or deletion of material in some copies, caused by alterations executed in the course of the original printing before public sale". But as we have just seen, this definition may be extended to include alterations made after the first issue, provided they have not appeared under a new title-leaf.

McKerrow distinguishes between "accidental" and "intentional" variants.[6] Accidental variants were produced in the hand-printed book mostly by the method of inking. The action of dabbing the type with ink-balls was apt, if the forme had been insecurely locked, to pick up loose type, and a number of sheets may have been printed before this mishap was noticed. Even then a printer would not always replace the missing type with the right sorts, and so the printed text would present variations between one copy and another. Accidents of a similar nature resulting from an upset forme could also cause variants, but these are all of minor importance compared with alterations made intentionally during the course of printing.

The slow process of operating a hand press gave ample opportunity for errors to be corrected by the printer or author, or for the latter to

[6] R. B. McKerrow. An Introduction to bibliography for literary students (1928), Ch. 6.

23

make last minute changes to the text. If printing had already commenced, the sheets already machined were left in their original state and only those to be printed at the time of correction would be altered. The possible importance of such variants to the textual critic or literary students is obvious, and one aim of descriptive bibliography is to record the existence of variant texts found in different copies of the same edition or the same issue of a work.

PART II

FIFTEENTH CENTURY BOOKS

CHAPTER 3

Bibliographical Study

As was shown in the previous chapter the bibliographical study of xv century books has been concerned with their identification and classification by country, town and press of origin. Analysis has been directed towards establishing a true account of the development of early printing with incunabula treated as specimens of printing and the art of the book rather than as important literary texts. Little attempt has been made to examine early printed books for the accuracy with which the author's copy was transmitted into print or for the continued purity of text through subsequent editions. The reasons for this stem partly from the nature of the texts themselves and partly from the evidence, or rather lack of evidence, afforded by these books.

The vast majority of incunabula were written in Latin, seldom in the vernacular. Pure literature formed only a small part of the published output, the emphasis being on theological and scientific subjects. The literary works that were produced were mostly *editiones principes* of classical authors whose writings had existed in manuscript form for many years. Few contemporary works of permanent literary value were offered to readers in the new form of the printed book. The interest and pride shown in national literature, which has been the spur to much bibliographical study of later works has not, therefore, been generated by xv century printed material and, consequently, bibliography has seldom been called upon to support literary studies of this period.

The early printers based the design of their books on the only model they knew—the manuscript book. As a result, the first books were printed without title-pages, and this, coupled with the reluctance of many printers to sign or date their books, has concentrated bibliographical study on the problems of identification. This work is now almost complete, and with the recent discoveries of Dr. Allan Stevenson concerning the more accurate dating of book papers, the orderly arrangement of yet undated and unassigned incunabula may soon be speedily effected. This task of identification has been so difficult and prolonged that little attempt has been made to differentiate extant incunabula beyond grouping by edition. The more subtle analysis of determining issues and variants is yet to be tackled. In any event, the very nature of many incunabula will present difficulties if detailed analyses of texts are to be made. Frequently they are a mixture of print and calligraphy. Paragraph divisions and initial letters were often left by the printer to be added by the rubricator who could never achieve the consistency of printed copies and would, indeed, vary his work to meet the special requirements of the book's purchaser. In these instances to establish an "ideal copy", the basis of all true bibliographical description, would be well nigh impossible.[1] Nevertheless, with the near completion of the initial task of identification, it is to be expected that future bibliographical study will turn to textual problems, perhaps at first in certain subject fields. However, much more needs to be known of the working methods employed by the earliest printers before the results of textual analysis can be revealed and explained.

It should not be assumed that because bibliographies of incunabula do not record such details as issues and variant states their descriptions have not involved much analytical investigation. Nothing would be further from the truth. But instead of an examination of the text to explore its progress from manuscript to print, emphasis has been given to such pieces of evidence that aid identification and provide a fuller appreciation of early printing history. Detailed typographical notes are included in most descriptions for the evidence afforded by early type and the way it was set on the page often provides the best means of assigning a book to its printer. Much of this study has been carried out in the great national libraries, holders of the largest collections of xv century books. Partly because each library is mainly concerned with its own collection, and partly because of the extreme rarity of many

[1] Bowers. *op. cit.*, p. 324.

incunabula, bibliographical descriptions of these works are based more often than not on the examination of works in a single collection and not on the characteristics of an ideal copy. For these reasons Professor Bowers prefers to call the results of such work "bibliographical catalogues" rather than descriptive bibliographies.

CHAPTER 4

Characteristics of Fifteenth Century Books

The invention of printing in *c.* A.D. 1450 did not revolutionize the design of the book. The printed book, at least for the first fifty years or so, was the manuscript book mechanically produced. This was the only book known to readers and the printer would have been taking an unnecessary commercial risk by manufacturing and marketing a completely new looking counterpart. The physical make-up of the manuscript book, therefore, determined the production methods adopted by the early printers and many of their publications now prove, at first sight, difficult to distinguish from their manuscript contemporaries.

Format

The codex form of the book, constructed from a series of folded sheets, had been in existence from the iii or iv century A.D. Some old codices made of papyrus exist in which all the sheets have been placed one on the other and brought together by a single fold. This produced an awkward looking book with a very ungainly fore-edge which, when trimmed, resulted in the inside leaves being narrower than the outside ones. Papyrus, however, was neither tall enough, nor sufficiently flexible, to permit a second fold to be made, but with the increasing use of parchment or vellum as the main writing material different formats were obtained by folding the sheets more than once. Even so, vellum, being a hard permanent material, tends to resist folding and the common formats of the manuscript book were either folio (folded once) or quarto (folded twice). Each folded sheet, or quire, was sewn through the fold and joined with its fellows to make a loosely-constructed book, eventually to be made more solid and compact by the practice, introduced from about the x century, of sewing the quires to leather thongs or cords. In order to reduce the amount of sewing more than one sheet was often used to form each quire. The common form of the manuscript book was a folio in 8's with each quire consisting of 4 sheets each folded once to give 8 leaves. The same result could be obtained in a different way. The scribe could take two large sheets of vellum, place one on top of the other and then fold them together, first parallel to the longer side and then parallel to the shorter side. When the leaves were cut the result would be the same, a quire of 8 leaves.

In writing a manuscript book a scribe using the single-fold method would write straight through the quire from the first to last page. He could do the same with his multi-folded sheets if he postponed writing until after the folds had been cut, but if he wrote on the sheets in uncut form he had to arrange the position and sequence of his pages on the sheets so that when these were folded and cut, the pages would be in their proper order. When the early printer produced books with formats smaller than folio he had of necessity to impose his type-pages in a similar way.

The actual make-up of printed quires or gatherings also followed manuscript tradition. Gatherings in folio books were usually constructed of a number of sheets of paper—five was popular in the very first years of printing, but this was subsequently reduced to four. Even quarto gatherings were usually formed by bringing two sheets together. But one difference may be noted: frequently, particularly in early books with lengthy texts, the printed gatherings show much greater irregularity in their make-up than was the case with manuscripts. This was caused by the practice of printing a book in parts simultaneously on a number of presses. Many xv century printers owned more than one press and to produce a large book quickly they would divide its printing amongst a number of pressmen. Unfortunately it was often difficult to estimate accurately the amount of paper each part would occupy and we find in these books gatherings with less or more than the usual number of leaves where the calculations had gone astray. Moreover, many early printed books exhibit gatherings made-up alternately of a different number of leaves, as for instance, 10, 8, 10, 8 . . . ; or a tripartite arrangement of, say, 8, 4, 4,

8, 4, 4. Husner's edition of the *Rationale* of Duranti (B.M. Catalogue of books printed in the xv century, I.B. 1048) contains a sequence of 24 gatherings made up of 10, 8, 6, 8 repeated six times. No satisfactory explanation has yet been advanced for this somewhat strange practice.

The vast majority of xv century books are either of folio or quarto format even though by now vellum had given way to paper and not until Aldus Manutius introduced his small octavo series of classics in 1501 was there a genuine attempt to reduce the size and weight of the printed book.

Register

With the sort of complicated arrangement of gatherings mentioned above it is not surprising that some form of checking device was necessary for the printer, binder or owner, to determine easily whether his book was complete or not and whether the sheets had been gathered in the correct order. This was provided by the 'register' which gave a list of signatures designating the sheets of which the book was composed. It is sometimes found at the end of the text or, alternatively, on a blank page or half-page at the front.

To begin with the first words of gatherings and sheets were listed rather than signatures. They were set down in columns and Haebler suggests that the subsequent change to listing by signature was dictated almost entirely by the amount of space the printer had at his disposal. If he had a page or greater part of it, then he would keep to the old form and tabulate the catchwords, but if he were more limited he merely listed the signatures with a statement of the size of each individual gathering.[1] Eventually the register was simplified to the extent that following a simple row of signature letters a general statement was added merely summarizing the number of leaves or sheets to be found in each gathering.

The register seems to have originated amongst Roman printers and its use was widespread in Italy, extending from there to France and Spain. But it was by no means universally adopted in the xv century, in

---

[1] Konrad Haebler. The study of incunabula, (1933 repr. 1967), p. 59.

fact it seldom appeared in English and German books. It is found sporadically and with decreasing frequency until the end of the xvi century.

Signatures

Manuscript books as early as the viii century contain signatures but the practice of marking the quires was not universally followed during the Middle Ages. Where it was used, the scribe, after completing the writing of each quire, would sign it with a letter or symbol as an indication to the binder of the correct order for binding. These signatures were usually added near the edge of the leaf and, consequently, in most manuscripts have been cut away during binding in trimming the edges. As we might expect some early printers followed this practice but since it was difficult to set up a single piece of type at some distance from the type-page, signatures were usually added by hand after printing. For this purpose a lower-case alphabet of 23 letters was used, omitting i or j, u or v and w, except that quite often double forms of r and s are found. If one alphabet proved insufficient for the book, a second was added usually in upper-case. The first to print signatures along with the text was Johann Koelhoff the Elder at Cologne in Nider's *Exposition Decalogi*, (1472). Other printers followed this lead and within a dozen years or so the practice had been fairly widely adopted. The way in which the gatherings were signed varied according to local practice but in the early years not only the first leaf was signed, but all the leaves in the first half of the gathering by adding the figures 2, 3, 4, etc. after the signature letter. Sometimes the signing included the first leaf after the sewing in the centre of the gathering, yet on the other hand, in smaller formats, e.g. octavo, it was quite common for the sheets alone to be signed so that we might find in an octavo only the first, or if the gathering was constructed of two sheets, the first and fifth leaves, have signatures. Because the binder followed the order indicated by the signatures in arranging the gatherings for sewing, the printer was usually careful to avoid mistakes in signing. It is for this reason that bibliographers use signatures rather than page numbering when referring to particular places in a book.

Catchwords

Catchwords although less common in printed books than signatures begin to appear from the early 1470s, at first in Italian publications. They also are a continuation of scribal practice for catchwords were used in manuscripts in the xi century and it was not uncommon in later books for the scribe to add at the end of a quire the first word to appear at the beginning of the next quire as a guide to the binder when collating the quires in their correct order.

When first inserted in printed books they occupied the same positions and must have had the same purpose. That they appear at the same time as the first printed signatures but are seldom found in the same book with them reinforces this view. Their extension to the first leaves of sheets forming a gathering also enabled them to be used as a check that the sheets had been assembled in the right sequence. Later, in the early years of the xvi century, they appear even more frequently, generally at the foot of every page, their purpose being to enable the reader, particularly when reading aloud, to pass without hesitation from one page to another. It is possible too, that the printer when imposing would find in them a quick means of positioning the type-pages correctly in the forme. Although modern readers have no use for catchwords, except perhaps at the foot of typewritten pages, their presence in former centuries was much appreciated for they continued to appear in printed books until the latter part of the xviii century.

Foliation

Although the numbering of leaves was fairly common in later manuscript books there was no immediate continuation of this practice in the printed book. Some early incunabula, it is true, contain leaves numbered by hand, but for printed foliation we have to wait for its appearance in Rolewinck's *Sermo ad festo presentacionis Beatissime Marie*, printed by Ter Hoernan in 1470. This was but a year or so before the introduction of printed signatures and as many books at first contained either one or the other but seldom both, it would appear that foliation was used for a time in place of signatures and vice-versa. It remained comparatively uncommon throughout the xv century and gradually gave way in the following century to page numbering. Yet it lingered on in legal, religious and other of the more conservatively produced books.

In addition to foliation we also find column numbering in books with pages set in two or more columns and sometimes this was used in place of numbering the leaves. Column numbering was by no means widespread, being far less common in German than in Italian books. Pagination was practically non-existent in incunabula and Haebler[2] is able to give only one example of its use—in Perottus, *Cornucopiae*, printed by Aldus Manutius at Venice in 1499. As intimated above, both foliation and pagination in early printed books were frequently done very carelessly and one can only assume that the printers of those days regarded these refinements as being of little real importance.

Title-page and colophon

The identification of modern books is an easy matter. In the vast majority of cases the title-page will provide all the information required, but following manuscript practice the first printed books were without title-pages. The earliest known example dates from 1470 in the book mentioned above printed by Ter Hoernan at Cologne. In a few lines of consecutive text it gives the name of the author, the title of the sermon and the date of printing. Before this time some printers had sought protection for the first page of text by printing it on the verso of the first leaf, leaving the recto to form an outside cover. From 1470 this became general practice and it is not until 1476 that we find another title-page, this time including the place of printing and the names of the printers responsible. It appeared in the *Calendarium* compiled by the German astronomer Johannes Regiomontanus and printed by Erhardt Ratdolt and his two partners at Venice. The more enterprising printers could see the value of printing a title-page as it supplied an advertisement to the contents of the book, but it is only from about 1510 onwards that it forms a regular feature of the average publication.

The xv century reader was introduced to the name of the work

---

[2] K. Haebler, *op. cit.*, p. 72.

usually by the "incipit", the first words of the text, or else by the "explicit" at the end of the book. This latter feature of the manuscript was in effect the author's or scribe's colophon. After completing his wearisome task of copying the text, he would generally end with a note praising God that he had finished the book on a particular day, sometimes including the title, and occasionally adding his own name, although this was by no means common. An early printer often gave similar information on the last page of text including the place of printing as well in his colophon. In trying to identify xv century books, one should, therefore, look for the colophon. It might be expected that printers would be quick to recognize the commercial value of adding their names to the colophon, but probably the majority of incunabula are not signed. Hirsch[3] quotes the results of a statistical survey carried out by E. von Kathen of the entries in volumes I-VII of the *Gesamtkatalog der Wiegendrucke* covering about 20% of all xv century books. This shows that of books printed before 1480, 57·4% were not signed, in the next decade, 53% and in the last decade of the century, 45·3%.

Gradually, as we have seen, the matter in the colophon was transferred to the title-page and having lost its purpose the colophon disappeared from use. But printing practices die hard and we still find a number of books printed in the early part of the xvi century containing both title-pages and colophons, and even later a colophon was occasionally included in a book of which the title-page had already been printed to show a change in publishing arrangements.

Type

The most obvious debt that the first printed books owed to their manuscript predecessors is apparent in the design of types. The style of handwriting prevalent in a particular district quite naturally became the model for the founts of type cast by local printers. Furthermore, just as different hands had been used for copying various kinds of books: the most formal hand, upright and angular, for Bibles and service books; a less formal hand for theological and legal works; and a slightly sloping cursive hand for less important works including those

3 R. Hirsch. Printing, selling and reading. Wiesbaden, Harrassowitz, (1967), p.25.

in the vernacular, so too printers rigidly held to these conventions. The first types were gothic, but before long they were joined by roman, an open, more legible type based on the hands of the humanist scholars of Italy who, copying earlier manuscripts of the ancient writers, followed the Carolingian miniscule hands of the pre-gothic era. Roman was used particularly as a vehicle for the dissemination of the new learning, and it would have been unthinkable for a humanist printer to have set an edition of Virgil in a gothic type.

Not only were early types designed from currently fashionable xv century book-hands, but the composition of each fount was based on scribal practice. To save time in the laborious task of copying texts and to economize in the use of parchment and paper, over the long years of the Middle Ages scribes had devised a very abbreviated, almost shorthand, way of writing. Vowels were omitted, prefixes dropped, case-endings abbreviated, and prepositions and conjunctions indicated by the substitution of special signs which were well understood by readers. These were all readily adopted by printers as normal setting practice and were, indeed, valued for the flexibility they gave in adjusting lines of type to an even length.

The printer's case was made even more complicated by the provision of ligatures. In cursive and even semi-formal book-hands the scribe frequently joined his letters when writing. Although considerable difficulty must have been experienced in their casting, these ligatures were considered essential by many printers and were copied in type-form. An extreme example is afforded by the first italic types cut by Francesco Griffi for Aldus Manutius which included 65 ligatures in the fount.

By the xvi century, however, both abbreviations and ligatures had disappeared from most founts of type in a general desire for greater legibility in printing. Hirsch has shown[4] that the development of the humanist script and subsequently the spread of roman types coincided with an increase in reading amongst the middle classes who required a more legible script than the highly cramped gothic book-hands. It was, in fact, the roman founts which were the first to be freed from abbreviations and ligatures, although the trend is also noticeable in the gothic types.

4 R. Hirsch, *op. cit.*, pp. 24–5.

From the evidence available at the present time it is believed that type-founding as an industry distinct from printing did not exist in the xv century. Early printers designed, cut and cast their own types or else employed skilled craftsmen to do it for them. Founts of type were at times sold to other printers and certainly worn types were disposed of in this way or left to successors, but the general rule of "one type, one printer," has provided the bibliographer with an excellent means of attributing unsigned books to their printers. The time and labour involved in the manufacture of type made this item of a printer's equipment the most expensive. Impecunious printers were invariably short of type and even important ones during the early years managed with a comparatively small amount. Caxton, who was reasonably well-off had, in all, only eight founts, and his successor Wynkyn de Worde continued to use some of them after Caxton's death. Less fortunate printers were pleased to obtain types that had been in use for a number of years and finally discarded. De Worde gave one of Caxton's founts to Hugo Goes of York who printed with it in 1509, and John Scoler of Oxford was another recipient of type from de Worde. Evidence from both the adoption of new founts and the deterioration of old ones forms a valuable aid to the dating of early undated books.

Lay-out

The lay-out of the page also followed manuscript practice. Almost all Bibles and liturgical books apart from the psalter were printed in double-column MS style even when the type was large enough to be set full measure. But the strength of this tradition is best seen by the way in which early printers arranged a commentary along with the text. The latter is set in the centre of the page, sometimes in two columns, in normal sized type and the commentary is made to form a frame around the text in a smaller type. Apart from the intricacies in actual setting, it must have proved very difficult to estimate the amount of space required by each setting especially as every page would have involved a separate calculation. Yet the practice had been mastered as early as 1460 by Fust and Schoeffer in the Clemens V, *Constitutiones*.[5]

5 Cited by Haebler. The Study of incunabula, p. 91.

38

The use of the footnote method relegating subsidiary matter to the bottom of the page was only gradually adopted during the first half of the xvi century.

Early printers also followed the closely-packed arrangement of words on the page that is a feature of the manuscript book. The scribe restricted the amount of spacing between words and lines to a minimum and introduced a new paragraph not by indenting on the next line but by the use of a paragraph mark "**⁋**" on the same line of text just completed. The first printed books exhibit the same crowded appearance but the desire for greater legibility gradually resulted in more liberal spacing and better paragraphing.

Rubrication and decoration

The pages of the manuscript book were frequently embellished with coloured initials and borders. In the more expensive books these were illuminated, i.e. painted in various colours with the addition of gold, or perhaps, silver. In the cheaper MSS the initials and headings along with paragraph marks, etc., were rubricated, i.e. painted or written in a single colour, generally red but occasionally blue.

In the early years of printing, apart from a few notable exceptions, the printer did not attempt to mechanise either method, and colour when added to the book was introduced by hand in the traditional manner. E. P. Goldschmidt has pointed out that this most probably was not done immediately after printing. It was contemporary practice to dispatch printed books in sheet form packed in barrels to various European book centres. The assembly of the sheets into completed copies, including the addition of all hand-painted initials, borders and rubrication marks was done on arrival with the result that "the place of imprint of the book gives no clue at all for the local origin of all subsequent ornamentation".[6] The exceptions mentioned above were the experiments that took place in printing the *42-line Bible* (*c*.1455), which was probably planned and partly executed by Gutenberg himself, and the Latin *Psalters* printed by Fust and Schoeffer in 1457 and 1459. The Psalters contain initials in red and blue which are now considered to have been printed from metal, not wooden, blocks.

[6] E. P. Goldschmidt. The Printed book of the Renaissance. C.U.P., (1950), p. 10.

Each initial was formed of two sections which were separately inked, reassembled and printed at the same time as the text. The result reflects the care and skill with which this elaborate procedure was executed, but because of the costs involved in time and labour these experiments were obviously impracticable for normal commercial publications and so were discontinued.

As a guide to the rubricator, the printer often inserted the appropriate lower-case letter, or "director", in the space left for the initial. Later, woodcut initials set up in the forme with the type and printed in black and white took the place of these rubrics. Similarly, there are examples of printed books in which the designs of border decorations were printed in outline from woodcut blocks. Both practices saved the illuminator or rubricator considerable time and labour as their subsequent colouring was a comparatively easy matter.[7] A few years later both the initial letter and the woodcut border were considered perfectly acceptable in their black and white state and by 1476, Erhardt Ratdolt had used some fine woodcut borders in his books printed at Venice.

There was much printing of the text in red and black particularly in liturgical books. Exactly how this was done has not been satisfactorily resolved but two possible alternatives suggest themselves. The first involved separate settings of the types to be printed in black and red and it would appear from the evidence of incomplete impressions that the red usually preceded the black. The major difficulty, of course, was to ensure that when the sheets were put through the press for the second colour correct register was obtained, and some unsuccessful attempts may be spotted by an overlapping of colours in the finished book. For the second method the type was set altogether in the chase in the normal fashion but the two printings were accomplished by masking off with pieces of stout paper the type not required in the colour being printed. Where the masks had slipped during presswork we find that adjacent types were inked in the wrong colour. Haebler believes this to be less common than the first method since it was only suited to books in which printing in red was kept to a

---

[7] A reproduction of a woodcut border designed for colouring accompanies an article by A. W. Pollard, "Woodcut designs for illumination in Venetian books, 1469–73" in Bibliographica, vol. III, (1897), pp. 122–8.

minimum.[8] Other methods of colour printing are mentioned by McKerrow[9] including hand-stamping words in red in spaces purposely left in an otherwise black page. By the end of the century, however, apart from the lavishly produced liturgical books of Germany, most printers had settled for a single colour. The emphasis and contrast formerly provided by red or blue was by this time obtained by the use of larger or bolder types selected from the greater variety of founts now possessed by the majority of printers.

Illustration

Although printers were able to make almost perfect facsimile copies of book-hands and thus preserve the appearance of an unillustrated book, they were unable for technical reasons to emulate the glories of the mediaeval illuminated manuscript. Some finely printed books, it is true, were embellished with miniatures, but these were added after printing had been completed. As E. P. Goldschmidt has stated[10] the earliest illustrated books copied a particular kind of MS: "the cheap, trade-produced paper manuscripts current in Flanders, Burgundy, Alsace and Western Germany. That was the merchandise the printers intended to supplant, and so, naturally, these were the models they set out to imitate." They were mainly popular works with crudely drawn, hastily coloured illustrations, the designs of which may, in some instances, have been printed from woodcuts. Certainly, when illustrations were introduced into the printed book, for the first twenty years or so they consisted of simple black on white outline designs from woodcuts and were intended to be coloured by hand. The pedestrian task of filling in the colour could be handed over to less experienced craftsmen who could not be entrusted with the skilled work of illuminating the precious pages of the more costly manuscript books. This may explain why so much colouring of xv century woodcut illustrations is crudely executed. The deliberate policy of many early printers to produce cheap books for a class of public who could not afford illuminated vellum manuscripts was also a contributory

[8] K. Haebler, *op. cit.*, p. 132.
[9] Introduction to bibliography, App. 6, pp. 329–36.
[10] E. P. Goldschmidt. *op. cit.*, p. 40.

factor. It was not long, however, before book illustration became more self-sufficient. From about 1470 the woodcut developed its own methods of shading, first with closely-drawn parallel lines and subsequently with cross-hatching to introduce modelling and tonal effects. As in the case of rubrication, the hand-colouring of illustrations became less essential and disappears from most books by the end of the century.

The woodcut lent itself to the illustration of printed books because, like type, the lines which print stand up in relief from a cut-away background. They were thus suited to printing alongside type, and the thickness of the blocks themselves—about $\frac{7}{8}$ in.—made them a convenient height for this purpose. At the first known attempt at printed book illustration, Albrecht Pfister printing at Bamberg the first edition (1461) of *Der Ackermann aus Böhmen* by Johannes von Saaz, left spaces for the subsequent insertion of five full-page woodcuts. In the second edition two years later, it is clear that the text and illustrations were printed together.

If treated with care woodblocks yield a considerable number of impressions. Because of their comparatively high cost, however, early printers tended to print from them after they had shown signs of deterioration. The designs became worn with broken and frayed lines occurring particularly in the surrounding framework, though such blocks would probably be repaired from time to time. Printers also economised by using the same block in many different contexts often in the same book. One of the most lavishly illustrated books of the xv century, the *Nuremberg Chronicle*, printed by Anton Koberger in 1493 contains 1,809 illustrations and decorations printed from only 645 blocks. 270 kings are depicted by only 44 different woodcuts, 2 blocks of a papal synod illustrate 22 quite separate assemblies, 22 views of cities represent 69 actual places, and so on. Blocks were also handed down or sold from one printer to another, and those with artistic merit frequently openly copied by other printers. Very exact copies could be made from transferring the design of the original block onto a new block for cutting, although many poorer copies are in reverse, being made from the simplest method of copying: impressing the original directly onto another block. It is possible that metal casts were occasionally made to reproduce copies, though they seem to have been more frequently adopted for duplicating woodcut decorations and ornaments which could be used much more often than the illustrative cut. As we shall see, the provenance and deterioration of woodcut illustrations can be of assistance to the bibliographer in dating the books in which they appear.

Binding

The typical xv century book, whether written or printed, was bound in wooden boards covered in a strong leather, generally of calf or pigskin. Decoration was added in the form of lines, tooled in blind, which divided the cover into a series of compartments. These were frequently ornamented with individual stamps from engraved metal dies. Many designs were used, some abstract, others of plant and animal forms. A few books towards the end of the century were tooled in gold, following the introduction of this method of decoration into Naples by Moorish craftsmen in the 1480s. Of more practical use to binders, who by now were endeavouring to keep pace with the increasing flow of printed books, was the panel stamp, which was introduced about the same time. By using a press to exert the pressure demanded by its size, the binder was able with one impression to decorate a binding with a large design covering the central portion of the cover.

As in the case of illumination and rubrication, bindings should not be attributed to the place of printing, nor to the date of publication, if known. Conversely, knowing where a particular book was bound seldom throws any light on where and when it was printed. Only in those cases where it has been established that a printer also maintained a bindery can such assumptions be made. The value to the bibliographer of a study of bindings will be considered in more detail in the next chapter.

The introduction into the printed book of the various features considered in this chapter, has often been of assistance in assigning dates to undated material although it should be realized that, because we find an innovation adopted by one printer or in common use in one centre of printing, it does not follow it was known to printers working in other localities. By the end of the xv century, through improvements in trading channels and the establishment of book agencies in many European centres, practice in the trade was becoming stabilised, but before this time printers were working in comparative isolation and made advances in technique independently of each other.

CHAPTER 5

Evidence from Materials

We can now turn to the evidence which xv century books present in the materials of which they were constructed and in the methods employed to fashion these materials into printed books. In following this course we shall have to omit any discussion on the importance of collateral evidence, for example, the contemporary records of many kinds which have been examined for information concerning printers and where they worked. Sometimes the date of a book can also be suggested by relating a passage in its text to some historical event. A neat piece of deduction of this nature may be followed in Paul R. Baumgartner's account[1] of his investigation of *Cocke Lorelles Bote*, an anonymous Tudor poem printed by Wynkyn de Worde. For the purpose of analysis, however, our concern is with the book solely as a material object and we shall concentrate on evidence which leads to the identification and dating of incunabula since these two problems have formed the major part of the bibliographical study of this period.

Paper

Up till the end of the xviii century paper was made by hand by pulping rag material, mostly of linen origin, into a fibrous suspension in water. This "stuff" was formed into sheets of paper by the action of the vatman in scooping up a sufficient quantity onto a mould. This was a wooden frame with a bottom of interwoven wires through which the water drained but which supported the wet paper sheet. The sheet was turned out onto a felt blanket, pressed to exclude surplus water and subsequently sized to prevent the absorption of ink. The wires of the

[1] "The Date of Cocke Lorelles Bote". Studies in Bibliography. Vol. xix, (1966), pp. 175–81.

45

mould were of two thicknesses: those running parallel to the long side of the frame were thin and closely spaced, whilst those running at right angles were thicker and from three-quarters to one inch apart. From as early as A.D. 1282 paper-makers fashioned designs out of fine wire and threaded them into the network of wires at the bottom of the mould. These designs form the watermarks in paper which, like the wire-marks, are visible when the paper is held up to the light. The origins of watermarks remain somewhat obscure and a number of theories have been postulated to explain their significance. However, it seems reasonable to suppose that certain designs were favoured by their makers and soon assumed the role of trade-marks. Sometimes paper-makers fashioned watermarks of their initials, occasionally adding dates, but more often than not their designs were less personal. In the early years simple shapes such as stars and crosses were popular, but in time the designs became more elaborate and artistic: in the xv century a bull's head was frequently used. Although at a later date some of the designs were attributed to particular sizes of paper, as for instance the "fools-cap", it is very doubtful whether they were originally fashioned for this purpose. In fact, we find the same designs in different sizes of paper and the number of designs has always far exceeded the various sizes.

A watermark appears usually, but not invariably, in the centre of one half of a sheet of paper, so when the sheet is folded once to make a folio, it is found in the centre of one of the leaves so formed. In a quarto book the watermark is cut in half by the fold and in an octavo it is found in quarters at the top of the inner margins of four of the leaves. It gets proportionately dismembered in smaller formats and becomes progressively more difficult to identify. In many cases it is trimmed away completely by the binder, or else remains perversely hidden near the fold in a tightly bound book.

Watermarks have been studied for the evidence they provide for the date and place of manufacture of the paper in which they are found. Bibliographers have been greatly assisted in this work by Charles Moise Briquet's remarkable book, *Les Filigranes*, published in 4 volumes in 1907. Briquet, in the preparation of his book, investigated the contents of 235 archives and libraries on the Continent choosing wherever possible those that were or at one time had been near a paper-mill. He confined his study of watermarks from the date of their first appearance in about 1280 to the end of the xvi century, examining mostly archival material rather than printed book papers. He traced over 44,000 watermarks, selecting 16,112 to appear in *Les Filigranes* where they are arranged in chronological order under their design or subject-matter. This tremendous pioneering achievement has been criticized for a number of reasons, but it became the basis for all subsequent research. When the second edition was published in Leipzig in 1923 the text was unaltered, a tribute in part to his scholarship, but also to the fact that no-one had improved on his labours.[2]

Unfortunately, for dating incunabula the work has its limitations. Very seldom does one find a watermark in Briquet that corresponds exactly with the one being examined, and there are so many marks similar in design that bibliographers have tended to be wary of attributing book-papers to a particular mill and of assigning definite dates to their manufacture. Identification is made more difficult by the very practice of paper-making which, to ensure continuous production, demanded the use of a pair of moulds (each with its wire-form) by the vatman. The two watermarks inevitably show some differences because of their method of construction and frequently these differences are greater than between moulds of different pairs. When Dr. K. Th. Weiss pointed this out to Briquet in 1915, he admitted that he had overlooked the possibility of distinguishing between mould pairs.[3] It is a matter of some importance in bibliography that twin watermarks should be paired off otherwise the slight divergencies in their designs might lead one to suppose, quite wrongly, that they belonged to different stocks of paper. Moreover, their appearance and reappearance in books provides much more irrefutable evidence for dating than does the identification of a single mark.[4]

Briquet, as a result of his researches on paper used for writing

[2] A new edition, rearranged with much additional material by Dr. Allan Stevenson, was published in 1968 by The Paper Publications Society, Amsterdam.

[3] Alfred Schulte. "C. M. Briquet's work and the task of his successors". Monumenta Chartae Papyraceae Historiam Illustrantia. Vol. 2: The Briquet Album, (1952), p. 55.

[4] Allan H. Stevenson. "Watermarks as twins". Studies in Bibliography. Vol. iv, (1951–2), pp. 57–91.

purposes, concluded that between the manufacture of the paper and its subsequent use, a period of between four and fifteen years could lapse depending on the popularity of its size. Exceptionally large papers were used infrequently and with these the time-lag might extend to as long as thirty years. Of more importance in dating is the need to ascertain how long each particular pair of moulds were in use. This would depend on how often they were required which, in turn, would be determined to some extent by the various types and sizes of paper made by the mill. If manufacture were restricted to one or two sizes only, the moulds would probably need to be replaced annually, but if many varieties were produced, the life of a single pair of moulds would be prolonged. Perhaps the greatest limitation of Briquet's work for the study of incunabula is that he examined few printing papers. As these were often of different sizes from writing papers they could not be made from the same moulds and thus would show different watermarks. Some mills towards the end of the xv century concentrated exclusively on printing papers and their omission from Briquet is a gap which has not yet been filled by subsequent research.

Even when the identity of the paper has been established and the date of its manufacture ascertained from Briquet, one is still left with doubts of the actual date of its use by a printer. Although stocks of paper would probably be used up quickly to avoid storage problems and the possibility of deterioration, it is seldom that we have any corroborative evidence of this. Often all that can be said with certainty is that the book under investigation could not have been printed before the manufacture of the paper! Pollard, writing in 1908 shortly after the publication of *Les Filigranes* pointed out that "evidence from paper is not free from uncertainty" and, in the first volume of the British Museum *Catalogue of books printed in the xv century*, that

> only here and there has the use of paper with not merely similar but identical watermarks been accepted as contributory evidence for grouping together two or more quartos so thin that the same batch of paper may reasonably be supposed to have sufficed for them all.[5]

On the other hand we have the famous case, mentioned on page 11, of watermarks providing evidence which led to the proper dating of a batch of falsely dated quarto editions of certain Shakespearian plays.

[5] p. xv of The Introduction.

Since Briquet subsequent studies have added much to the store of information on the history of papermaking and watermarks: Louis le Clert on the papers produced near Troyes; Nicolaïs' study of paper-mills in S.W. France; Heawood on English watermarks; Churchill on watermarks of xvii and xviii centuries mostly in Dutch papers; and the volumes of the Paper Publications Society edited by E. J. Labarre, are all major contributions. Their value to a bibliographer, however, suffers from the same limitations imposed by using Briquet—the necessity of making a comparison with a watermark reproduced from a mere tracing. But recently a new technique has been evolved which is likely to alter most previously held opinions on the accuracy of watermarks as evidence. Dr. Allan Stevenson has made use both of microfilm positives (which can be enlarged on a screen) and β-radiography for accurate comparison. The latter method uses radioactive isotopes which measure differences in paper thicknesses and reveal the thinner portions corresponding to the watermark design and chain-lines as black lines on a light background.[6] This technique not only accurately reproduces the exact form of the watermark but also reveals quite clearly the "sewing-dots"—little bulbous points in the wireform where fine copper wire was used to sew the form to the bottom of the mould. Each wireform would be sewn at a number of places and it would be extremely unlikely for the exact position and size of the dots ever to be duplicated in another watermark even from the same pair of moulds. It follows that marks found to be identical must have originated from the same mould, and by noting the position of the sewing dots it is possible to identify an individual watermark with a great deal of confidence.

By using this accurate method of identifying watermarks, Dr. Stevenson has evolved a new technique of dating based on the theory that "slight variations in old watermarks must be regarded as important, inasmuch as they often represent the variant states of identical marks and thus may have considerable value as bibliographical evidence". With a mould in continual use its wireform is bound to suffer damage.

---

[6] The information given here is derived from Dr. Allan Stevenson's own account "Paper as bibliographical evidence". The Library. 5th Series. Vol. xvii, (1962), pp. 197–212.

Wires become broken and even lost, their shape distorted and the whole form works loose and has to be resewn to the mould. Dr. Stevenson has managed to trace through the resulting watermarks the life-history of wireforms from their pristine state when new to a battered and distorted appearance in old-age. In studying these changing forms, continuity is provided by the sewing-dots which retain their relative positions even when the wireforms are dragged out of place. Some new dots may appear from time to time as a result of resewing but their appearance is explained by some previous mishap to the wireform. Dr. Stevenson has found it possible to recognize an identical mark in a very late state of distortion when only a few characteristic dots remain.

This new technique has made much more possible the accurate dating of book papers and Dr. Stevenson has applied it to a number of controversial datings of incunabula, including the *Missale speciale Constantiense* (the Constance Missal), and certain block-books. The Missal has been variously dated c. 1450 and c. 1454–7 mainly on the evidence of its type, but Dr. Stevenson by examining the watermarks and identifying them with paper used in dated books is of the opinion that it was printed in 1473.[7] Similarly, he places the first edition of the *Apocalypse*, the earliest of the block-books, in 1451 (earlier than the Mainz Indulgences and the earliest editions of the *Biblia Pauperum* and *Ars Moriendi* probably in 1465 and 1466 respectively).[8]

Much more research needs to be undertaken on the life-history of individual watermarks. In Italy Roberto Ridolfi has distinguished thirty-eight varieties of a single watermark found in Florentine incunabula and has, as a result, been able to suggest dates for certain undated editions.[9] But for any general application the quantity of marks to be studied combined with the painstaking nature of the research involved offer a heartbreaking prospect. Nevertheless, the

[7] Allan Stevenson. The Problem of the Missale Speciale. Bibliographical Society, (1968).

[8] Allan Stevenson. "The Quincentenniel of Netherlandish blockbooks". B. M. Quarterly. Vol. xxxi, (1967), pp. 83–7.

[9] Roberto Ridolfi. Le Filigrane dei paleotipi: saggio metodologico. Firenze, Tipografia Giuntina, (1957).

Centro per lo Studio dei Paleotipi in Florence has started the tremendous task of recording all watermarks that occur in printed papers before 1500. Whether this will be emulated by other interested organizations remains to be seen, but, at least for dating individual items of importance, the work of Dr. Stevenson has extended the bibliographical evidence that can be obtained from a study of watermarks.

Types

Early types afford evidence of greater value than that normally obtained from paper and it has been from a classification of typeforms that bibliographers have brought off their greatest successes in assigning books to their printers. As has been shown, the majority of xv century printers designed and cast their own types, or else had them made to their requirements. Particular founts can, therefore, be associated with individual printers and books which do not bear their printer's name may frequently be assigned by identifying their typefaces. This simple fact conceals the long and detailed study that was necessary to classify xv century types, a study made more complicated by the fact that a printer might well sell founts to others or pass down types to his successors. Because of this seeming crack in the "one type, one printer" theory, doubts have been expressed on the value of the work of Bradshaw, Proctor and Haebler in identifying and listing xv century types, but all subsequent research has only served to vindicate their method and to support the now well-established view that types can provide a most reliable guide to printer and date.[10]

The use of type as bibliographical evidence demands a great deal of comparison. Where a type used for an undated book can be identified with that found in a number of dated books, the book can be placed within, or close to, their first and last dates. The greater the proportion of dated to undated books by a particular printer will increase the probability of correct assignment and sometimes the inclusive dates are closely defined by clear evidence of a change to a

---

[10] Haebler points out that a second owner frequently did not use his acquired fount without renovating some of the sorts or recasting them on a different body. *See* The Study of incunabula, pp. 104–5.

3

different type. Some printers melted down an existing type in order to cast a new one. In these cases their publications form neat chronological groups and the placing of an undated work within its appropriate group is comparatively easy. There are more instances, however, of a well-used fount having some of its sorts replaced from time to time and thus its complete renewal is spread over a period of months or years. Much detailed examination is necessary to extract evidence of dating from these founts, but the results may in the end be more exact, for sometimes it is possible to trace where a new sort is used for the first time and to watch the gradual disappearance of its battered predecessor until its final discard.[11]

This kind of evidence was used by Proctor in his investigation of the xv century books in the British Museum and Bodleian Libraries. His *Index* was based on the identification, listing and comparison of types and provided the first clear picture of the development of xv century printing. Subsequent work at the British Museum, although correcting Proctor's mistakes, has largely verified his accuracy and the *Catalogue of books printed in the xv century* is arranged in "Proctor order". It provides excellent facsimiles of types which may be used for the purposes of comparison but the most comprehensive handbook for this purpose is Haebler's *Typenrepertorium der Wiegendrucke*.

"Haebler" is not an easy book to use. It is a highly detailed classification of xv century types based partly on characteristics of design and partly on size. Design is represented by facsimiles of 102 forms of the capital "M" for gothic types and "Qu" for roman, a distinction being made whether the latter is printed as two separate letters or as a logotype. Haebler selected these letters as key forms since they both underwent the most numerous changes in design. The size of each fount is provided by the measurement in millimetres of twenty lines of type set solid taken from the base of the first to that of the twenty-first line above. The work is divided into two sections: the first containing the types of Germany and countries directly influenced by early German printing, and the second those of Italy, the Netherlands,

[11] A. W. Pollard *in his introduction to* vol. I of the B.M. Catalogue of books printed in the xv century, p. xvi. For an example of the replacement of sorts in a type fount *see* Frank Isaac "Types used by Wynkyn de Worde 1501–34". Library, 4th ser., IX, (1928–9), p. 395.

France, Portugal and England. Under the respective countries towns are listed alphabetically, with printers arranged in chronological order. The types used by each printer are indicated by a series of symbols and numbers together with their 20-line measurements. Where the "M" or "Qu" forms may prove insufficient to identify a particular fount, some lower-case letters (especially the h-form) and such sorts as the hyphen, marks of rubrication, etc., have been mentioned. The two indexes, one of gothic, the other of roman types, are essential in using the book, and with practice and care it is possible with the aid of Haebler to identify the type used in a particular xv century book as well as to identify a fragment of printing of unknown origin.[12]

Relief blocks

Evidence from the relief blocks, whether of wood or metal, used by early printers to provide decorations or illustrations in books, is similar to that afforded by type. Although within certain limits blocks can provided information concerning printer and date, their usefulness varies considerably. Identification with a printer depends on the sole use of a block by that printer or, at least, a clear indication of its ownership by only a few. It follows, therefore, that the more insignificant the block or the poorer the quality of its execution, the greater its value to the bibliographer for it was less likely to be bought or copied by other printers. On the other hand, a block of some artistic significance was frequently copied and in the latter part of the xvi century well-designed metal blocks were cast in quantity from a matrix. They were thus made available to a number of printers and so are of little use as evidence for identification.

As in the case of types, where we find a block appearing in a number of dated books, the first and last dates provide limits within which an undated book containing the same block may be placed. A series of blocks was often cut to illustrate a particular book and to find their occasional and apparently haphazard appearance in other books would indicate a subsequent use. A more exact determination of date, however, is frequently provided by the gradual deterioration of a block, not from an apparent wearing-down of the design, which may have

[12] Margaret B. Stillwell. Incunabula and Americana, 1450–1800, (1930), p. 53.

been due to bad inking or a lack of care in making-ready, but from evidence inherent in the block itself. A woodblock in the course of time breaks or cracks or is attacked by woodworm which drill neat round holes appearing as small white circles in the finished print. Obviously a woodblock impression marred by a wormhole may safely be assumed to be of a later date than a similar impression without the hole. Cracks which appear as white lines when printed are not so trustworthy for they can vary in size according to the dryness of the block and how tightly they were locked up in the chase: there are examples of cracks which disappear in later impressions. More acceptable evidence is afforded by breaks in design especially when they are not checked over a long period so that progressive "states" of deterioration may be identified. One should be on the look-out for possible repairs, however, particularly in the framework surrounding the design as breaks here were more noticeable to the printer and subject to his frequent attention. With metal-cuts lines tend to bend out of position rather than to break off completely. The best example of accurate dating from a metal-cut showing progressive distortion is that provided by the printer's device first used in 1496 by Richard Pynson. From 1499 the lower edge begins to bend upwards until in 1513 it breaks away completely and, presumably, the block was then destroyed.

Blocks used for book decoration generally provide more useful evidence to the bibliographer than those cut for illustrations. They were not so restricted to a particular use and could, therefore, be successfully repeated in a great number of books. They often lasted for long periods, their life-histories being traceable from printer to printer, and from their state at any time the date of printing may often be deduced. Title-page borders, especially those framed with rules, were particularly susceptible to damage and often provide assistance in dating. On the other hand, woodcut initials which, because of their small size, do not show wear and tear very clearly, are not very helpful. Perhaps the best evidence of all comes from printers' devices for their very purpose links a book to its printer. They often passed through a succession of printers, but although their appearance at the time of transfer may not resolve the difficulty in assigning a particular book to its true printer, they were quickly altered to indicate change of ownership by the substitution of new initials or mottoes. The classic example is Wynkyn de Worde's continued use of Caxton's device as a basis for his own numerous designs. Printers sometimes adopted new devices themselves and even if attached to a particular design they might alter it in some way. If the date of change-over or alteration is known, books in which varying states of the device appear may often be dated with precision.

Illustration blocks do have one advantage over those used for decoration. They are mainly representational in character and their method of treating subjects or depicting costume which, even of biblical characters, often followed contemporary fashion, may suggest the place of origin and the date of cutting. Allowance must always be made, however, for the transfer of blocks between printers working far apart from each other. A. M. Hind considered that evidence of origin could also be ascertained by the way in which woodcut illustrations were subsequently coloured and in his *An Introduction to a history of woodcut*, (1935), gives a preliminary list of colours with notes on their use in particular centres.[13]

Bindings

The relatively small value of bookbindings in assigning a book to its printer or to its date of publication has already been touched upon. For many years bindings were not connected with publishing but were solely a means of subsequent preservation. In fact it is not until after 1825 that edition binding was introduced as a result of using cloth as a binding material. In the xv century books were issued in sheet form and dispatched all over Europe in an unbound condition. It was left to their buyers to decided whether and what kind of binding was required. E. P. Goldschmidt[14] has shown that whereas printers settled in the great trading cities, Venice, Augsberg, Nuremberg, Paris, etc., the centres of bookbinding were established in those places where books were most read and appreciated—the university towns. He gives as an example the university town of Erfurt which was very insignificant for its printing, but where there were at least twelve bookbinders who signed their bindings in full.

[13] pp. 167–9.
[14] Gothic and Renaissance bookbindings, (1928), pp. 44–5.

Bibliographers may, however, wish to identify a binding, and the method of decoration combined with the use of particular tool designs does form characteristic styles which are attributable to certain regional localities. But such identification is a matter for the expert, for the history of bookbinding, like that of typography, is really an independent study. All the bibliographer should attempt to give in his description, unless he has made a special study of the subject, is some account of the general appearance of the binding and of the designs of the tools used.

Apart from styles of decoration, old bindings have sometimes provided evidence of their origin from the materials that were used. Paper-linings have enabled a bindery to be associated with a particular press. We know, for example, that Richard Pynson must have had a bindery attached to his printing office because his earliest books had their covers lined with leaves printed by Machlinia whom he succeeded about 1488. Vellum particularly, was treasured by binders, no doubt because of its durable nature, and fragments were often used for a backing into which the sections were sewn. They too may provide evidence to suggest the origin of a binding.

A careful examination of old bindings has sometimes yielded fragments which prove to be the only surviving leaves of otherwise lost incunabula. Most of the Donatuses and other examples of the earliest Dutch printing have survived as linings to covers of other books, and a glance through E. Gordon Duff's *Fifteenth century English books*, (1917), will reveal other instances of a similar nature. For example, the two surviving leaves of the *Doctrinale* of Alexander Grammaticus printed in Oxford by Theodoric Rood and Thomas Hunte were found in the binding of a copy of *Godscalci Preceptorium*, printed by Anton Koberger at Nuremberg in 1505. Almanacks and *Prognostica* which were usually printed on one side of the leaf only were particular favourites of binders. Being published annually they were of no value when the year was over and unsold copies were often used as cover linings. In this state they survived the fate of their more successful fellows and now provide the only information we have of this type of publication in the xv century.[15]

[15] K. Haebler. The Study of incunabula, pp. 210–2.

Contemporary manuscript notes written on the inside covers or fly-leaves of books by their owners can be of special value because they may reveal a date after which the book could not have been printed. A well-known example is afforded by the notes inserted in the *42-line Bible* now preserved in the Bibliotheque Nationale, which state that Heinrich Cremer, vicar of St. Stephen's at Mainz, finished rubricating and binding it on 24th August, 1456. Similarly the controversy over the first book to be printed in Italy was decided by an owner's inscription in the undated edition of Cicero's *De oratore* showing that it preceded the *Lactantius* dated 1465.

CHAPTER 6

Evidence from Methods

The early years of printing were a time of experiment and improvement. Individual printers were learning by trial and error how best to operate their equipment. Improvements in technique would sometimes be made to enhance the appearance of their books, but more often they resulted from a search for a simpler and cheaper method of working. From this it is reasonable to assume that once a printer has made certain improvements he would not revert to his earlier methods. Evidence, therefore, of such advances provides a general guide to the dating of a printer's output.

Composition

The nature of printing from moveable type necessitates locking-up individual letters into a solid mass. Each line of type, therefore, either has to be fully justified or else spaced-out with non-printing material to an even length to provide the rigidity required. At first printers were content to follow the normal manuscript practice of leaving lines unjustified, merely filling in the gaps with spacing material. It was obviously more economical, however, to fill each line to the full with type, apart from the improved appearance that would result from having a clean right-hand edge, and progress towards justification was generally made within a few years of starting to print. Once the principle had been accepted that lines ought to end evenly, a printer would be unlikely to return to uneven endings, so we may assume that a book with justified lines is later than one by the same printer where the lines are uneven. This can only be regarded as a generalisation for, during the period when the practice was variable, justification would depend on the habits of the individual compositor and it is not always possible to assign a precise date to the adoption of regular line-endings by a particular office.

The work of a compositor is obviously affected by the nature of his copy, and in the very earliest period of printing it may well have influenced his line spacing. He would naturally prefer to work from a previously printed text for if he were setting type of a similar size, the layout and spacing were already done for him. Often rather than adjust the spacing when copying from a book with irregular line-endings, a compositor would slavishly follow the original. Because of this, McKerrow[1] has pointed out the danger of assuming that when a book is known to have been reprinted line for line from a printed copy, the version with the irregular line-endings is the earlier, and notes:

> that if in a book with irregular line-endings we find lines which would have admitted the first word of the following line, we can be practically certain that we have to do with a reprint.

When the compositor has had the benefit of a printed or a carefully written manuscript book as copy, problems of casting-off are also considerably reduced. The result is noticeable in the regular way in which the gatherings of a book are made-up. When, however, a compositor was working from a badly laid-out MS or from an author's complicated or hurriedly written copy, difficulties arose in calculating the number of pages the copy would occupy when set in type. This difficulty was made greater in the early years of printing by the fact that presswork was a much slower process than composition. Until the 1470s, pages were printed singly and to produce a lengthy book a number of presses were brought into use: the *42-line Bible* is reckoned to have been printed on six presses. The type to be printed by each press was set up separately and, as we saw on page 31, the problem was to divide the copy in such a way that each part when set in type occupied a number of complete gatherings. A bad or complicated copy could well result in miscalculations which are evidenced by irregularities in the make-up of the gatherings such as the addition of an extra fold or leaf. In time, printers became more experienced and overcame these difficulties more easily, so, as a general rule, we may

---

[1] *Introduction to bibliography*, p. 56.

assume that excessive irregularities in gatherings, particularly in lengthy books, may well be evidence of very early printing.

Press-work

The composing and printing of each page singly was superseded in the 1470s by setting pages in pairs (for folios) and arranging them side by side in the forme so that they could be placed together on the bed of the press. Even then printing can be said to have been by single pages because a separate pull of the lever was required to bring the platen down on each page. It is better, however, to think of this method as printing "two pulls to the forme", and it would appear that this was the accepted procedure until the introduction of the iron press in 1800.[2] Printing two pulls to the forme was much quicker than the former method because after the first page was printed, the position of the forme was altered merely by moving the carriage to bring the second page under the platen. Previously, after printing all the required copies, the page of type had to be removed from the press, replaced by the next one to be printed, and the sheets of paper laid on in a new position to receive its impression. Once a printer had learnt the new method, he would be very unlikely to revert to printing pages singly. Evidence of a change in practice can, therefore, be an aid in dating. Single-page printing may be deduced from changes in different copies of a book between the relative positions of pages that would normally be printed in the same forme. The necessity of moving the paper after printing each page, unless done with great accuracy, would result in the type-pages being printed out of parallel with each other. With two pulls to the forme the paper stays in the same position relative to the type-pages, but the pressure of the platen on one half of the sheet may drag the other half slightly across the inked type causing a slur which is sometimes noticeable in the finished book. Evidence from type-impression can also determine the method used. The blow from the platen would force the type to bite into the sheet of paper and leave a raised impression on its verso. This would only disappear when, on perfecting the sheet, the verso was printed. By a careful examination of the printed leaf it is possible to determine which page was printed

[2] McKerrow, *op. cit.*, p. 61.

first and which second. If in a gathering all the rectos show the same state of printing it must have been done by pages, for both rectos and versos are imposed together when printing by formes and are not separated in the printing.[3]

Early printers were able to perfect their sheets with surprising accuracy. Pin-points were set in the tympan to pierce the paper and hold it in position, and to ensure that when the paper was reversed and placed so that the points went through the same holes, perfect register would be achieved. The first printers used a great number of points: in the *42-line Bible* there were as many as ten to each leaf, four at the top, four at the bottom and two in the outer margin. Gradually it was found that fewer pin-points were just as effective and they were gradually reduced to four, from four to two and finally abandoned completely. The number of holes found in a sheet can offer a useful guide to dating the work of an individual printer, although they are normally only visible at the head and tail of the fold in loosely bound folios or at the four corners of the sheet. In smaller formats they have usually been trimmed away by the binder.

The adoption of other techniques may also provide some indication of the date of publication. The addition of signatures and catchwords, as well as the use of lower-case letters to guide the rubricator, all involved the compositor in extra work but were justified by the dividends they paid in the finished book. Without their assistance the binder might well have gathered the sheets in the wrong order for sewing, or the rubricator mistaken the correct initial letter he had to paint in the space provided. Once their benefits were established they would not be discarded afterwards by the printer, unless, as in the case of rubrics, they were superseded by an acceptable alternative.

Evidence deduced from methods of working is of most value when the output of an individual printer is under consideration because of its direct application to the body of material being studied. Its value is less when applied to the more extensive output of a country or town, for although certain practices may be attributed to a group of printers working in a certain locality, it is not to be expected that they would all have changed over to new techniques at the same time.

3 Haebler. The Study of incunabula, p. 82.

Incunabula have been studied with an increasing application of scientific method for over 100 years by the uncovering of internal evidence of the kind discussed here. In addition, contemporary sources, documents, letters, etc., have helped to build up a large fund of information that is now available to the present-day bibliographer. For instance, biographical data concerning an early printer may be of particular value in dating one of his publications. If the extreme dates of his activity are known or, more specifically, when he was printing or publishing at a particular address, the field of investigation is narrowed and a lead may be given to a more exact dating from internal evidence. Information from all sources has been accumulated in the major bibliographies of incunabula (described in chapter 8) which form an almost complete survey of the development of early printing. Over 40,000 separate editions are known of books printed before 1500 and there can be few others left in the world today which remain unrecorded. But in the larger libraries the study of incunabula continues, some books have so far defied all efforts to assign them to a particular printer or date, and others are being re-assessed in the light of new facts which have come to light since they were last examined. In the following chapter we shall consider this task of identification.

CHAPTER 7

The Identification of Incunabula

The process of identifying a xv century book requires not only a close examination of the book itself, but also recourse to the published bibliographies and catalogues of incunabula. These must be consulted at various stages of the investigation in order to verify one's findings. We need to know the author and title of the work and, so as to establish the particular edition to which the copy belongs, its printer and the date and place of publication. It would be unusual for all these facts to be yielded up by the book itself and the bibliographies must be checked to fill in the missing details. A full identification is not complete without a thorough collation of the book, not merely to discover whether all its leaves are intact, but also to ascertain how it was constructed. This may prove the only clue by which the copy may be assigned to its proper edition when two editions were published within a few months of each other. The procedures for identification are now considered in more detail.

As most xv century books are without title-pages, it is best to turn to the colophon for evidence of printing and perhaps for the author and title. At once it will be realised that there are certain prerequisites for collating early printed books. The majority of colophons are in Latin and many contain the contractions and abbreviations beloved by the mediaeval scribe. A working knowledge of these is valuable as is the ability to decipher the unfamiliar letter-forms of some Gothic founts. One must expect the place of printing to be Latinized and the less obvious forms, e.g. Argentina (for Strassburg) and Rothomagum (for Rouen), should be checked in lists provided by McKerrow[1], Stillwell[2] and others. The name may be given in the genitive or ablative case and may well exhibit minor variations from the normal spelling.

[1] R. B. McKerrow. An Introduction to bibliography, App. 7, pp. 337–40.
[2] M. B. Stillwell. Incunabula and Americana, 1450–1800, (1930), pp. 228–48.

Interpreting the date can prove difficult since it appears in a variety of forms. The year may be a combination of numerals and words. Saints' Days are often used for calendar dates, and one must remember that the Old Style calendar was in use with its New Year's Day on 25th March. Even this was subject to local variation.

Authors' names are usually recognizable because the majority of xv century printed books contain works written by classical or long-established mediaeval writers, but they often appear in their mediaeval form, with birthplaces used as family names, and in a variety of spellings. Care should be taken not to mistake the name of a commentator for that of the author.

Frequently the colophon will not yield all the information desired and it is fortunate to find one as full as that found in the edition of *The Chronicles of England* printed by Gerard Leeu at Antwerp in 1493:

> Here ben endyd the Cronycles of the Reame of Englond with their | apperteignaunces. En-prētyd In the Duchye of Braband. in the towne | of Andewarpe In the yere of owr lord .M.cccc.xciij. By maistir Gerard | de leew. a man of grete wysedom in all maner of kūnyng: whych nowe | is come from lyfe vnto the deth/ which is grete harme for many a poure | man. On whos sowle god almyghty for his hygh grace haue mercy | A M E N | [Leeu's device]

Many are far less explicit, perhaps giving only one piece of information, e.g. "Impressum Venetijs" or, "Impressum per Richardū Pynson", and one would need to look elsewhere in the book for further details. Nevertheless, a full transcript must be made of the colophon, word for word and line for line, regardless of the amount of information it provides. Failing the colophon, the author and title might be given in the incipit or explicit; the printer might be identified by his device, traced from the place of printing, or, with the help of Haebler's *Typenrepertorium der Wiegendrucke* from the types used. Any clue likely to be of value should not be neglected.

Having obtained as much information as possible concerning author, title, printer, place and date of printing, the standard bibliographies of incunabula should now be consulted. These are arranged either by authors or else in "Proctor order" and so permit an approach to be made best suited to the known facts. Any entry which matches the information should be noted down along with the number reference of the printed description, e.g. "Hain 1100."

The task of identification is by no means complete when a matching entry has been found for we have to be absolutely sure that the copy in hand agrees in all its details with the full description contained in the bibliography. Before this can be done, however, the copy must be collated to discover how it was constructed and whether or not it is complete. This, in turn, involves determining the format, analysing the structure of each gathering and counting the total number of leaves.

The format is best ascertained by noting the direction in which the chain-lines run, whether vertically or horizontally across the printed leaves, together with the position of the watermarks. McKerrow[3] deals with this subject fully and it is sufficient here to note that if the chain-lines are vertical and the watermark is found whole in the centre of one of a pair of leaves, it indicates that the sheet of paper was folded once and the book is a folio. To reduce the amount of sewing required, gatherings in folio books were normally constructed of a number of folded sheets inserted within each other. In a folio gathering of three regularly folded sheets, the watermarks, if found on leaves 1, 2 and 3, would be absent from leaves 4, 5 and 6, and vice-versa, depending on the way the printer placed the sheets on the press. If the chain-lines are horizontal and the watermark is found cut in half in the centre of the inner margins of leaves 2 and 3, or 1 and 4, the sheet has been folded twice and the book is a quarto. In an octavo, where the sheet has been folded three times, the chain-lines are once again vertical but the watermark is cut in quarters and appears at the head of the inner margin, on leaves 1, 4, 5 and 8, or 2, 3, 6 and 7. Fortunately, with incunabula one is not often called upon to collate smaller sizes of books.

When establishing the format by this method allowance must be made for variations in the position of the watermark in the unfolded sheet—it is by no means always in the centre of one half—and for the possibility that the binder in trimming the edges of the leaves may have removed all traces of the marks at least from some of the leaves on which they should appear. The format, besides showing how the sheets were folded, also suggests how the type-pages were imposed in the forme. But before this can be determined precisely, it is

[3] Introduction to bibliography, pp. 164–74.

necessary to check the gatherings to see whether each was constructed of one or more sheets and whether all show a consistent make-up throughout the book. In this check it often helps to put oneself in the position of the printer and to follow his actions as closely as possible. A printer in setting-up a book from an author's manuscript would normally begin with page 1 of the text leaving the composition of the preliminaries until later. When he came to the end of the text he might find that he had not filled a full forme of type-pages and, not wishing to leave blank leaves in the finished book, might decide to set-up part of the preliminaries in the space left. Collation should, therefore, start with the first page of the text leaving the preliminaries until the end unless it is obvious from the signing that the book has been set up from a previously printed copy. In this case the first page of text may start, not on the first, but on an inner leaf of a gathering, or the signing of the gatherings will probably proceed regularly from cover to cover with no special marks used for the preliminaries. For example, of two copies of a book containing the same text, the one with signatures A–M⁴ is likely to be a later edition and perhaps a close copy of the one collated *² **² A–L⁴.

Of particular importance in collating are the blank leaves often found at the front and back of a book. It must be established by careful examination whether they form an integral part of the first and last printed sheets, in which case they must be recorded; or, whether they are binder's fly-leaves or end-papers and thus relate to the binding and not to the printed part of the book, in which case they are not recorded.

Rules for recording the order and size of gatherings have been set down and explained by Sir Walter Greg in his *A Formulary of Collation*.[4] They were later expanded and examined in great detail by Professor Bowers in his *Principles of Bibliographical Description*, (1949), chapter 9 and appendix III of which deal with the special problems of incunabula. It is not proposed here to consider the recommendations made by Bowers, although an outline of the essential requirements of collation formulary is given later in chapter 13. It should be noted, however, that Bowers' methods have not been universally accepted, and certainly the major bibliographies of incunabula which were

[4] *The Library*. 4th series. Vol. xiv, (1934), pp. 365–82.

published before 1949 differ considerably in their recording of collations. Two divergencies in particular can cause confusion when comparing them with a Bowers-made collation.

The first arises from the fact that the gatherings in incunabula were frequently left unsigned. Bowers recommends in describing such books that the gatherings should be numbered consecutively with arabic numerals, e.g. [1–23^{10} 24^8], on the theory that if one has no evidence at all to go on one cannot infer how the printer would have signed the gatherings. It will be found, however, that the usual practice in bibliographies of incunabula is to supply a lower-case alphabet of inferred signatures, e.g. [a–z^{10} aa^8], although there is no generally accepted practice and the B.M. *Catalogue of books printed in the xv century* varies its method from volume to volume. It is essential to check the method adopted by the respective bibliography before endeavouring to reconcile it with one's own collation.

The second divergence is found in the manner of recording gatherings which contain an odd number of leaves. In all bibliographies the number of leaves in each gathering is indicated by a superior number following the signature, e.g. A^8 B^4, etc. According to Greg and Bowers the numbers should always be even for they are meant to record the original state of the gathering made up of a number of folds. A gathering containing an odd number of leaves must have suffered some alteration either by an insertion or cancellation and this fact is recorded separately by the use of a plus or minus sign. For instance, a quarto gathering of four regularly folded leaves which has an extra leaf signed A5 added at the end is recorded: A^4(A4+A5). Similarly, a simple cancellation of a leaf is shown: A^4(—A3), indicating that the third leaf has been removed. It is important to distinguish an insertion from a cancellation in order to determine the original state of the gathering. A gathering with an odd number of leaves, say A^7, could in a folio book represent either a regularly folded gathering of 6 leaves with a single leaf insertion, or a regularly folded gathering of 8 leaves with a leaf cancelled. An inserted leaf would have been pasted or bound in with the folds of the gathering and some evidence of this should be looked for. Insertions or cancellations were frequently planned in advance by the printer and may or may not contain printed text. They are particularly prevalent in early printed books because, as we have seen, the usual method of setting-up a text was to divide it between two or more compositors. Difficulties encountered in casting off each part and miscalculations by a compositor would result on the one hand of having to cram a portion of the text into insufficient space, or on the other, of leaving pages blank when the text was too short for the space allotted. To overcome the first difficulty an extra leaf may have been added, and to avoid leaving unsightly blank pages in the middle of the printed text the printer may well have cancelled them. It is probably because of the frequency of such miscalculations in early printing, that one often finds in bibliographies of incunabula the use of odd superior numbers to indicate an altered gathering, e.g. A^9, or A^{8+1}. Neither example provides much information concerning the actual make-up of the gathering: the second shows an insertion but does not state where it occurs in the gathering, and the first leaves one in doubt whether an insertion or a cancellation has been made. The method recommended by Greg and Bowers is obviously more precise and explicit and whenever possible should be used in making one's own record of the gatherings.

After the gatherings have been examined and their make-up noted, the number of leaves recorded should be verified against an actual count of the total number present in the book. Their foliation should also be noted and checked against the count of leaves. Early printers were not greatly concerned with the accuracy with which they numbered the leaves and one frequently finds that their printed notation does not agree with the physical count. In such cases the correct total should be indicated in brackets following the notation, e.g. 40 leaves, ff. 1–20 23–30 32–43 [= 40]. With incunabula, of course, pagination does not have to be considered.

The collation and foliation should now be compared with that recorded in the various bibliographies. If they are found to differ from the printed descriptions it is as well to check one's own work again very carefully before assuming that the copy in hand comes from another edition of the work. If the comparison is the same, then one can reasonably be certain that the copy has been properly identified, but to make absolutely sure the analysis of the copy should continue with an examination of the type-page and of the types, ornaments, devices, etc., used.

The type-page is described by recording the number of lines to a typical page and by recording its vertical and horizontal measurements in millimetres. Double-column printing is also noted for as we have seen this was common in the xv century, printers often adopting this more complicated method of setting even for a short text requiring no such treatment. In recording the lines to the page, a selection of pages should be examined to ensure that the number stated represents a typical page, and in order that any variations may be noted. If the number varies frequently throughout the book one may note the inclusive figures, e.g. 30-34 lines. *Der Gesamtkatalog der Wiegendrucke* uses the word "wechselnd" (variable) for such practice, but gives "20-21 z" where a slight variation is noted on a few pages only. The *B.M. Catalogue* indicates a selected page and continues with the dimensions of the area covered by the type, giving the vertical measurement first, e.g. 3^a: 33 lines, 143 × 90 mm., or where the pages also contain marginal printing, 3^a: 33 lines and marginalia, 143 × 69 (90) mm. Considerable variations in the same book are specifically indicated, for instance, the last description continues with the measurements of another page, 18^a: 42 lines of smaller type, 142 × 90 mm.

An accurate description of the type itself is a very difficult matter since the identification of early types requires a long period of acquaintanceship with incunabula. Even with the aid of Haebler the task is by no means simple and for the non-expert it is probably wise merely to indicate the general style of typeface, e.g. gothic (perhaps venturing to textura, rotunda, bastarda, etc.), roman, and greek. An indication of the size of type used, can however, be given by the distance in millimetres covered by 20 lines set solid following Haebler's method of measuring from the base of the bottom line on the page, i.e. omitting descenders, to the base of the 21st line counted up the page. The distance may be found to differ slightly on other pages of the book owing to the variable shrinkage of the paper—it was invariably dampened before printing—and, where different papers are used in the same book, to a change of quality. One may either note the average measurement from a number of pages, or by taking the height of the type-page (which has already been measured) multiplying by 20 and dividing the product by the number of lines on the page. The identification of early types was first undertaken on a large scale by Robert Proctor who numbered each printer's types chronologically according to their first appearance. This method was adopted by Haebler for his *Typenrepertorium* and Haebler's enumeration has been used by subsequent bibliographies, e.g. by the *GW* where we find following the number of lines to the page a typical statement: Typen: 1,2,5. This is not particularly informative to readers unable to refer to Haebler, and from the third volume the compilers added the 20-line measurement in millimetres, e.g. Typen: 1:83G, 2:110R—the G and R standing for gothic and roman. The compilers of the *B.M. Catalogue*, in striving for the utmost accuracy, have taken the average measurement from every book in the Museum in which the type is used, and we find it identified quite simply by this, e.g. Type: 118.

A full picture of a xv century type-page is not complete without mention of the woodcut-initials, borders, illustrations, and rubrics present. Apart from their contribution to the art of book decoration they are often valuable for the evidence they provide on the date and origin of printing. Of particular value in this respect are the printers' devices, and these, with all the other decorative features just mentioned, are always noted in bibliographical descriptions. In analysing the copy under examination their position in the book should be indicated by reference to folio number or signature. The standard catalogues and bibliographies treat these features with varying degrees of fulness, but they should be checked for corresponding locations and descriptions.

After a careful and successful comparison of all the recorded details, one is now entitled to conclude that the copy in hand corresponds with a given description and the appropriate number reference can now be assigned to the copy, e.g. "Hain 1100", "GW 1900", etc. Alternatively, one should equally be confident of stating "not Hain 1100" if a matching entry has not been found. In any event it is as well to verify one's findings with more than one bibliography in case some minor variation is found which might indicate that the copy is from a different issue of the work.

The analytical procedure given above has been aimed at identification and consequently has concentrated on establishing and recording the kind of information necessary for an accurate comparison to be made with the printed descriptions in standard bibliographies. At the same time, the notes made on the copy will be valuable in writing a detailed bibliographical description of one's own. It must be remembered, however, that a true description is of an "ideal copy" of an edition and consequently cannot be compiled without a full analysis of as many other copies of the same edition as possible. It is not proposed here to deal with description of incunabula, and the student is referred to Bowers' *Principles of Bibliographical Description* for a detailed explanation. But because any bibliographical study of the period involves frequent references to the descriptions found in the standard bibliographies, these will now be considered in more detail.

CHAPTER 8

Bibliographies of Incunabula

(i) Hain, Ludwig.   Repertorium bibliographicum.   Stuttgart, 1826–38.   2 vols. in 4.

"Hain", although published over a century and a quarter ago, is still of value to bibliographers both for the accuracy and wealth of description it provides and because it often acts as a starting place for further research. The entries, which are numbered consecutively, list over 16,000 incunabula and are arranged in alphabetical order of authors. Those marked with an asterisk were compiled by Hain himself from the books under his care at Munich, whereas the other entries rely on the researches of earlier xvii and xviii century bibliographers and from information supplied by his contemporaries. As one might expect, the marked entries contain more description than the others.

Each entry consists of an assigned heading comprising the author and brief title followed by transcripts of the incipit, major section-titles and the colophon. Reference to the positions these occupy in the book is made by folio number, e.g. *F 1 a* followed by the title-caption indicates that this is to be found on the recto of the first folio. When the title-caption is printed on a subsequent leaf, the form *F 1 a vacat* is used and the transcript made with the appropriate folio reference. The colophon or explicit transcript is preceded by the words *In fine* and is made in full in the style of type used in the original with line-endings indicated by ‖.

The colophon is followed by the collation of the book given in a series of initials and abbreviations, e.g. the collation of Hain 5530 is stated as: *s. l. a. et typ. n. f. g. ch. s. f. c. et pp. n. 2 col. 42l. 304ff.* This may be expanded into: sine loco, anno et typographici nomine, folio, goticis characteribus, sine signatoribus, custodibus et paginarum numeris, 2 columnae, 42 lineae, 304 folia, and translated as: without place, year and printer's name, in folio, in Gothic characters, without signatures, catchwords and page numbers, 2 columns, 42 lines to the page, 304 folios. Hain added a note in brackets at the end of this particular collation to the effect that the book was printed by Ulrich Zell at Cologne. A convenient list of the Latin abbreviations used by Hain will be found in Miss Margaret Stillwell's *Incunabula and Americana*, 1450–1800, pp. 223–5.

It should be noted that Hain gives no locations for any of the books listed in his bibliography nor does he refer to other authorities even for those entries which he did not compile himself.

(ii) Copinger, W. A.   Supplement to Hain's Repertorium bibliographicum. London, 1895, 1898, 1902. 2 vols. in 3.

Even though Haebler considered Copinger's *Supplement* next to Hain the "most necessary book for the student of incunabula", it should be used with great caution. Part I, which contains nearly 7,000 corrections and additional collations to the works listed in Hain, was severely criticized in a review published in *Bibliographica*, vol. II, (1896) because of the many errors it contained and the absence of quoted authorities. In this first part, Hain's original numbering is followed and the entries are normally referred to by later authorities as "Hain-Copinger", or "H-C". For instance, H-C 4152 relates to the same number in Hain as augmented by Copinger.

Perhaps chastened by the criticism Part I had invoked, Copinger somewhat apologetically explained his intentions for Part II:

> What has been attempted in Part II is to indicate the existence of Incunabula not mentioned by Hain, and to supply just that information which must be forthcoming before the actual collating of the works can be taken in hand. In a large number of instances collations are given, but this is not the professed object of this work, which may perhaps best be described as a catalogue on an extended scale, with Bibliographical particulars. It is intended to be merely introductory to something better—rather to indicate sources of information than to give the actual collations which must subsequently be made.

Consequently, the entries, which in style resemble Hain's, refer to other authorities. Copinger retained some of Hain's abbreviations, using *s.l.* (without place of printing); *s.t.n.* (without printer's name);

s.a. (without date), and introduced *sine notâ* if all these were absent. The collation is given before the transcripts of incipit and colophon and, whereas Hain collected undated editions in no particular order before the entries for dated editions, Copinger based his order on the number of lines to the page, adopting the rough and ready rule that a smaller number of lines and a larger number of leaves are probably indications of an earlier edition. The numbering of entries in Part II is Copinger's own and an entry here is usually referred to by later authorities as "Copinger", "Cop.", or just "C", followed by its number.

The publication of Copinger's *Supplement* was, however, redeemed by the inclusion, at the end of Part II, of Burger's *Index*, or, to give it its full title:

> (iii) Burger, Konrad. The Printers and publishers of the fifteenth century with lists of their works. Index to the Supplement to Hain's Repertorium Bibliographicum, etc. 1902.

This is a very painstaking and useful work by someone who regarded it as "a labour of love to me, which has been much delayed, as I could attend to it only after the day's toil was over". Each printer is arranged by his self-adopted form of name in alphabetical order, with his works arranged in chronological order followed by those issued *s.a.* and *s.n.* The entries, for ease of reference, have been kept more or less to a single line and thus often afford a short-cut in tracing an obscure title. In compiling them, Burger included not only books listed by Hain and Copinger but those from other sources such as Proctor, the first volume of Pellechet, Haebler's *Tipografía Ibérica*, etc. He relied much on Proctor's dating, and appended a list of books which bear a date but have no indication of printer and place of printing. He apologized in his Foreword for omitting about 2,000 books which appeared without printer's name, place and date, and also for not including a list of printing places with the names of their printers and publishers, but referred readers requiring this information to Proctor's *Index*. Nevertheless, Burger's *Index* remains the best brief chronological record of the output of each xv century press.

(iv) Reichling, D.   Appendices ad Hainii-Copingeri Repertorium bibliographicum. Additiones
et emendationes. Monachii, 1905–11.
Suppl. 1914. 8 vols.

A further step towards a complete listing of xv century printed
books was taken by Reichling when he published his *Appendices*
giving notices of additional incunabula and correcting certain entries
in both Hain and Copinger. The main work was published in six
fascicules with two sequences running through them in alphabetical
order of author with anonymous works entered under their titles.
One sequence contains works not known to Hain or Copinger numbered consecutively throughout; the second additions to the descriptions
contained in Hain and Copinger, each entry being preceded by the
appropriate numerical reference to "H" for Hain, "H(C)" for Hain
and Part I of Copinger, and "Cop" for Part II of Copinger.

Because the two sequences alternate through the six fascicules,
the indexes contained in fascicule 7 are essential for easy reference.
They provide author and, for anonymous works, title indexes to
both sequences, quoting for (a) the Reichling number in arabic
numerals, e.g.

Festivalis liber   Lond., Pynson, 1495   179

and for (b) the fascicule number in Roman with arabic numerals to
indicate the page, e.g.

H(C) 13243 Polo, Marco: delle mara-
          vig lie del mondo   Ven., de Sessa, 1496, 13.Jun.
                                III. 153.

Further indexes provide an alphabetical list to both sequences,
each with its printers listed in chronological order of first printing.
The supplement, published in 1914, carried additional entries and a
general index combining in one alphabet the items listed in the preceding fascicules. In all, the work added some 2,100 editions not known
to Hain or Copinger, and amplified about 3,400 of their descriptions.
It is regarded as a much more authoritative work than Copinger
since Reichling did at least examine the works he described.

(v) Pellechet, M. L. C. Catalogue général des incunables des bibliothèques publiques de France, 1897–. 3 vols. only.

As the title indicates, this is a census of xv century printed books contained in French libraries. Unfortunately it was never finished, the third and last published volume ending the alphabetical sequences of authors at "Gregorius". Mlle. Pellechet died in 1900 after only the first volume (A—Biblia) had appeared and the work was continued by M. Louis Polain, who improved on its standard of accuracy and gave much fuller collations. When quoting extracts from the books Mlle. Pellechet used the Hain method of reference from the folio number but also added a reference by signatures when these were present. The work remains useful because of the additional information it gives of French incunabula which were not very extensively covered by Hain.

(vi) Duff, E. Gordon. Fifteenth century English books. Bibliographical Society, 1917.

This is the standard bibliography of English incunabula and represents some 28 years' work of locating, examining and describing books in libraries scattered all over the country. 431 separate editions are entered and Duff records that about one half of the books chronicled are now known only from single copies, from a leaf or two, or even from fragments of a leaf. The work is arranged alphabetically by author, or by title if anonymous. The collation of each edition is given before the transcripts of its major sections which are followed by locations of copies and occasional brief notes of interest concerning the work. A typographical index is included which lists the types used by each printer together with a list of printed books with an indication by number of the type(s) used in each. Duff did not make a re-examination of the types being content to follow Proctor's classification and enumeration; on the other hand, his work is made more useful by a large number of facsimiles.[1] Occasionally, when assigning dates to undated books he neglected to indicate by a question mark the possibility of error.[2]

[1] V. Scholderer. "Early printed books". *In* The Bibliographical Society 1892–1942: studies in retrospect, (1945), p. 39.

[2] F. S. Ferguson. "English books before 1640". *Ibid*, p. 52, footnote.

(vii) Gesamtkatalog der Wiegendrucke. Leipzig, 1925–38. Vols. 1–7 only.

This tremendous undertaking to record with full descriptions all editions of incunabula known to the xx century was, unfortunately, not finished before the Second World War put an end to its further compilation, although an attempt is now being made to resume publication. It is much more comprehensive than Hain: in the section of the alphabet "A to Eigenschaften" 9,255 books are entered compared with Hain's 6,554. In addition much more collational information is provided and, unlike Hain, it quotes other authorities and lists the location of copies. It is in a straightforward alphabetical sequence of authors, or titles for anonymous works, each entry being consecutively numbered.

The description of each incunabulum contains:

(a) a general bibliographical note, consisting of author's name (with brief biographical details), short title, editor, translator, etc., place of printing, printer, publisher, date and format.

(b) the collation, recording the number of leaves, its quires, signatures (for books without signatures an alphabetical sequence is supplied in brackets), catchwords and arrangement of the page, e.g. number of columns and lines, and the occurrence of headlines and marginalia. The types, initials, borders, rubrics and printer's devices are, as far as possible, described in accordance with Haebler's *Typenrepertorium der Wiegendrucke*, and from the third volume the measurement of 20 lines together with the kind of type (R = roman, G = gothic) is added. Title woodcuts are specially mentioned and maps are noted in every case; information on music printing and printing in colours is included.

(c) the transcript of the title, caption headings and colophon in roman or gothic following the original.

(d) references to sources, e.g. Hain, Copinger, Reichling, Proctor, Duff, B.M. Catalogue, etc., with reference to facsimiles.

(e) the locations of all known copies whenever their number does not exceed 10, otherwise a selection is given.

Scholderer has commented that in *GW* the allocation of printers, dates and types to unsigned incunabula is sometimes questionable because its method of compilation did not permit the simultaneous examination of all the works of any given press.[3] For purposes of identification, on the other hand, the *GW* is the most obvious source of reference (within its alphabetical limits) after Hain.

> (viii) Incunabula in American libraries: a third census of fifteenth century books recorded in North American collections. Compiled and edited by Frederick R. Goff. N.Y., Bibliographical Society of America, 1964.

Three censuses have now been published recording at different times the xv century books contained in American collections. The first arose from a proposal of the Bibliographical Society of America in 1904, but was not published separately until 1919. It had appeared serially between April and December, 1918, in the Bulletin of the New York Public Library. It recorded 13,200 copies of 6,292 incunabula in American ownership. The second census, compiled by Miss M. Stillwell in 1940 was a greatly enlarged publication consisting of 11,132 titles and locating 35,232 copies. This soon established for itself a world-wide reputation for the accuracy of its compilation and is generally referred to in other bibliographies and catalogues as "Stillwell". The third census reflects the ever-increasing wealth of American collections, which by 1964 contained 47,188 copies of 12,599 separate incunabula.

The three censuses are in the nature of short-title catalogues giving the minimum amount of information sufficient for the identification of each edition listed. The entries are given in roman, which with the brevity of each description makes for easy identification. They are frequently used as a short-cut to the more detailed descriptions provided by other authorities to which the last census refers very fully.

The books are arranged in a single alphabetical sequence of author and title if anonymous. The form of author's name is based on that used by Hain, unless both the *B.M. Catalogue* and *GW* agree

3 V. Scholderer. "Early printed books". *Ibid*, p. 41.

on a different entry. Collected works precede individual titles which are also arranged alphabetically. The various editions of each title are in chronological order and those in Greek and Latin are entered first followed by translations. Works in Hebrew are treated as a separate category under the heading "Hebraica". After the brief title comes the imprint in the usual form of place, printer and date, together with the format. The collation is not given. Various notes follow the entry, when considered necessary, giving brief details of publication or printing, added works, references to other authorities and the locations of copies. At the end of the book a cross-reference list of variant author-forms and entries is provided together with an index of printers and publishers, a feature not included in the earlier Censuses.

> (ix) Proctor, Robert. An Index to the Early Printed Books in the British Museum: from the invention of printing to the year MD with notes of those in the Bodleian Library. 2 vols. K. Paul, 1898–9; 4 Supps. 1899–1902

The importance of this work in extending our knowledge of the earliest printing has already been stressed. Proctor had intended that his *Index* should include books printed before the end of 1520 as he considered that the initial period of printing ended at this date rather than at the more arbitrarily chosen date of 1500. After 1520 the output of books was suddenly increased by the flood of controversial works published during the period of the Reformation. Unfortunately Proctor died in 1903 having indexed only the xv century books and those printed in Germany by 1520, and it was left to Lieutenant-Colonel Frank Isaac to continue the work. His sections covering Italy, Switzerland and Eastern European countries were published by Bernard Quaritch in one volume in 1938. Isaac simplified the entries somewhat and used modern terminology to describe types, e.g. Textura, Rotunda, Schwabacher, etc., but followed the same arrangement as that adopted by Proctor.

Proctor's aim was to illustrate the early history of printing by listing in chronological order all xv century presses and types. Thus the development of printing may be traced through the books printed in the various countries and towns by individual presses. As a guide to the entries, a list of towns arranged in the order in which printing was first practised is placed at the head of each country, and under each town a chronological list of all the presses which worked there precedes the entries for the books themselves. Proctor's great achievement was his identification of the types used. This enabled him to assign the majority of the books without any printer's name to their respective printers. The 450 or so books that defeated him he placed at the end of the entries for each town, or if they proved even more intractable, under their country. Each printer's type is listed and numbered by the chronological order of its appearance. The size of most Roman types and many others is given by noting their height in millimetres of 20 lines. Unfortunately he measured from the base of the first line, without taking the descenders into account, to the upper edge of the lower-case letters of the 20th line, ignoring the ascenders. The measurement thus falls short of the full distance owing to the omission of the bottom descenders and top ascenders and cannot be used as a basis for measuring fewer lines than 20 when these are not available. Later, in his Supplements, he realised his error and recommended that the measurement should be taken from the base of the first to the base of the twenty-first line.[4]

The entries for individual books are kept to the minimum necessary for identification, each book being described by a short title in the briefest intelligible form. The format is given but no further collational details. It must be remembered that this is merely an index and for further information Proctor provided the heading under which each book is to be found in the British Museum Catalogue, together with references to Hain or to Campbell's *Annales de la typographie Ne'erlandaise du XVe siècle*. At the end of Part I (which lists the xv century books) is to be found an index in alphabetical order of places, printers and publishers, and other indexes of authors arranged by their Hain or Campbell numbers and in alphabetical order. In Part II (books printed in Germany 1501-20) Proctor confined himself to the books contained in the British Museum and provided a type-

[4] Haebler. The Study of incunabula, p. 33.

register containing every fount of type mentioned in the text arranged in their various classes with measurements. This is followed by 67 facsimiles of the more important types—a feature which was also provided by Colonel Isaac in the sections published in 1938.

(x) Catalogue of books printed in the xvth century now in the British Museum. 9 vols. to date, 1908 –.

Although still unfinished after sixty years the *B.M.C.* is recognized as the principal work of reference for all incunabulists. Initially under the general editorship of A. W. Pollard and later under that of Dr. Victor Scholderer with Messrs. L. A. Sheppard and George D. Painter jointly responsible for the last published volume, it stands as a great tribute to British scholarship. The wealth of the collection at the British Museum together with the care taken to ensure that the collational information given for each entry is of an ideal copy, makes this work not merely the catalogue of a single collection but a general bibliography of the period.

The work is arranged in Proctor order under countries, towns and presses in their priority of printing. The volumes published to date are:

Part I Xylographica and Books printed with types at Mainz, Strassburg, Bamberg and Cologne. (1908).

Part II Germany: Eltvil—Trier. (1912).

Part III Germany: Leipzig—Pforzheim, German-speaking Switzerland and Austria-Hungary. (1913).

Part IV Italy: Subiaco and Rome. (1916).

Part V Venice. (1924).

Part VI Italy: Foligno, Ferrova, Florence, Milan, Bologna, Naples, Perugia and Treviso. (1930).

Part VII Italy: Genoa. Unassigned addenda. (1935).

Part VIII France, French-speaking Switzerland. (1949).

Part IX Fascicule I—Holland. Fascicule II—Belgium. (1962).

The first volume has a general introduction and a review of the evidence used for identification and dating by A. W. Pollard. General surveys of national printing are to be found in Vol. III (German by A. W. Pollard); Vol. VII (Italian by V. Scholderer); Vol. VIII (French by V. Scholderer); and Vol. IX (Dutch and Belgian by George D. Painter). Each volume contains plates of type facsimiles giving their sources and the average measurement adopted in the body of the catalogue for each of the types reproduced.

The greatest part of each volume is, of course, concerned with descriptive entries of the books in the library. Each entry consists of four parts:

(a) the heading, with author's name, short title of the book and its stated or conjectured date;

(b) the description with quotations from the title, incipit, colophon and other important passages;

(c) the collation of an ideal copy;

(d) notes on the particular copy described.

The quotations from the title, etc., are all printed in roman following the original as closely as possible but transliterating capitals to lower-case in accordance with the simplified method of transcription (see page 179). The rejection of quasi-facsimile transcription for these passages certainly results in a more attractive page which is easier to consult and doubtless has the considerable advantage of reducing costs, but its value for the comparison of other copies is thereby reduced. Line-endings are indicated by a double vertical stroke "||" and an additional stroke is added to indicate larger spaces.

The collation begins with the format followed by the signature formula. Unsigned gatherings are indicated by placing inferred signatures within brackets. The number of leaves and columns is shown as are also the number of lines and the measurement of a stated page. The types in which the book is printed are indicated by the average measurement of 20 unleaded lines. This notation by measurement, e.g. type 91 signifying that over 20 lines it measures 91 mm., enables the type to be visualized reasonably accurately—something that is not possible with Proctor's system of numbering types in chronological order of their first appearance. Notes are also given of the pinholes used (for the earliest books), the presence of initials, printed guide letters and headlines. References are made to Hain's *Repertorium* and other authorities and occasionally a contents note is added as well as a statement of the relation that the book bears to other editions of the same work.

4

Part III

SIXTEENTH TO EIGHTEENTH

CENTURIES

CHAPTER 9

Bibliographical Study

We move now to the period of book production which has received most attention from critical bibliographers. Their studies have been directed in particular to the printed works of the xvi and xvii centuries, largely as a result of the pride felt on both sides of the Atlantic in a common literary heritage. The first high plateau of English literary achievement was reached in Elizabethan times and the continued demand for critical editions of Shakespeare and his contemporaries led, as we have seen, to the development of the "New Bibliography". Since the early years of the present century the scope of bibliographical study has widened to include later periods of English literature, the xviii century especially providing a rich field for investigation yet presenting at the same time particular problems of its own.

The nature of the study, as a consequence, has been closely linked with textual criticism and the problem of the transmission of text from author's manuscript to printed book. The bibliographer has endeavoured to distinguish for the literary editor and critic the most authoritative printed text of a writer's work. In fact, the aim goes further than this. It is the nature of the author's manuscript which is the real goal of critical bibliography, the need to verify the words written by the author himself: for in the production of a printed book the work of many people, some of whom had little education, was interposed between the author's copy and the printed page. Moreover, in the days of hand printing, the demand for a reprint invariably necessitated a new setting of the type. Each edition was normally copied from its immediate predecessor with the risk of increasing deviation from the original. It is this direct but ever diverging descent that emphasizes the importance of the first edition as the best claimant to textual authority, unless, of course, it is known that a later edition was revised by the author himself.

A bibliographer, in examining the life-history of a particular work of this period, begins his studies in much the same way as if dealing with incunabula. Identification and dating are still a first necessity, and the value of placing editions in their correct order of publication so as to evaluate the authority of their texts is obvious, but the investigation has to be carried much further than the edition stage. The need to arrive at the most correct text involves the detailed examination of all evidence, often involving a page-by-page comparison between copies of two or more editions and between copies of the same edition. Where differences are found it then becomes the duty of the bibliographer to offer reasoned explanations for their presence. Drawing on his knowledge of contemporary printing methods, he has in many instances produced incontrovertible evidence to explain the cause of certain textual variants. His success in this sphere has during this century altered considerably the appearance of Elizabethan texts from their xix century editions which were produced without the benefit of bibliographical research. In other instances, the differences in the early editions of a text may not be explained so conclusively and alternative possibilities may suggest themselves. Yet again, variants in other works remain unexplained and may never be resolved through lack of bibliographical evidence. Their existence, however, remains a challenge to bibliographers who are constantly applying the findings of the latest researches into contemporary printing and publishing practices to their particular field of investigation. In this respect the study in recent years of xviii century practices has often led to a better understanding of those of earlier periods.

During the xvi century the book threw off the shackles imposed by its manuscript predecessor and took on the appearance of its modern counterpart. The commercial advantages of an informative title-page soon became obvious to the more progressive printers of the earliest part of the century. Books were no longer left unsigned and the printer's device was introduced as a self-advertising trademark. The author's name was given more prominence and the title of the book was set down with boldness and clarity on its own page.

Admittedly there were exceptions brought about by a desire on the part of some printers to conceal certain information. During the Reformation, for instance, many Protestant publications were printed with false imprints to escape the harsh penalties that could be expected from unsympathetic authorities. There were always examples, too, of printers who altered dates and titles to make an old book appear a new one, or, as was probably the case with the Pavier quartos, to avoid suspicion when infringing copyrights. Nevertheless, the problem of identification and dating for the vast majority of xvi to xviii century books has proved less arduous than for incunabula, and the first two centuries at least, have been thoroughly charted by Pollard and Redgrave,[1] and by Wing,[2] in their Short-title Catalogues.

The problem of textual analysis requires the bibliographer to distinguish between separate issues and variant states of the various editions of a work. In this investigation his study is less concerned with the materials of which the books were made than with the methods adopted by printers in their production. Printing-house practices have to be followed very carefully from the decision by the master-printer on how the work should proceed to the individual actions of the compositor and pressman. The need for an understanding of this was noted by McKerrow in the early years of this century:

> Until some curious inquirer makes a thorough investigation into all the technical details of Elizabethan printing, and from this and a comparison of handwritings arrives at some definite statement of the relative probability of various misreadings and misprints, emendation must remain in the same state as medicine was before dissection was practised.

Since these words were written, subsequent study, McKerrow's own being not the least important, enabled F. P. Wilson to write[3] in 1945:

> we are now able to stand by the elbow of an Elizabethan compositor and see what sort and what size of paper he was using; what founts of type and whence they were derived; what devices, title-page borders, and ornaments; how he set up

[1] A. W. Pollard and G. R. Redgrave, *comps.* A Short-title catalogue of books printed in England, Scotland and Ireland, and of English books printed abroad, 1475–1640. Bibliographical Soc., (1926).

[2] Wing, D. G., *comp.* Short-title catalogue of books printed in England, Scotland, Ireland, Wales, and British America and of English books printed in other countries, 1641–1700. 3 vols. N.Y., Index Society, (1945–51).

[3] "Shakespeare and the 'New Bibliography' ". *In* The Bibliographical Society 1892–1942: studies in retrospect, (1945), pp. 92–3.

his type and what was the method of imposition; how much if he were a skilled man he could compose in one day and how many presses he could keep busy at this rate of composition; if he and another compositor were working on the same book, at what point the one succeeded the other; whether he read his copy or had it dictated to him.

Some of the evidence which has supplied this information has come from a study of the books themselves, the rest from external sources, e.g. parallel studies by other bibliographers, from contemporary documents relating to authors and printers, and perhaps most important of all from printing manuals which give an authoritative account of trade practices. The earliest and most significant, being itself a source for many later manuals, is Joseph Moxon's *Mechanick Exercises,* vol. II, (1683). Although of a comparatively late date, it is considered, because of the conservative nature of the printing trade, to be generally applicable for all but the earliest period of hand-printing.

CHAPTER 10

Printing Practice

The nature of the copy

The purpose of any printing is to re-duplicate a single copy-text without alteration. If this aim had been achieved with any constancy in the period of hand-printing, bibliography would probably never have developed beyond the stage of identification and dating. But alterations are found between copies and they spring from a number of causes. They can result from an intentional change made by the author or publisher, or from mistakes occurring at some stage in the transmission of the text from script to print. But the first source of any deviation from the author's intended words may lie in the nature of the copy itself.

Although it may be assumed that the majority of first editions were composed in type directly from the author's manuscript, the copy which often arrived in the printer's office was sometimes far removed from the author's hand. Many books first enjoyed a limited circulation in manuscript form from which copies were made from time to time, any one of which might have formed the ultimate copy for the printer. This applied not only to the *editiones principes* of the early period of printing, but also to many later books, for we read in a number of prefaces that the work was written initially for a small circulation only, for which manuscript copies were no doubt made from the original. Greg[1] informs us that some sermons were compiled from notes taken by a system of shorthand, and the theory has been advanced that the text of some of Shakespeare's plays is derived from this method of composition. In fact, Elizabethan printed drama, the original texts for which were written to be spoken rather than printed, is particularly bedevilled by the variety of copies used by the printer,

[1] W. Greg. Collected papers. Clar. P., (1966), p. 275

some two or three stages removed from the author's manuscript. If the shorthand theory has lately fallen into discredit, the printer's copy of Shakespeare is now thought to have come severally from transcripts of his original manuscripts (or foul papers), some credited to Shakespeare himself and some to other hands; from copies prepared for the actual stage performances (prompt-books), or from transcripts of these; and one play, *Richard III*, is thought to have been reconstructed from memory. All these are in addition to those plays considered to have been set directly from the original manuscripts. An author sometimes directed that a copy should be made, perhaps to render the manuscript more legible for the licenser or in realisation that his own handwriting might prove a source of error to the printer. Simpson[2] cites the example of Henry More, the Platonist, who admitted to "scribling ill favouredly" and who frequently mentioned the transcripts he found necessary to have made of any work he sent to the press. It is obviously important that the bibliographer should endeavour to discover the nature of the printer's copy in each case so as to be able to assess its relationship with the author's original manuscript.

Bibliographical study has shown that, in general, the compositor carefully followed copy and the previously held conviction that he was an ignorant and careless workman is not supported by the comparison of his work with the few pieces of copy that have survived. Where mistakes were made in composition the fault did not always rest with the compositor but can often be attributed to the poor quality of the copy he had to follow. H. S. Bennett has cited[3] certain observations made by authors themselves to support this fact:

> Authors will even acknowledge that their manuscript was "verie darke and enterlined, and I loth to write it out againe". What Henry Holland called his "ragged hand" went straight to the press without any attempt on his part to make a fair copy, while Chettle tells us that he had to transcribe Greene's work which "was il written, as sometimes Greene's hand was none of the best". We read of copy that was "eyther blotted or obscurely penned" or "not legible in sundrie places" so that the printer was forced to admit to faults by which the book is made "obscure in places, or to read contrarye to the Authors meaning".

In his earlier survey[4] Mr. Bennett relates how Andrew Borde confessed

---

[2] P. Simpson. Proof reading in the sixteenth, seventeenth and eighteenth centuries. O.U.P., (1935), p. 36.
[3] H. S. Bennett. English books and readers, 1558-1603. C.U.P., (1965), pp. 286-7.
[4] H. S. Bennett. English books and readers, 1475-1557. C.U.P., (1952), p. 205.

that he wrote *The Pryncyples of Astronomye* (1547), an octavo with 58 pages of text, "with one olde pen with out mendyng".

The subject matter of the text was sometimes another cause of trouble to the compositor, especially if of a highly technical nature, e.g. legal or scientific. Books written in foreign languages also brought occasional apologies from the printer—"the Compositor understandes no Italian". Simpson tells how[5] the translator of Lavater's *Of ghostes and spirites walking by nyght* (1572), having compiled a list of "Faultes escaped in the Print", writes:

> Although some of our Printers be not Homers, neyther seene in Greeke nor Latine, nor sometime exactly in Englishe, yet they can nod and take a nap, as well as any Homer...

Planning the work

The master printer, on receiving copy, had to take certain decisions which are now the responsibility of the publisher as well as those which related particularly to the printing of the work. Apart from questions of format, types to be used, the binding up of certain copies, etc. (with which we are not at present concerned), he would also be faced with the perennial problem of publishing—how many copies should he print? This is a difficult enough decision to face today with its market surveys and statistics, but must have been even more so in earlier times. It is a matter about which we know very little, but from an order issued by the Stationers' Company in 1587 which requires that, with the exception of Bibles, primers, catechisms and similar books printed in non-pareil and brevier (the equivalent of 6- and 8-point types), the number of copies from one impression should not exceed 1,250 to 1,500, we are given a rough idea of the size of the normal edition. Of course, many books of limited appeal were produced in smaller quantities than these, but their totals would fluctuate considerably and are of little value in making a general assessment.

In planning the progress of the work through his printing-office the master printer's decisions would, in the first place, be determined

---

[5] P. Simpson, *op. cit.*, p. 34.

by the number of presses he owned and what other printing he might have in hand. Compared with their more prosperous Continental rivals (Christophe Plantin had 25 presses working in 1576), English printers kept modest establishments. Christopher Barker, Queen's Printer and a leading member of the trade, at the end of the xvi century operated only five presses. Yet even so, the Star Chamber thought fit in a decree of 1615 to limit the number of presses in London. Excepting the King's Printer, who was not mentioned, of the nineteen other printers working at the time, fourteen were permitted to have two presses each, and five were restricted to one each. This number was subsequently modified by a further decree in 1637 permitting no more than two presses to any printer unless he had been Master or Upper Warden of the Stationers' Company, in which case he was allowed three, and unless a printer for some special reason was given express permission by the Archbishop of Canterbury or the Bishop of London. From this it is reasonable to assume that in Elizabethan times the normal complement of the majority of printing-offices was only two presses.

Other factors affecting the organisation of the work were the rate at which type could be set and the sheets printed. The two operations, if an even flow of work were to be achieved, had to keep pace with each other, for the normal practice was to print each sheet as soon as the type had been set and the pages imposed, and to distribute the type immediately after all copies of the sheet had been printed. According to Moxon one press worked by two men could print on one side only 250 sheets an hour. The working day was one of twelve hours with about two hours' break for meals, and so, unless for some reason there were stoppages longer than for minor adjustments to the press or for a few corrections to be made, an average day's output was 1,250 perfected sheets. This figure is confirmed in a remarkable way by one Joseph Baretti who was in Madrid in 1760. As cited by Updike[6] he mentions in his *Journey from London to Genoa* visiting "a large printing-office in the Calle de las Carretas [*sic*], a street so called, and chiefly inhabited by printers and booksellers".

[6] D. B. Updike. Printing types. Vol. II. (2nd ed.), p. 85, footnote. I am indebted to Mr. J. Mosley, Librarian of St. Bride Printing Library for drawing my attention to this source.

Speaking of the fifty workmen employed there and the rate of production he says,

> I asked two fellows at one press, how many sheets they could work off in a day, and was answered five and twenty hundred, which I thought a pretty good number, especially as they were none of the most muscular men.

One has to accept here that "five and twenty hundred" relates to impressions, i.e. single sides of a sheet. Accepting this figure, and 1,250 copies as being the size of an average edition, it would appear theoretically possible in Elizabethan times for all copies of one sheet to be printed in a single day. When this is stated at the rate of one impression every 15 seconds, however, there is little allowance for make-ready, corrections, washing the forme, etc.

Have we any evidence that the compositor could keep up with this rate of working? Moxon[7] certainly suggests he could by stating:

> It is Customary in some Printing-houses that if the *Compositer* or *Press-man* make either the other stand still through the neglect of their contracted Task, that then he who neglected, shall pay him that stands still as much as if he had Wrought.

From a study of Edwarde Allde's printing practices, McKerrow[8] concluded that in Elizabethan times books could be set up, under pressure, by a single compositor, or by two compositors working alternately, at the rate of one sheet, 8 quarto or 16 octavo pages, per day, although he went on to apply this quantity to a much reduced rate of printing than that outlined above. While McKerrow's estimate of the rate of composition may be accepted in the light of the scanty evidence we have on this subject, there were certainly many books, which, because of the nature of their copy or the special care taken with their production, took much longer to set up in type. For example, Greg in considering the printing of the First Folio[9], has shown that to set and distribute one sheet must have taken a compositor two full working days of twelve hours each, and that, given an edition of 1,000 copies, two compositors were required to keep up with the pressman. The allocation of the text between two or more compositors was

---

[7] J. Moxon. Mechanick Exercises; ed. by Herbert Davis & Harry Carter. O.U.P., (1958), p. 328.

[8] R. B. McKerrow. "Edwarde Allde as a typical trade printer". The Library. 4th series. Vol. X, (1929–30), p. 143.

[9] W. W. Greg. The Shakespeare First Folio. Oxford, (1955), pp. 456–7.

common practice whenever two presses were available for working either to keep employees fully occupied or to speed-up production. Evidence of this has often proved of importance in the study of many xvi and xvii century texts because the finished product was to some extent affected by the intelligence and habits of the individual compositors concerned.

Composition

The attitude of the compositor towards his copy is obviously a matter of profound significance in the study of texts. It used to be thought that by far the majority of unlikely readings in early printed editions were caused by ignorant and careless compositors. More recent investigations into compositorial practice have modified this view and, as we have just seen, some authors were not entirely free from blame. Undoubtedly there were many inferior workmen who were directly responsible for a number of the errors found in printed texts, but sometimes changes were made deliberately to rectify the author's own mistakes, or in adhering to certain house rules laid down for compositors to follow. The basic job of the compositor was "to follow copy". Moxon[10] states categorically:

> For by the Laws of Printing, *a* Compositor *is strictly to follow his* Copy, *viz. to observe and do just so much and no more than his* Copy *will bear him out for; so that his* Copy *is to be his Rule and Authority.*

Yet he goes on to add

> But the carelessness of some good Authors, and the ignorance of other Authors, has forc'd Printers to introduce a Custom, which among them is look'd upon as a task and duty incumbent on the Compositor, viz. to discern and amend the bad Spelling and Pointing of his Copy, if it be English...

Moxon's statement of the compositor's responsibilities has been substantiated by Greg's investigation[11] of a manuscript in the British Museum containing Cantos xiv-xlvi of Ariosto's *Orlando Furioso* translated into English verse by Sir John Harington. The copy which is in Sir John's own handwriting was used by Richard Field in setting up the original edition of the work in 1591. After comparing the copy

---

[10] J. Moxon, *op. cit.*, p. 192.

[11] W. W. Greg. "An Elizabethan printer and his copy". The Library. 4th series. Vol. iv, (1923), p. 102–18.

against the printed text, Greg came to the conclusion that the compositors had a recognized standard of spelling and punctuation which was certainly more uniform than that of most writers of the day. However, they were apt to follow the author's spelling whenever they came across a word with which they were unfamiliar. Greg was careful to point out that the standards maintained by Richard Field were not necessarily followed by lesser printing-houses and that with inferior craftsmen changes would result more from mistakes than as a consequence of deliberate policy. On the other hand they would also have been more influenced by their copy and transferred more of the author's spellings to the printed text.

Printing has always had a stabilising effect on spelling and punctuation. From a business efficiency point of view it was good practice for a master printer to insist on certain rules of composition being followed, for a compositor can work much more quickly observing a standardized procedure. Sometimes, however, an immediate need would cause the house-practice to be abandoned, as, for example, when the compositor had to squeeze in or space-out matter at the end of a section or to justify a line. In these situations the flexibility of spelling acceptable in his day gave him the opportunity of contracting and expanding words to make the necessary adjustments.

If the compositor had a certain licence to alter the author's spelling to conform to house-practice, yet, on the other hand, tried to follow copy, particularly when setting up a highly technical passage or one containing unusual words, how are we to discover the author's original spelling? Unfortunately, it must be admitted that, although intelligent deductions can be made from a knowledge of contemporary authorial and compositorial practices, the problem is really insoluble, unless, of course, the author's manuscript has survived. But the effect the compositor can have on a text does not only relate to spelling. Carelessness, a lapse in concentration, or a misunderstanding, perhaps through limited intelligence, can result in words being omitted, added, or changed, or even being set in the wrong order. These are called respectively by the textual critic, omissions, interpolations, substitutions and transpositions. With these kinds of error the character and idiosyncracies of the individual compositor are directly related and it is with this aspect of printing that modern bibliographical investigation has been increasingly occupied. Changes in the spelling of the same words in different parts of a printed text have enabled two or more compositors to be identified, and once this has been established, their individual practices can be noticed (see page 127). From these observances certain deductions can sometimes be made concerning certain doubtful readings. From an examination of spellings in the setting of *Macbeth* for the First Folio, T. Satchell in 1920 distinguished two compositors, whom he designated "A" and "B". E. E. Willoughby in his extensive study on the *Printing of the First Folio*, (1932), found that these two men had had a hand in setting parts of other plays in the Folio and concluded also that "there was another pair of compositors at work" ("C" and "D"). Charlton Hinman in *The Prentice Hand*, (1957) added another compositor "E", an apprentice, who from the number of errors he made obviously had great difficulty in dealing with manuscript copy. By 1955 Greg in *The Shakespeare First Folio* was writing "It is already apparent that a study of the habits of compositors will in future not only influence editorial procedure but may even affect basic assumptions respecting the nature of the text".[12]

The compositor set the type in a composing stick which, when full, he emptied on to a galley, a shallow tray used for assembling type into pages. The modern galley holds two or three pages of type matter, but in Elizabethan times the galley accommodated only a single page at a time. When the page had been made up the catchword and signature (if required) were added at the foot and the running-title at the head. The whole assembly was then tied up with cord to await imposition. When sufficient type-pages had been composed to print one side of a sheet, they were imposed in such a way that the printed sheet, after being perfected, could be folded so that the pages would appear in their correct order. The type-pages were separated from each other by crossbars of spacing material and surrounded by more spacing material or furniture (pieces of wood or metal below type height) to enable them to be locked up in a metal frame or "chase" by means of wedges and quoins. The completed assembly is known

[12] Note E, p. 466.

technically as a "forme" and two formes were required, one to print each side of the sheet.

Until recently it was assumed that for a first edition a compositor would almost inevitably set the pages of type in seriatim order. With a quarto gathering, for example, he would begin with page 1 and work through to page 8. In addition to being the logical way of following copy it was always held that a compositor would set the whole amount of matter required to fill a gathering before commencing to print. It is true that since the last page is always imposed alongside the first, the outer forme is completed last, and the inner forme is ready to go to press first—immediately, in fact, after the penultimate page has been set. But a printer who had insufficient type to complete the setting of a whole gathering before printing would be asking for trouble.[13]

For these very good reasons the seriatim order of composition must have been the usual practice but, as first demonstrated by William H. Bond[14], a compositor might occasionally set and impose the pages of one forme at a time to avoid the danger of running out of sorts. To work in this way he needed to cast-off the amount of copy for the pages of the other forme of the gathering. To take the example of a simple quarto gathering again, where pages 1, 4, 5 and 8 occupy the outer forme and pages 2, 3, 6 and 7 the inner, he would set page 1, cast-off pages 2 and 3, set pages 4 and 5, cast-off 6 and 7, and finally set page 8. In this way the printer needed to have only 2 or 3 formes in type at a time to provide a continuous flow of work for both compositor and pressman, whereas the seriatim order requires 3 or 4 formes in type at a time. Of course, when a compositor composed type for a page-for-page reprint he worked whenever possible from a printed copy of the previous edition and could then set seriatim or by formes, whichever method he found more convenient. The evidence for setting by formes is considered in the next chapter.

Imposition

Schemes of imposition relating to various formats have been described in McKerrow and other textbooks and need not be repeated

[13] McKerrow. Introduction to bibliography, p. 32.
[14] "Casting off copy by Elizabethan printers: a theory". P.B.S.A. Vol. 42, (1948), pp. 281–91.

here. It should be noted, however, that in his diagram of type-pages imposed for a quarto[15], McKerrow has shown the two formes incorrectly placed in relation to each other. Moxon in his illustration of imposed type-pages (Plate 26) places them on their sides with the inner forme above the outer, as follows:

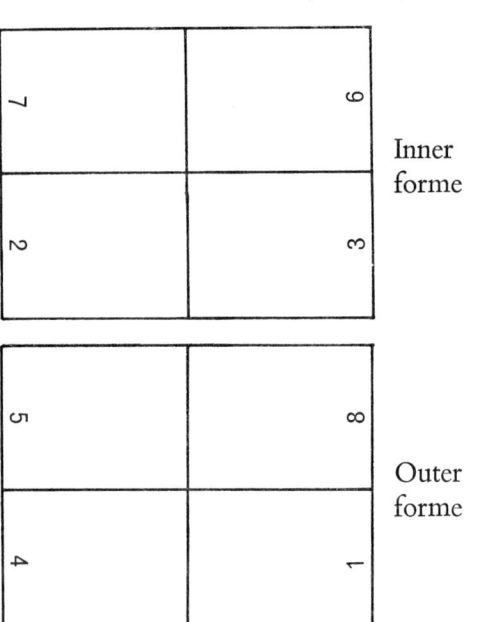

Inner forme

Outer forme

Bowers has shown[16] that this arrangement is essential when perfecting to enable the sheet to be turned end for end so that the pins in the tympan go through the identical holes in the paper and give a true register.

Further evidence substantiating Moxon's arrangement is provided by the way in which headlines were normally transferred from forme to forme. The headline added to the top of the page in most books to accommodate the running-title usually remained constant throughout the book or a large section of it, so once a set of headlines had been provided for the type-pages in the first forme, it was used over and over again in subsequent formes. The headlines were, in fact, considered as part of the skeleton—the furniture surrounding the type-pages. To save time, the compositor avoided constructing a new skeleton for each forme and repeatedly used the original one. This practice also ensured that the type-pages were consistently registered, and Moxon gives very clear instructions to the compositor

[15] Introduction to bibliography, pp. 16-17.

[16] "Headlines in early books." English Institute Annual, 1941. N.Y., Columbia Univ. Pr., (1942), p. 190.

to place each piece of the skeleton in precisely the same position in the new forme as it had occupied in the old. The relative positions of the headlines on their transference from forme to forme is of great importance bibliographically because of the information they afford on the method of printing (see page 129).

Some books are found in which the number of leaves per gathering is only half that normally expected from the format. For instance, octavos are found with gatherings of 4 leaves and sextodecimos with 8 leaves. This is the result of half-sheet imposition. It was used both to save type, since printing could commence earlier, and, as suggested by McKerrow, to "facilitate the economical distribution of work between compositor and pressman". Even if the entire book was not constructed of half-sheets, the procedure was frequently adopted for the last gathering when the amount of copy left to be composed was insufficient to fill a whole sheet.

There were two methods of half-sheet imposition. In the case of an octavo, the more usual one was for the printer to take the first 8 pages only and to impose them as for a gathering in 4's in one chase. After printing and perfecting, the sheet was cut in two to obtain two identical gatherings each of 4 leaves. The lay-out of the single forme would be as follows:

A3		A2
4	5	6	3
1	8	7	2
A		A4

The alternative, but less common, method requires the outer formes of two consecutive gatherings in 4's to be imposed together in one chase and printed, the sheet turned end to end and perfected from the inner formes of the two gatherings (see overleaf). By this method two separate gatherings (A and B) are printed each with half the normal number of leaves.

It will be apparent that either method of half-sheet imposition requires a different set of type-pages to be arranged in the forme than for full-sheet work. This fact is of significance when variant formes are being examined and in tracing the transfer of headlines from forme to forme.

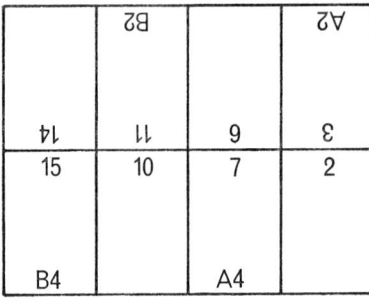

Outer formes of A and B
in 4's in one chase

Inner formes of A and B
in 4's in one chase

Presswork

Whatever the method of imposition, it was normal for printing to begin immediately the first forme had been composed. The forme was placed on the bed of the press and inked with two leather balls; the paper placed in position on the tympan; the frisket lowered over the paper which in turn was brought down on the type; the whole wound under the platen and the lever pulled. Until about 1800, because of the relatively small size of the platen, two pulls were required to print a forme, so that after the first pull the carriage with its forme of type and paper had to be wound further under the platen in position for the second pull.[17] After the impression, the platen was raised, the carriage wound back, the tympan and frisket opened and the printed sheet taken off and stacked ready for perfecting. It was usual to print

[17] There were a few exceptions to this procedure. If a small size of paper was used, the printer could arrange his type and paper at right-angles to the normal method so that they would be covered by the platen. Only one pull to the forme would then be required. See D. Foxon, "On printing 'at one pull' and distinguishing impressions by point-holes". The Library. 5th series. Vol. xi, (1956), pp. 284–5.

the inner forme before the outer because the composition of its type-pages was completed first, but there are examples of books which show from the relative position of their running-titles that the outer formes were the first through the press.

The method of inking by dabbing the forme with two leather balls whose surfaces were well covered with ink sometimes resulted in the displacement of type. If the type-pages had been insecurely locked and the sorts were loose in the chase, there was a likelihood that at least one sort, sticking to an ink-ball, would be lifted from the forme. If it went unnoticed and was not immediately replaced, the printed page would be missing a letter, and if, as was sometimes the case, the gap was filled by any sort ready to hand, a minor variation in the state of the text would result (see page 119).

While the presswork continued the next forme would be prepared and if the work had been evenly allocated, the compositor and pressman were able to work in unison and avoid wasting each other's time. As soon as the required number of impressions of a forme had been taken, the type would be distributed so as to be available for further composition. We have seen that on distribution the skeleton of the forme was saved and transferred to a forme being prepared for the press. If it were transferred to the very next forme, e.g. an outer forme used to perfect an inner, some delay would inevitably ensue while the pressman rinsed the wrought-off forme and the compositor transferred the skeleton. However, even though there was this delay, the use of one skeleton was common practice before the Restoration and Bowers has suggested[18] that the method was adopted because only three men were required, the compositor, the pressman and his assistant, whereas the preparation of two formes whilst one was being printed would probably have involved an additional compositor. This second procedure, however, enabled the second forme to be locked-up for the press whilst the first was being printed and for a third to have its type-pages positioned on the stone ready to receive the skeleton from the first forme after all the copies required from it had been pulled. With this method two skeletons would be needed each with its own

[18] "Notes on running-titles as bibliographical evidence". The Library. 4th series. Vol. xix, (1939), p. 324.

set of headlines: one set would be used in the inner forme of each sheet in the entire volume, and the other set in the outer forme. As there was no delay in effecting the transfer it is not surprising that the two skeleton method became more common by the latter part of the xvii century.

By using two skeletons, the work of the pressman was speeded-up, but not that of the compositor who still had to impose the same number of formes. But if the pressman, when working with one skeleton was able to keep ahead of the compositor, as, for instance, when he was printing a small edition, then there was no advantage in improving his speed with a second skeleton. This was first pointed out by Dr. Hinman[19] who concluded that two sets of headlines will appear in a book printed on a single press only if the edition was large enough for composition to have kept ahead of presswork. The number of sets used, therefore, can give a very rough idea of edition size.

Until comparatively recently it was thought that after being printed on one side the sheets had to be dried before being perfected. McKerrow,[20] for example, mentions the drying of sheets on strings or wooden battens fixed across the room when the first side had been printed as well as after the sheet had been perfected. Professor R. C. Bald,[21] who questioned this statement, referred to Moxon for corroboration but there discovered[22] that the sheets after receiving their first impression were immediately stacked in a pile which was turned upside-down as soon as the new forme was at the press ready for perfecting. On asking a present-day printer which was correct, Bald was told that both were, as it depended on the quality of the ink: a cheap ink dries quickly and would not set-off, whereas the best quality ink dries much more slowly and would easily set-off. As the average quality of English ink, at least in Moxon's day, was poor, Bald had no hesitation in accepting the procedure outlined by Moxon rather than that of McKerrow. In further support of Professor Bald

---

[19] "New uses for headlines as bibliographical evidence". The English Institute Annual, 1941. N.Y., Columbia U.P., (1942), p. 209.

[20] *Op. cit.*, p. 23.

[21] "Evidence and inference in bibliography". English Institute Annual, 1941, (1942), p. 179.

[22] Mechanick Exercises; ed. by Davis & Carter, p. 296, etc.

it can be argued that hanging sheets out to dry the ink after printing the first side would be unlikely if only for the reason that the drying of the paper itself would be hastened. Hand-made paper required damping for printing—a long and tedious process—and one which the printer would avoid repeating, if possible, when perfecting the sheets. It would appear that the quick drying qualities of poor ink were a decided advantage in working the sheets.[23]

It is now generally accepted that Moxon's description of the process was followed by the majority of printers. Sheets were, therefore, perfected in the same order in which they had been printed on the first side. This, as we shall see (page 119), is a matter of some importance in considering textual variants found in different copies of the same edition.

Proofs and corrections

A consensus of available evidence seems to show that it was not the custom during the xvi and xvii centuries for proofs to be sent to an author for his corrections. Unless he was indisposed and "confined to his chamber", he was expected to attend regularly at the printing office to check the composition of the sheets. To read every sheet the author would need to make a daily visit and to time his arrival so as to approve the first pulls taken from the formes before the working of each sheet was commenced. We find evidence of this in a number of books of the period in which the printer has added a note of explanation for the errors contained in the text. For instance, in *The Droomme of Doomesday*, translated and collected by George Gascoigne, and printed by Gabriell Cawood, (1576), we read:

An aduertiſement of the Prynter to the Reader.

VNderſtand (gentle Reader) that whiles this worke was in the preſſe, it pleaſed God to viſit the tranſlatour therof with ſickneſſe. So that being vnable himſelfe to attend the dayly proofes, he apoynted a ſeruaunt of his to ouerſee the ſame. Who (being not ſo well acquainted with the matter as his maiſter was) there haue paſſed ſome faultes much contrary vnto both our meanings and deſires. The vvhich I haue therefore collected into this Table. Deſiring euery Reader that vvyll vouchſafe to peruſe this booke, that he vvyll firſte correct thoſe faultes and then iudge accordingly.

[23] Mr. J. Mosley confirms from personal experience of hand-press printing that worked damp sheets can be piled on each other without danger of set-off. He believes this is made possible because the type bites deeply into the damp paper. The risk of set-off was increased when printing with large types (double pica and upwards) and it was the custom in these circumstances to interleave the sheets with blank paper.

That this was common practice may be seen from other examples collected by Mr. Percy Simpson and published in his *Proof-reading in the sixteenth, seventeenth and eighteenth centuries*, (1935).

If the author's visit was delayed and he was late in arriving at the press, he would probably find that the printing of the next sheet had already commenced. As the majority of printers of the xvi and early xvii centuries were restricted to one or two presses, none could afford to delay printing whilst waiting for the author to appear. Furthermore, they were unwilling to destroy the uncorrected sheets already printed before the author's arrival, but stacked them in the same pile as the corrected sheets. This explains why we find variations in the text between different pulls of sheets or formes in copies of the same edition of a book. Verification of the regular attendance at the press by the author and of the mixture of corrected and uncorrected sheets is seen in a note to the reader[24] from the printer of William Gouge's *The Whole Armor of God*, (1616):

> I haue taken the best care that I could to set foorth this worke in the best manner that I could for true Printing: yet I cannot denie that some faults haue escaped on some copies: such diligence hath been vsed by the Author in correcting his worke, that so oft as his leasure permitted him, he came himselfe to the Presse, and as he found a fault amended it, so that there are very few faults but are amended in most of the Bookes. If therefore thou meete with any slippe that may make the sence obscure, compare thy Booke with some others, and thou maiest finde it amended.

Reading a pull at the printing-office was not perhaps the ideal method for an author to check for corrections. If printing was continuing he would be concerned that any mistake he had found should be corrected as soon as possible, and so probably gave his instructions after a single reading. This may explain why in many books further errors were discovered while the sheets were still being worked. Printing would again be halted temporarily and the necessary corrections made. In some books of the period we find a progression of variants, proof that the press was stopped a number of times before all copies of a sheet had been printed. For corrections to be found in only a few copies of an edition implies that the error in the sheet had not been discovered until quite late in the run.

In the absence of the author it would appear that the master-printer himself or an employee checked the work of the compositor.

[24] First cited by E. E. Willoughby in The Library. 4th series, vol, xi, (1930), p. 104.

Exactly how far he went to match it with the author's manuscript, or whether he was concerned just with the corrections of literals, is not known, but the number of books in which variants are found suggest that some degree of responsibility was accepted by the printer. Even so, errors slipped through and are often found listed in the book to enable the reader to make his own corrections. John Beale, the printer of *The Whole Armor of God*, mentioned above, was obviously insufficiently troubled even to do this, for the last sentence of his note suggests that the reader himself should track down copies of the book containing corrected sheets to amend the errors in his own copy! A printed list of errors was preferred by printers to the printing and pasting-in of small errata-slips, no doubt because of the time this would have involved. Similarly, the printer resisted making alterations by hand although some books exhibit this form of correction. The author was sometimes responsible for these, particularly in presentation copies, but when made by the printer, Simpson[25] suggests they were probably the result of compulsion.

A more extensive error, for instance the suppression of a whole passage through fear of reprisals from the authorities who were active during this period in rooting out any suggestion of heresy or sedition, would involve a cancel. The offending leaf or leaves would be deleted and replaced by the corrected text printed either on a separate sheet, or, if the decision to cancel was made during printing, on spare leaves not required at the end of the book or in the preliminaries. The evaluation of variants and detection of cancels is considered in the next chapter.

[25] P. Simpson. Proof reading in the sixteenth, seventeenth and eighteenth centuries. O.U.P., (1935), p. 30.

Chapter 11

Analytical Bibliography

As we have seen, the major purpose of the bibliographical study of books printed during the xvi–xviii centuries has been to establish, so far as possible, the author's authentic text. The results of individual studies, depending on their scope, are either reported in the journals of the various bibliographical societies, or published as full-scale critical bibliographies. The highest aim of the latter is to provide as complete a picture as possible of the life history of each work examined. The process involves, to begin with, analysing as many copies of each edition of each work as is practicable in order to discover the differences between editions and between copies of the same edition; and, secondly, recording the results in the form of a bibliographical description of an ideal copy of each edition and issue with explanatory notes concerning the existence of variant copies.

A good deal of evidence can be obtained from an analysis of a single copy of a book, but this cannot be relied upon to furnish an accurate description of the whole edition. As many copies as possible must be examined to determine and describe the characteristics of an "ideal copy" so that a standard of reference may be established against which all other copies of the same edition may be collated. Most of the work of analysis demands, therefore, a comparison of copies, and at once we are confronted with one of the major difficulties facing bibliographers. Copies of the texts needed for analysis will be scattered among libraries of institutions and private individuals in many parts of the world so that a physical comparison of one copy with another is frequently impossible. If one is fortunate enough to be able to take a "control" copy around with one, a copy which exhibits so far as is known all the characteristics of an ideal copy, then the difficulty is overcome. But the possession of a control copy for each edition of the works to be studied generally presupposes a large personal collection. It may be possible in some cases to borrow copies for this purpose, but bibliographers have to rely mainly on keeping extensive descriptive notes of the books examined. The trouble with taking notes is that they often prove inadequate when some new feature is discovered, for example, a previously unknown variant. It may then prove necessary to retrace one's steps to ensure that the variant has not been overlooked in copies already collated.

One way of overcoming the drudgery of detailed note-taking is to equip oneself with a microfilm reproduction of the book to act as the control copy. This, it must be admitted, entails expenses beyond the reach of many bibliographers, particularly since a portable reader is a necessary accessory for use in those libraries not possessing microfilming equipment. Professor Bowers, who spent some ten years compiling a descriptive bibliography of Restoration drama, was fortunate in being subsidised by two universities which enabled him to carry around a complete microfilm of every edition and issue of the plays with which he was concerned. He reported to the Bibliographical Society[1] on the advantages he found in using microfilm:

> This method of comparison is not only, curiously, faster than the conventional way of comparing copies against one's notes, but it is to the highest degree more accurate. I need hardly say that in this process I have been able to discover reimpositions, partial resettings, new closely reprinted editions, and miscellaneous variants to an astonishing number and to an extent which, according to my experience, would have proved impossible by any other method. Not the least valuable, I estimate, has been my ability to detect the making up of copies from sheets or leaves of various editions and thus to warn my readers where they are and of what they are composed. Conversely, if no record to this effect is found in my listing of the copies, the user of any recorded copy can be assured that it is the assigned edition for every leaf. I believe this method of comparison against a constant control is good scientific bibliography and is, in fact, the only safe method to employ.

Not many bibliographers will be in the same fortunate position as Professor Bowers and will probably have to rely on extensive notes made of the relevant details of each copy. However, the acquisition of photostat or xerographic copies of title-pages and other important features can, for a reasonable outlay, reduce the amount of descriptive note-taking.

[1] "Purposes of descriptive bibliography, with some remarks on methods." The Library, 5th series. vol. viii. (1953), p. 6.

The orderly arrangement of the results of one's analysis is best accomplished by classifying the copies of each work examined into editions and issues noting any variant states that exist of each. We need now to consider the evidence which enables the bibliographer to determine the characteristics of each group.

Edition

An edition consists of the total number of copies printed from a single setting of type. Whereas in modern times an edition may run through a number of impressions printed either from standing type or from a copy made of the original setting, during the period of hand-printing it was not usual for a printer to keep his type standing. He distributed his type immediately after printing partly because he could not afford to keep his most valuable asset locked up awaiting a possible reprinting, and partly because of the laws of the Stationers' Company which, as we have seen, limited the number of copies of an edition to between 1,250 and 1,500. The need for further copies of a book, therefore, almost invariably entailed re-setting the type, and as a result the more popular books ran into a number of editions whereas nowadays they would merely have been reprinted.

The bibliographer is mostly concerned, therefore, with the identification and orderly arrangement of distinct editions, but occasionally he might come across a book which shows a new setting of type mixed either with type kept standing from a previous printing, or with the old sheets which had never been issued. The question that has to be answered is whether both of these examples should be classified as a new edition or as a new issue of the existing edition.

The first mixture—from standing type and reset material—usually results from a decision to print additional copies taken either before the first printing was finished or immediately after completion but before the type of the last sheets had been distributed. The type kept standing was, therefore, normally restricted to the final sheets of the book or to the preliminaries if they had been printed after the text. The reset material would in these cases cover the greater part of the book and, taking this into conjunction with the intention of the printer, which was to print a new edition, we are justified in considering this category of book as constituting a separate edition. Printers sometimes used standing type illegally to overcome the limitation on the number of copies permitted from one edition. Type relating to various isolated parts of the book was left standing and concealed in the midst of newly set matter, so avoiding much distribution and resetting. This deliberate flouting of the laws of the Stationers' Company was very difficult to detect, and if such copies can be detected now, they are, according to Bowers, best classified as new editions.

In the second mixture, new sheets are combined with old. This normally resulted from a substantial addition to or continuation of the text being appended to the old sheets and issued with a new title-page. McKerrow prefers to classify this type of book as "a new issue with additional matter", whereas Bowers calls it a new edition. McKerrow's argument[2] is that "there is no new edition of what was originally printed, since we have merely the remainder of the old sheets; nor can it be a new edition of the added part, for that never appeared before". It is apparent that McKerrow in reaching his conclusion was thinking of the two separate parts of the book and not of the result as a whole, and as Bowers points out[3]

> there is difficulty in McKerrow's classification. For example, if in such a book the original sheets of the first part were finally exhausted and reset, to carry forward McKerrow it would still not be a new edition since the original setting of the second part would logically under such circumstances become re-issued sheets; and the cycle continues.

The methods of identifying and dating an edition, as discussed in the previous chapter on incunabula, may be applied to hand-printed books of the xvi-xviii centuries and need no repetition here. Mention should be made, however, of the work of Mr. R. A. Sayce who, in the *Library* (March, 1966), suggested methods for the placing and dating of printed books based upon a comparison of compositorial practices as exhibited by over 2,800 books mainly of the xvii and xviii centuries. Mr. Sayce, who acknowledges Mr. Giles Barber's pioneering article[4] in this field, has discovered that certain printing localities followed

[2] McKerrow, *op. cit.*, p. 178.

[3] Principles of bibliographical description, p. 111. For a more detailed consideration of edition, pages 108–13 should be consulted.

[4] "Catchwords and press figures at home and abroad". Bookcollector, vol. ix, (1960), pp. 301–7,

distinctive practices particularly in the way books were signed, catch-words set, pages numbered, press-figures added and dates composed in imprints. For example, he concludes, *inter alia*, that the use of inverted parentheses ")(" for signing preliminaries is a peculiar characteristic of German and Basle printing; the inclusion of catchwords only on pages other than those bearing signatures is mostly indicative of Lyons printing in the xvi century; page numbers found enclosed in ornaments are almost exclusively German; press numbers are almost certain proof of English origin and in composing dates the use of commas instead of full stops, e.g. M,DCC,LII is quite frequent in xviii century London books. The value of these findings is that the placing and dating of books may be achieved without a specialized knowledge of the history of printing, but Mr. Sayce admits that a wider survey is required to substantiate his findings.

In order to show the history of a particular text it is necessary for the bibliographer to place the various editions of the work in their order of publication. In the majority of cases this is merely a matter of arranging by date, but when an edition is undated, or two editions bear the same date, then the problem requires further investigation. As a general rule, an edition other than the first was set up from a copy of the preceding edition. If the earlier one was a well-planned piece of printing, the compositor of the later edition would save himself much time and labour by following the original setting as closely as possible. This was naturally the usual procedure and in consequence copies from two editions are often difficult to differentiate at first glance. There are certain kinds of evidence, however, that enable them to be separated and which may, for convenience, be grouped according to the sequence of actions performed by the second compositor:

(1) lay-out and casting-off.

(2) following the original page setting.

(3) selecting types for the resetting.

(1) The great advantage to the compositor in following a copy of the previous edition is that the work involved in determining the dimensions of the type-page and in casting-off to estimate the amount

of paper required is already done for him. Providing he has the same size of type available he will know the measure of the type-line, the number of lines to the page and the number of sheets required for the book. But he is in a position to make certain economies—he would doubtless be instructed to make them by the master printer—which were not practicable for the original compositor. In the first edition it may not have been possible to calculate the exact number of sheets required to accommodate the text, and we often find odd leaves or half-gatherings at the beginning or end of a book which cost the printer just as much to work as a full sheet. But the second compositor could adjust the size of his page, either by increasing the measure or the number of lines, to fit the text into a given number of whole sheets. Thus when we find two copies of a book, one of which is collated A—P⁴Q², and the other A—P⁴, the second is likely to be the later edition. The method adopted by the second compositor in fitting his text may generally be ascertained by an examination of the type-pages.

In the same way the compositor of a later edition can, if he wishes, alter the way in which the gatherings were signed. The original compositor almost invariably began setting his type with page 1 of the text, leaving the preliminaries until later, since on many occasions they were the last to be completed by the author. The compositor would either sign the first gathering of the text "A", leaving the preliminaries to be signed with an arbitrary symbol, e.g. "*", or he could take a chance on the final length of the preliminaries and allocate "A" for them, signing the first gathering of the text "B". The first alternative was the safer method, for if the preliminaries proved too long for one gathering, the compositor could always double-up on his signing, e.g. **, ***, and still maintain a recognizable sequence. If he had signed the preliminaries "A", however, he would be forced to introduce a different method of signing the second and subsequent sheets. He might, for example, resort to lower-case letters, when the collation of his book might appear as A⁴ a—b⁴ c², B—K⁴ L². The second compositor, however, could simplify the make-up of the book and clarify the order of gatherings for the binder by signing them A—N⁴. McKerrow[5] formulated the general principle:

[5] McKerrow, *op. cit.*, p. 190.

that an edition in which the signatures are all of one alphabet, beginning with A and proceeding regularly, is likely to be later than an edition in which the preliminary leaves have a separate signature.

(2) When following the original setting, the compositor may have decided to copy it strictly line-for-line, or he may have wished to give himself a little flexibility in working and have copied only page-for-page. In the latter case he would not worry about making an exact resetting so long as he finished the page with the same word as the original and could use the same catchword at the bottom. Evidence in two copies of a book of the same page-endings, even though the line-endings are dissimilar is proof enough that one copy is a resetting of the other, for no two compositors working from a manuscript would achieve such a parallel result throughout the length of a book.

In establishing the order of editions we can sometimes take advantage of the second compositor's errors in copying. Occasionally he misread his copy in such a way that the cause of his mistake is self-evident, as, for example, with an alteration in paragraph division. If in his copy the last line of a paragraph was almost full, it would be easy for a compositor not to notice that a new paragraph was intended and to carry on setting type without a break. Similarly, he sometimes repeated hyphenated words unnecessarily. If owing to slight variations in spacing during composition the position of a hyphenated word had moved from the end of a line in its original setting to, say, midway along a line in the second setting, the hyphen should obviously be omitted as it no longer serves any purpose. Sometimes, however, an unthinking compositor would retain the hyphen, offering us strong evidence that the copy in which it appears was printed from a direct resetting of the other. Evidence can come not only from mistakes in resetting, but also from unsuccessful attempts on the part of the second compositor to correct errors in the previous edition (for examples see McKerrow, pp. 198-9).

When an exact reprint has been made line-for-line, it is not only very difficult to establish the order of the two editions, but equally to distinguish one from the other. However, although his copying of the original setting of the text may be immaculate, the second compositor would have no reason to follow the exact positioning of a signature at the foot of a page. He would doubtless set his own signatures in accordance with his usual practice and so separate editions may sometimes be recognized by the different positions occupied by signatures relative to the last line of the pages on which they occur.

(3) Additional evidence may be offered by the type itself. In the xvi and xvii centuries, italic and swash capitals were often used indiscriminately, hence the second compositor might well have selected a swash capital when copying an italic capital in the original setting and vice-versa. Furthermore, unless the second setting was done very soon after the first, it is unlikely that all the types would still be available. The use of different initials and ornaments, in particular, frequently enables two editions to be distinguished. If the substitute type, etc., was of a larger or smaller size than the original, the second compositor would have to crowd-in or space-out his matter to maintain a page-for-page setting. In a comparison of two copies of a book, therefore, one having a normal setting on a particular page, but the second showing an awkward spacing of the type near the foot, the first copy may be taken to belong to the earlier edition and the second to a new edition closely reprinted from the former. Evidence of copy-fitting was used recently to establish which of two editions of Caxton's printing of *The Dictes or sayengis of the philosophres* was the earlier. Mr. G. Legman[6] demonstrated that edition II was printed from edition I because when the two are compared page by page, the next-to-last line on various pages in II is seen to have been loosely set, or the final line to have been crowded, in order to make each of these pages end evenly at the last word on the corresponding pages in I. To a compositor spacing was most important and he had one advantage denied to his modern counterpart—the choice of altering the spelling of a word. He could usually find some acceptable alternative spelling which would either fill out his space or reduce the matter to be set. This would differentiate two editions and, with the additional evidence of awkward spacing, might help to establish the order in which they were printed.

[6] "A Word on Caxton's *Dictes*". The Library. 5th series. Vol. iii, (1948), pp. 155–85. But see also Curt F. Buhler. "Some observations on *The Dictes and Sayings of the Philosophers*". The Library. 5th series. vol. viii, (1955), pp. 77–88.

5

For further explanations and additional evidence the reader is referred to McKerrow's *Introduction to bibliography*.[7] In particular, he should note the ruler method for determining whether or not two copies of a book belong to the same edition. McKerrow recommends laying a ruler so that it runs from one full stop to another ten or twelve lines apart on a selected page in one copy and noting the letters cut by the edge. The same procedure is repeated on the corresponding page of the other copy and the two sequences of letters compared. If they are the same, both copies must be from the same setting of type; if not, they are from two separate editions providing, of course, the page chosen for the investigation does not happen to be a cancel in some copies.

Issue

As may be seen from the definition given on page 22 "issue" is a term which relates to the act of publishing as well as to printing. When an edition is put on sale for the first time, the copies so marketed form the first issue of that edition. In many cases they will remain the only issue. Other copies of the same edition however are sometimes found with a different title-page and possibly with some alteration to the preliminaries or to minor parts of the text. These copies form a new or second issue of the edition and were there further similar alterations in other copies involving in each case a new title-page then subsequent issues would be formed.

The reasons behind a new issue are many, some representing genuine attempts to improve the contents and to bring a book up to date, others, perhaps, not so honourably conceived. New material which had come to light after the first copies of the edition had been published, may have been set up as an appendix to the main text or added to the preliminaries. In some cases the publisher may have wished to correct a passage containing a gross error, or may have been forced to suppress another lest it should give offence and invoke an action for libel. The copyright of the book may have changed hands after its initial appearance, and the new owners would no doubt wish to draw attention to the new publishing arrangements by means of

[7] pp. 180-99.

an altered imprint. A change in the bookseller may have been noted in the same way. On the other hand, a publisher may have wished to stimulate the sale of a book, pretending it had been revised, by cancelling the original title-leaf and re-issuing the remaining copies with a new one bearing a later date, perhaps with an improved title.

Other circumstances in the printing-office sometimes resulted in copies of an edition being altered in such a way that the bibliographer finds it convenient to classify them as a new or re-issue. For example, when a printer found that he could not make up additional copies of a book because the required number of sheets was lacking, it was necessary for him to reset the type involved. If the demand for these additional copies had come some time after initial publication, he could most probably issue them with a new title-leaf to bring the book up to date. These copies constitute a new issue. Occasionally printers would cautiously print far less copies of a book than the 1250 or so they were allowed, being prepared to keep the type standing for a second run if the demand warranted. By the time the formes were put on the press again, some type may have become pied or even accidentally distributed. Any resetting would usually be insufficient to justify calling these copies a new edition and they are accordingly classed as a new issue.

Copies of a book were, and still are, occasionally produced in a special form to appear simultaneously with the ordinary commercial edition. They may comprise impressions on large paper, or contain additional illustrations, or again, may be printed from a re-imposition of the type-pages in a different format, e.g. from quarto to folio. These and other examples are fully examined by Bowers[8], but generally, since they are printed from the same setting of type and do not constitute a new edition, and since they appear at the same time (or roughly so) as the normal trade copies and therefore are not a re-issue, they are best regarded as a "separate issue".

It should be clear from the foregoing that a re-issue should be suspected if some copies of an edition exhibit a different title leaf. Minor alterations, e.g. to dates, or to the name of printer, publisher and bookseller, were, however, sometimes made during the course of

[8] Principles of bibliographical description, pp. 80–108.

printing by stopping the press and changing the type in the forme. Such copies do not form a re-issue but merely exhibit a variant state of the title-page. In the case of a variant title, the leaf on which it is printed will still be conjugate with its partner in the first gathering, but in a re-issue, the original title-leaf would have been deleted and a new one added. This would normally have been tipped-in on the stub left by the deletion and evidence of this should always be sought after. Of course, the whole of the first gathering including the title-leaf may have been cancelled and a new one substituted, but in this case the preliminaries as well as the title would no doubt have undergone some alteration. In any event, the preliminaries should always be checked when a re-issue is suspected for evidence of matter added to, or substituted for, the original, or even for a straightforward deletion. Similarly, where a re-issue has been established, it is as well to check through the text for some evidence of re-setting following the methods previously outlined under '*Edition*'.

Evidence of new or substituted matter may come from the nature of the paper. It may be of a distinctly different quality, texture or colour, and probably the best clue for ascertaining the priority of issues is obtained from this and from variant watermarks. If in one issue the paper shows consistently the same watermark throughout each copy, but in another issue the preliminaries are printed wholly or in part on paper bearing a different watermark, then the latter may be considered the later of the two. This and further evidence obtainable from paper is discussed more fully on page 122.

Variant state

The third category of bibliographical classification is the "variant state", "state", or "variant"—the terms are synonymous. Variant states form part of an edition or issue and are copies which exhibit some minor alteration to the text not found in other copies. The alteration was made during the course of printing, or occasionally, as we have seen, after publication providing the printer considered its importance insufficient to warrant a new title-leaf. The accepted definition of variant state was given on page 23 and it remains to examine this a little more fully and to note some conclusions of importance to textual studies that have been drawn about the presence of such alterations.

McKerrow grouped variant states according to whether they were made by accident or intent. As we have seen, accidents sometimes occurred during the course of printing which necessitated partial resetting. For instance, when type was "pulled" by inking three states of the text were often produced: the state before the accident, the state after the type had been dislodged but before it had been noticed by the pressman, and finally, if the missing types were eventually replaced by wrong sorts, by sorts of the wrong fount, or reset in the wrong order, a third state was formed. Obviously, the state with the correct text is usually the earliest.

Another cause of this kind of variant was an accident to the type in the forme. It may have become loose and pied through the pressure of printing or the forme may have been upset when it was unlocked for correcting. Here again an incorrect resetting would result in a variant state in the copies subsequently printed. Accidental variants, however, when they can be established as such, are of minor importance to the editor or textual critic: it is those made intentionally that are significant.

We have seen that type in the forme was often corrected whilst it was at the press after an early pull had been checked by either author or printer. The press would be stopped, the forme unlocked, corrections made and printing resumed. From the considerable evidence we have of variant states in different copies of the same edition, it is clear that printers seldom made any attempt to separate uncorrected sheets from those corrected. It is of the utmost importance, of course, for an editor or textual critic to know which is the corrected text particularly when it is known that the author was in the habit of attending the press to check proofs. In many cases the corrected state will be obvious, for instance, where a spelling mistake has been rectified, punctuation improved, or grammar corrected, but in others it may prove very difficult to determine. Such decisions are really beyond the responsibility of the bibliographer, for his function is limited to revealing the presence of variants and only when there is incontrovertible supporting evidence should he point out which are corrections.

In all other cases the verdict should be left to the textual critic. However, there is one important fact which is relevant to such considerations. Only one side of a piece of paper can be printed at a time and so the unit of printing, and correcting, is the forme and not the sheet. It is reasonable to assume, therefore, that if a variant is found on one of the pages printed by the inner forme, say page 2 of a quarto, and it is obvious that this represents a correction, variants found on other pages printed from the same forme (3, 6 and 7), are also corrections. But this reasoning cannot be extended to variants found in pages printed by the outer forme (1, 4, 5 and 8 in a quarto), as they were produced by a different set of of circumstances and at a different time. In fact it is completely fortuitous if the whole sheet in some copies is in the corrected state because a corrected forme may be backed by either a corrected or uncorrected one depending entirely upon when the corrections were made.

An added complication is sometimes the degree of correction, for on some occasions the press was stopped more than once and a forme may exist in three or more states. A. K. McIlwraith[9], for example, found on examining the first quarto edition of Massinger's play *The Bondman* (1624), that of the 22 formes used in its printing, 5 exist in three states (evidence of two stoppages), and 2 in four states (three stoppages).[10] McIlwraith also found that in five sheets out of six the distribution of corrected and uncorrected states of the text was consistent with the conclusion of Professor R. C. Bald that all copies of a sheet would normally be perfected in the order of their first

[9] "Marginalia on press-corrections in books of the early 17th century". The Library. 5th series, vol. iv, (1950), pp. 238–48.

[10] This may have been due to the hasty reading of a pull by the author in his concern to have any mistakes corrected as soon as possible (see page 106), but Charlton Hinman has postulated another possible reason. In his investigation of 80 copies of the First Folio, he found evidence that pages 281 and 292 had been proof-read. These pages had been imposed side by side in the forme, but whereas page 292 displayed some proof-reader's marks, page 281 did not. Hinman suggests that the reason for this anomaly lies in the probability that "the proof-reader handed his corrections to the compositor as soon as he had read one page of an impression taken from the forme for proofing purposes and then used another impression as proof for the second page. Such a procedure is entirely plausible, since it would obviously save considerable time". *See* Charlton Hinman, "Mark III: new light on the proof reading for the First Folio of Shakespeare". Studies in Bibliography. Vol. III, (1950–1), pp. 145–53.

printing, and not with the supposition made by McKerrow that sheets were collected more or less haphazardly for perfecting.

Other alterations, if they can be proved to have been made during printing, or at least before publication, may be classified under the heading of variant state. The possibility of a stop-press alteration to an imprint or title has already been mentioned when considering '*Issue*', but another case of variant title may be cited. Mr. G. W. Cole has shown[11] from evidence found in a book dated 1629 that a missing leaf in a gathering instead of being blank, as may be suspected if nothing appears to be missing from the text, may have contained an alternative title of the same setting as that found in the book but with a different publisher's or bookseller's name in the imprint. This would be an instance of a book whose publication was financed by two booksellers and purposely printed with two title pages. Each title-page would bear the name of only one of the booksellers: in those copies sent by the printer to one bookseller the second leaf would be cancelled; for the other bookseller the first title-leaf would be cancelled and the second substituted in its place.

Further minor improvements and corrections which affect parts of the letterpress or make-up of the book but which do not incur a cancellation of the title-leaf are also classed as variant states. For information about these the reader is referred to Bowers's *Principles of Bibliographical Description*, pp. 42–77.

The detection of variants involves a painstaking collation of the text of a number of copies, and this for lengthy books is a task to deter even the most assiduous of bibliographers. Since the last war, however, for those fortunate enough to have access to one, the task has been lightened by the Hinman collating machine. This machine was developed by the American bibliographer, Dr. Charlton Hinman, with the primary aim of collating the 80 copies of Shakespeare's First Folio in the Folger Shakespeare Library. The results of his research are now available in his monumental *The Printing and proof-reading of the First Folio of Shakespeare*, (1963), in which he reveals *inter alia* many hundred new variant readings not previously known.

By a series of mirrors the machine enables two copies of a book to

[11] "Blank leaves or alternative titles". The Library. 4th series. vol. ii, (1922), pp. 272–4.

be compared page by page. Images of corresponding pages from each copy are superimposed on a final mirror facing the operator. Pages with identical settings form a single image but a variant or a re-positioning of type in one copy can be detected by an overlapping of its image on that from the second copy. Inspection is aided by means of a binocular eyepiece which enables the image to be magnified and damaged letters to be detected more easily than is possible by normal visual examination.

Not only are variants revealed by the Hinman collator, but print-ing from standing type may be distinguished in mixed issues and hybrid editions from newly set matter. It has also been used with success to detect variants in the pages of xix and xx century novels whose bulk had in the past deterred bibliographers from undertaking a full textual study of near-contemporary publications. Its importance lies in the far greater accuracy it achieves over normal methods of collating and the speed with which results are achieved. It made pos-sible the collation of 150 pages a day for the First Folio and a modern book can be collated at the rate of 40 pages an hour.

Other evidence

In addition to grouping the various works under investigation into edition, issue and variant state, the bibliographer will draw attention in his description to any features which throw light on the way a particular book was printed or published, or which may be significant to the study of the text. We shall now examine the informa-tion afforded by an investigation of some of these features.

(a) Paper

Although cheaper publications were occasionally printed on job lots of paper, as shown by the variety of watermarks found between their covers, most printers would ensure that they possessed a sufficient quantity of one kind of paper before commencing to print. It follows that when a contrasting paper, or paper bearing a different watermark is found in part of a book, we may assume that in the majority of cases that part was printed after the rest of the book. The only occasion when it could result from simultaneous printing was when two or more job lots of paper were used. Even here some facts may be deduced concerning the order in which the book went through the press as Dr. Stevenson has shown[12] from his investigation of a group of xvii century quarto plays printed by Thomas Cotes, 1639–40. Usually, however, the evidence points to a later printing, although how much later cannot be inferred from the paper alone.

In some cases where a printer had slightly underestimated the amount of paper required, he might have had to print the preliminaries on a different stock. If then the preliminaries are found printed on paper with a different watermark from that found on the text pages, it is sufficient proof that they were printed after the text, and the book may well be a first edition. Similarly, during or immediately after printing, an error may have been found in the text which was of sufficient importance to require the forme in which it appeared to be re-set. Sheets of contrasting paper or bearing variant watermarks should, therefore, be examined for the presence of such corrections. On a smaller scale, a single-leaf cancellation may also be detected from the use of different paper, or by evidence of its non-conjugacy with the leaf to which it is pasted. Such evidence may come from finding the watermark in an unexpected position, e.g. both sides of a fold in a folio, or from the non-alignment across the fold of the chain-lines in a quarto (see later under cancels).

The decision to cancel and substitute a leaf containing offending text may, however, have been made *after* instead of before publication. The longer the delay after the initial printing, the more likelihood there was that the printer would use a different paper. Variant watermarks, therefore, more frequently provide evidence of a new issue, mixed issues or the use of standing type. A new issue is evident from a variant watermark in the preliminaries and a new title-leaf; a mixed issue results from a printer lacking a number of sheets when a sudden demand called for more copies of a book, and his resetting of these to add to the old sheets in store. Similarly, certain copies of an edition may have been produced at a later time than the initial printing by a subsequent working from type standing for the purpose. In the latter

[12] A. Stevenson. "New uses of watermarks as bibliographical evidence". Papers of the Bibliographical Society of the University of Virginia. Vol. i, (1948–9), p. 151.

case the second batch of copies may have been printed throughout on entirely different paper than that used for the first. Evidence of lawful printing from standing type is very elusive and a variant watermark could provide the major clue to this practice.[13]

In an article "Chain-indentations in paper as evidence",[14] Dr. Stevenson has pointed out that grooves or indentations are left in the surface of all laid paper by the chain-wires. This is so whether the paper was hand made when the wires come in contact with the pulp as it rests on the bottom of the mould, or whether it was machine-made when they would be formed by the action of the dandy-roll. The indentations are clearly visible when a leaf is tilted towards the light or when artificial light is thrown across a page from a low angle. Their significance rests on the fact that they are present in only one side of the sheet and either correspond with the printed pages of the inner forme or else with those of the outer forme. Thus in a quarto gathering formed from a single sheet the indentations would be seen either on pages 1, 4, 5 and 8, or 2, 3, 6 and 7. This pattern would not apply, however, in gatherings made-up of a half-sheet or of more than one sheet, or in formats constructed by folding and cutting. But in a regular quarto, if any variation from the standard is found, e.g. indentations found on pages 1, 3, 5 and 8, then one of the leaves (in this case the second) must be a cancel or some other form of substitution. Of course, the presence of an inserted leaf may not always be noted in this way for there is an even chance that it would be printed with the indentations showing on the side of the leaf which conforms to the regular arrangement.

The comparative ease with which the indented side of laid paper can be determined makes this method of investigation very valuable, particularly when watermarks are absent. In addition to its obvious application to cancel hunting, a number of other uses are demonstrated by Dr. Stevenson as, for example, in determining whether a blank leaf at the front or back of a book is an integral part of the

---

[13] When variant watermarks are used to identify cancels, mixed issues or copies of books printed in part from standing type, it is important to establish with certainty that the variant relates to a different watermark and not to a twin (see page 47).

[14] Studies in Bibliography. Vol. vi, (1954), p. 181.

gatherings or just an endpaper; or, whether an engraved title has been printed on the same sheet as the printed title. In fact, wherever the question of conjugacy is involved it would appear that we have in chain-indentations a very effective bibliographical tool.

Whether it be from chain-indentations or from other characteristics both inherent or accidental, evidence from paper often affords the best guide to made-up copies, faked facsimiles and forgeries. A made-up copy is one which has had a missing leaf or more made good from another copy of the same edition. It is not necessary to question here the motive behind such an action, but although the paper would doubtless be of the same manufacture bearing an identical watermark, the position of the watermark, the non-correspondence of the chain-lines, or the incidence of chain-indentations may enable the inserted leaf to be detected.[15] Many facsimiles of printed books are honestly produced and contain some positive indication of their nature, but when the intention behind a facsimile was the production of a faked copy of the original, proof of dishonesty is often difficult to obtain. Faking is usually restricted to the insertion of a prepared leaf, or part of a leaf, to make the original book whole. A careful examination of the paper may bring to light some peculiarities which do not correspond with the original. Foxing, water-stains, grease-spots, etc., which penetrate a number of leaves may, on investigation, throw out the odd leaf, but the difficulty with a skilfully faked facsimile is that one's suspicions may not be sufficiently aroused in the first place to cause such tests to be made.

The classic example of a wholesale forgery being detected partly from a study of paper, was Carter and Pollard's investigation of the Wise forgeries, reported by them in *An Enquiry into the nature of certain xixth century pamphlets*, (1934). In this instance proof came from a scientific examination of the paper used by Wise to determine its raw materials. This was then compared with the dates at which

---

[15] *See* D. F. Foxon. Thomas J. Wise and the pre-Restoration Drama: a study in theft and sophistication. Bib. Soc., (1959). Foxon records how, with the help of Miss F. E. Ratchford, and from a study of stab-holes formed by sewing, the presence of worm-holes, stains and flaws in the paper, he confirmed the suspicion that Wise had stolen at least 206 leaves from early quarto plays in the British Museum to make-up not only copies in his own library but others that he sold to John Henry Wrenn.

certain substitutes for rag paper were introduced into this country in the xix century. It was not too difficult for Carter and Pollard to establish that any paper containing esparto must have been made after 1861 and any paper, at least for printed books, containing chemical wood, after 1874. But when these dates were checked against the Wise title-pages, 10 of the 27 pamphlets containing esparto were found to be dated *before* 1861, and 13 pamphlets containing a significant proportion of chemical wood were all apparently published *before* 1874.

(b) The Printer's measure

In early printing, compositors' sticks were not adjustable but were made in various fixed lengths to suit the common measures of type-pages. Being made of wood, even those intended to be of the same length would vary by up to 2 mms. This was an acceptable tolerance in normal practice for the difference in length was too small to be noticed in the printed line. It is, however, distinguishable by careful measurement, and when parts of a book are found to exhibit a different measure from the rest, it follows that two composing sticks were used. Now it would be unlikely for a single compositor to use different sticks to set various parts of the same book unless his work had suffered an interruption. Then, when he resumed setting, he might inadvertently have picked up the wrong stick. In such a case the change to the different measure could occur anywhere in the book, but once made would probably remain in use until the end. If the preliminaries were set in a different measure from the text, this too would point to the likelihood that they had been printed after the text and, accordingly, the book may be a first edition. Similarly, an insertion or substitution made some time after the text had been printed may have been set in a different stick and the change of measure would lead one to suspect a cancel. However, evidence from the measure alone is rarely decisive and a suspected cancel should be further examined for other features reflecting a separate setting and printing (see page 137).

It is believed that a compositor owned his own stick and the use of two sticks determined by change of measure can also point to simultaneous setting by two compositors. It was common practice for copy to be divided between two compositors either to supply two presses, or when a small edition was being printed to keep pace with a single press. In the first instance, the copy would probably be divided in half, in which case the change to a different measure appears only once approximately mid-way through the text. But when a small edition was being set, the sheets most likely would be set in turn by the two compositors and the different measures will be found to alternate from sheet to sheet. The identification of two compositors may be of great importance in the study of the text, and suspected pages should be examined closely for other evidence in the form of variant spellings, etc.

It will be appreciated that very careful measurement is required to distinguish the small differences in stick length and, even so, calculations may be upset by uneven shrinkage of the paper which can vary up to 2 mms. If the difference in measure is less than 3 mms. therefore, the suspected page should be examined further for the presence of variant spellings or other corroborative features, such as alterations in the headline, a change of paper, etc. For further information on this subject Fredson Bowers's paper *Bibliographical evidence from the printer's measure*[16] is recommended.

(c) Variant spellings and re-appearing types

Dr. Charlton Hinman has demonstrated[17] that spelling tests can be applied to distinguish the work of two compositors in setting different parts of the same book. Even though many of the better printers formulated their own house-rules for setting, including the observance of certain methods of spelling, any compositor of the xvi and xvii centuries, particularly if working in one of the less exacting offices would develop his own spelling habits. It is true that a compositor might vary his method of spelling in order to justify a line or because he was running out of a particular piece if type whose use he could obviate by adopting a different spelling. Nevertheless, these were

[16] Papers of the Bibliographical Society of the University of Virginia. Vol. ii, (1949–50), pp. 153–67.

[17] "Principles governing the use of variant spellings as evidence of alternate setting by two compositors". The Library. 4th series. vol. xxi, (1940–1), pp. 78–94.

breaks from his normal preferred method which can usually be determined from a full and careful examination of a text.

In the investigation of variant spellings the positions which they occupy is of vital significance. To relate their presence to the work of different compositors they must be found in those parts of a book which could reasonably be divided between two or more men. For instance, if the spelling of a particular word varies on the same page or in pages of the same forme, it cannot relate to the distinctive preferences of two men but must be either the work of a carefree compositor or, perhaps, one who occasionally follows the author's spelling rather than his own, or, indeed, one who finds it expeditious to adopt an alternative spelling in order to justify his line. But if variant spellings are found in distinct groups of pages which could well have been divided between two compositors then the evidence strongly supports this probability.

Although the position of variant spellings can distinguish the work of two compositors, it fails to determine which of the two set a particular group of pages and another test has to be applied. Each compositor would be likely to treat similar words in the same way, e.g. if he habitually spelt tarry as "tarrie", then doubtless he would spell marry as "marrie", and if he spelt chance as "chaunce", then he would most probably prefer "daunce" for dance. But without further investigation one cannot say that the man who set "chaunce" also set "tarrie". It is necessary to list the similarly constructed words exhibiting variant spellings and to make the most prevalent group, say, chance, chaunce, dance, daunce, etc., and to note exactly where in the text each of the two forms of spelling is found. If form A (dance, chance) is found in distinctly separate parts of the book from form B (daunce, chaunce), thus supporting the case for two compositors (x and y), then the other variant spellings found along with form A may be regarded the work of x and those in the same group of pages as form B may be assigned to y. As noted above, when the evidence from spelling is not conclusive, the deciding factor may come from corresponding variations in measure, or, when dealing with plays, in differences in the setting of scene-headings, stage-directions, etc.

Recently, however, a new theory has been postulated which after further testing might well prove very effective in assigning various parts of a text to their respective compositors. As with many recent studies it stems from the advances in bibliographical analysis made possible by the Hinman collating machine. Since its successful use by Dr. Hinman in recording the typographical minutiae of the Shakespeare First Folio, more and more attention has been paid by bibliographers to the evidence that can be extracted from a close examination of text-type. The theory has been put forward by Robert K. Turner, Jr., that the incidence of the re-appearance in different parts of a book of the same pieces of type would enable the various parts to be allocated to different compositors.[18] It is based, of course, on the assumption that the types set by each compositor would be distributed only into his type cases. Turner used his hypothesis to allocate different parts of the play *Albumazar* by Thomas Tomkis, printed by Nicholas Okes in 1615, to their compositors and found that his assumption concerning distribution was verified by the correlation of the typographical and spelling evidence in the setting of the text.

Even when it is clear that some types have been returned to the wrong case it may still be possible to assign different parts of the text to their respective compositors. For instance Turner, by tracing the re-appearance of types in the Beaumont and Fletcher Folio of 1647, found it possible to link parts of the text which lacked significant spellings with those that contained them and thus was able to make assignments "on the assumption that two segments of the text set from the same case would have been set by the same workman". He recognized that this assumption would not always be valid, for a workman could be relieved at times by another, but he felt it held good if no important discrepancies in spelling or typography were detected between the two segments under scrutiny.

(d) Headlines

We have seen that when type-pages were being imposed on the stone, they were fitted round the skeleton which had been transferred from a previously printed forme. As the headlines to the type-pages

[18] "Reappearing types as bibliographical evidence". Studies in Bibliography. Vol. xix. (1966), pp. 198–209.

were considered an integral part of the skeleton they too were transferred from forme to forme thus avoiding the necessity of resetting
them afresh each time. The significance of this practice to analytical
bibliographers was first explored by Professor Bowers and later
extended by Dr. Hinman. The study of headlines, in fact, has revealed
such a fruitful source of bibliographical evidence that Bowers considers a thorough bibliographical examination of the book to be
incomplete unless the sets of headlines are identified and any variations
in position and content have been explained.[19]

The skeleton of each forme contains a number or set of headlines
and to obtain any useful bibliographical evidence it is necessary to
identify a particular headline in a set, or to distinguish alternating sets
of headlines throughout a book, depending on whether one or two
skeletons were used. Each headline consists of the running-title flanked
by a number of quads and spaces. The running-title might show some
variation of setting, e.g. a difference in spelling or punctuation, the
use of a swash instead of an italic capital, the presence of broken letters,
etc., from other running-titles in the same set of headlines or from
its counterpart in a second or third set. In less obvious cases, Dr.
Hinman has shown that the amount of spacing material in the headline used before the running-title might vary since a compositor
would be unlikely to select exactly the same number and width of
quads and spaces in setting each headline in a set. Differences in measurement from the left-hand edge of the type-page to the first letter of
the running-title may, therefore, distinguish one headline from another.

Having identified a particular headline one can now establish the
use of one or two skeletons by noting the frequency of its appearance
throughout the book. The task is made easier if one knows in advance
where to look and fortunately the printer was nearly always consistent
in the way he transferred a skeleton from forme to forme. When using
a single skeleton in a quarto, for example, the transfer would be effected
as shown on the following page.

With two skeletons, the one used for the inner forme of the first
sheet would be transferred to the inner forme of each succeeding sheet
and that for the outer forme would be transferred to all subsequent

[19] "The Headline in early books". English Institute Annual, 1941. (1942), p. 188.

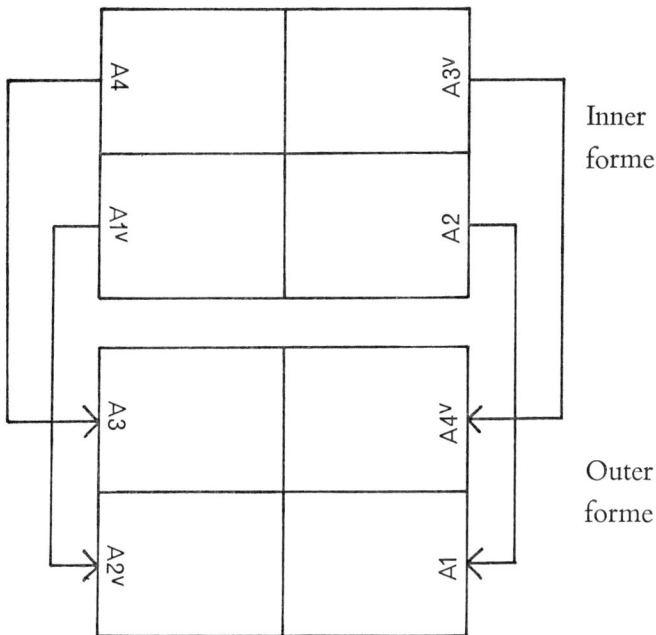

Inner forme

Outer forme

outer formes. Again a consistent procedure was followed so that the headline on B1 would normally appear on C1, D1, etc., and the headline of B1ᵛ would be used for C1ᵛ, D1ᵛ, etc. As suggested on page 104, the number of skeletons used can give a rough indication of the size of the edition, and Dr. Hinman has shown[20] that certain deductions can be made between the number of skeletons and the incidence of variants in both formes of a sheet. For other evidence, each headline throughout the book must be checked for variations either from its normal position or from its original setting. They can then provide a variety of information:

(i) the order in which the formes of both quired and unquired gatherings were printed. In a quired folio gathering, for instance, the headlines might show that the centre fold was printed first and that the printer then worked outwards to the fold containing the first and last leaves of the gathering. Similarly, in an unquired gathering, an

[20] C. Hinman. "New uses for headlines as bibliographical evidence". English Institute Annual, 1941, (1942), pp. 215–22.

incorrectly set running-title appearing in the inner forme may have been corrected on its transfer to the outer forme, thus proving that the inner forme was first through the press. Such a stop-press correction may also provide clear evidence of the priority of variant states of the text, the corrected form of the running-title appearing in the later state of the forme.

(ii) Fredson Bowers has demonstrated[21] that not only can headlines afford definite proof of half-sheet imposition, but also which method was used by the printer. For example, in a book collated A^2 B—T^4 U^2, it would have been possible for the printer either to set and print the two half-sheets together by imposing the inner formes of A and U together in the same forme and perfecting them by a second forme consisting of their outer formes, and then to cut the resulting sheet in half, or, he could impose the 4 type-pages of A in one forme, and the 4 of U in another and print them separately (both methods are explained on page 101). Bowers, by working out the way in which the headlines would have been transferred in either case, was able to provide the formula that can be applied to distinguish which method of imposition was chosen by the printer.

(iii) When an altered headline appears only once in a book and its position in subsequent formes is occupied by a repetition of its original setting a cancel is revealed. For example, if in a quarto in which two skeletons were used the headline which appeared on $B2^v$, $C2^v$, $D2^v$, shows a variant setting on $E2^v$, but reverts back to its original setting on $F2^v$, $G2^v$, and so throughout the book, then we may safely assume that E2 is a cancel.

(e) Line-counts and type shortages

In most books apart from those printed during the earliest years of printing, the number of lines to a full page remains constant throughout the text. Yet there are some books, and recent investigations suggest more than just a few, which contain pages with an irregular number of lines. Where there is no discernable pattern—the irregularities appearing at random throughout the book—it must be assumed that we are dealing with a particularly careless printer. When the

[21] "The Headline in early books". *op. cit.*, p. 188.

irregularities occur on the last pages of just a few gatherings at well-spaced intervals it is probable that we have evidence of copy-fitting. But in addition to these possibilities, Dr. William H. Bond discovered that a number of Elizabethan books were printed with too few or too many lines mostly on pages of inner formes and seldom in both formes of any one gathering. In an account of his investigations[22] he cites the example of Sir Philip Sidney's *The Defence of Poesie*, (1595), printed by Thomas Creede for William Ponsonby. This is a quarto of 35 leaves, normally with 32 lines to the page, but 8 pages, all in inner formes, are either overset or underset. Such a pattern of irregularity, he postulates, could result from setting pages by formes rather than consecutively.

In setting a quarto book by formes, the compositor would compose the first page of a gathering with the normal number of lines, cast-off pages 2 and 3, set pages 4 and 5, cast-off pages 6 and 7 and finally set page 8 (see page 99). The cast-off pages, i.e. where the amount of copy to fill the pages is estimated, all fall in the inner forme, and it is in this position in the books investigated by Dr. Bond that the line-counts differ. This practice of course implies that both formes of each gathering were not composed concurrently and to strengthen his theory Dr. Bond sought and found evidence from the headlines which confirmed this possibility.

Further support was given to this theory by the evidence obtained by Mr. G. W. Williams from other works printed by Thomas Creede which demonstrated that the compositor had exhausted his supply of type-pieces of a particular character during the course of his work.[23] Dr. Hinman had already demonstrated that the Shakespeare First Folio had been regularly set by formes and Williams by his investigations has shown that this method of composition was far more widespread than had been supposed. He based his theory on the evidence obtained from two observations: the number of type-pieces of a character appearing in a sheet or a forme and the presence and incidence of substitutions for this character when its supply had been

[22] "Casting off copy by Elizabethan printers: a theory". P.B.S.A. Vol. 42, (1948), pp. 281–91.
[23] "Setting by formes in quarto printing". Studies in Bibliography. Vol. xi, (1958), pp. 39–53.

exhausted in the course of composition. From this information he was able to demonstrate the order in which the pages of Thomas Creede's printing of *Epicedium: a funeral song upon the death of Lady Helen Branch*, (1594), a single sheet quarto, had been set. During its composition the compositor had run out of both the upper-case and lower-case "w" and had substituted "VV" and "vv" respectively. By noting the incidence of the original characters and of their substitutions on the pages of the sheet, Williams was able to prove that the setting was by formes, with the inner preceding the outer. In another example quoted in his article, he used the evidence of type-shortage equally as effectively to prove page setting in seriatim order.

McKerrow was aware that books had occasionally been set by formes, but he had assumed that the practice would only have been used for page-for-page reprints because the amount of copy to occupy each page in the sheet would only then have been known. The evidence he accepted for setting by formes was based on the reappearance of type within the same gathering of a book. He cites the example of certain initials appearing twice in the same gatherings (in opposite formes) of a Bible, a folio in sixes, printed by C. Barker in 1591. From this evidence he concluded that the compositor had set up either the three outer or the three inner formes of each gathering first. So sure was he that setting by formes was restricted to page-for-page reprints that he concluded[24]:

> when we come across a clear case of the same material (initial letters, ornaments, &c.) being used more than once in a gathering, we may infer, with little or no risk of error, that we are dealing with a page-for-page reprint of an earlier edition.

But the practice of setting by formes from a manuscript, with the distinct possibility of using the same type more than once in a gathering now considerably modifies McKerrow's dictum.

(f) Press-numbers

Many English books printed between 1680 and 1820 contain small figures or arbitrary symbols printed at the foot of one or more pages in some gatherings. The incidence of their appearance is seemingly haphazard for in some books only a few sheets are so marked,

[24] *Introduction to bibliography*, p. 31.

but in others they are found in either one or both formes of each sheet. Although press-numbers were first investigated by Dr. R. W. Chapman[25] some forty years ago, their original purpose remains obscure. The printing manuals of the day, which have frequently disclosed a possible solution to bibliographical problems involving the technicalities of the trade, remain somewhat obscure and even contradictory in their references to these numbers. It seems probable that their use varied from shop to shop depending perhaps on the number of men employed in each, and that no common practice was ever observed. Dr. Chapman formed the opinion that the numbers referred to individual presses and that a compositor would mark his work with a number to assign it to a particular press. The later investigations of Professor W. B. Todd[26] seem to indicate that the figures were used to designate men and not presses, and McKerrow's suggestion that they provided a basis for calculating the wages to be paid to each pressman was, therefore, probably correct. Mr. P. Gaskell[27] in supporting this theory has demonstrated the need a master-printer would have for a system of recording the number of sheets printed by each pressman and that the practice of marking the sheets themselves took the place of an elaborate form of bookkeeping that would otherwise have been necessary.

It is difficult, however, to square this with the haphazard appearance of the numbers—whole sequences of unnumbered formes are often found and no explanation that is generally accepted has yet been found for this phenomenon. Mr. W. E. Knott's theory[28] is that they designate the work of an unidentified press, the one used for the bulk of the printing, and that numbered formes relate to other presses which worked off the remainder. Dr. F. B. Kaye[29] considers that unnumbered formes represent the work of the press which is designated by the numbering of the formes immediately preceding or

[25] "Printing with figures: a note". The Library. 4th series. Vol. iii, (1922–3), pp. 175–6
[26] "Observations on the incidence and interpretation of press figures". Studies in Bibliography. Vol III, (1950-1), pp. 171–205.
[27] "Eighteenth-century press numbers". The Library. 5th series. Vol. iv, pp. 249–57.
[28] "Press numbers as a bibliographical tool". Harvard Library Bulletin, III, 2, (1949), pp. 198–212.
[29] Bernard Mandeville. The Fable of the Bees; ed. by F. B. Kaye, (1924), Vol. II, p. 395.

following, a theory which is supported by Professor Todd. In books where only one forme of a gathering is numbered, Mr. Gaskell has pointed out that both formes were probably printed by the same press, but the second figure was not inserted since it would have been quite straightforward to check on the work done from the single forme.

Whatever their original purpose and method of application, press-numbers are now recognized to be a valuable aid in detecting particular circumstances of a book's printing. They were usually positioned on or below the catchword line and were sometimes tied up with the type-page when the type was to be kept standing for a new impression.[30] Before the second printing, however, they would be replaced by new figures relating to another group of pressmen, and so copies from a new impression may be distinguished by a different set of press-numbers normally found in the same positions within the formes. Of course, the numbers may have been dropped before the type-pages were tied up, in which case the new numbers in the second impression would not only be different but would occupy different positions. The same would, however, result from a new setting of type, so it is not possible to distinguish between a new edition and a new impression on the evidence of press-numbers alone.

Professor Todd has also demonstrated their value in detecting books made-up of old sheets left over from a previous impression mixed with newly set sheets. These books may have resulted from a decision taken in the course of the first impression to print additional copies of the remaining sheets in anticipation of a second edition. The sheets already printed and for which the type had been distributed would obviously have to be reset and a copy from the second edition could be distinguished from the first by the alteration in the number and position of the press numbers contained in the reset sheets.

Press-numbers can also be used to reveal the format of a book which is otherwise in doubt. Professor Todd has demonstrated that in distinguishing between two methods of half-sheet imposition, only one figure is present in each gathering when a single forme on one press is used. But sometimes in the two forme method, involving

---

[30] For re-impression from standing type in the xviii century, see Chapter 14.

possibly the use of two presses, either two figures are revealed in one half-sheet only, or else one figure will appear in a particular forme of one half-sheet and the second in the obverse forme of the other half-sheet.

Yet another instance of the use of press-numbers is in the detection of cancels which is considered in the next section, but the examples quoted above are sufficient to indicate the significance now attached to these figures as bibliographical evidence. Unfortunately their importance was not appreciated until comparatively recently and the earlier bibliographies of xviii century books paid little attention to their presence. Now they form an essential part of any bibliography which aims to provide a definitive description of the books in which they appear.

(g) Cancels

The practice of stopping the press to make corrections was adopted only when the minimum of resetting was involved, and a different treatment was required for more extensive errors. These could not be allowed to stand in even a few uncorrected copies, so a replacement in the form of a new leaf, or sometimes a whole sheet, was printed and substituted for the faulty original. It was found more convenient not to make such a radical change during printing but to wait until the impression of the faulty sheet was complete before setting and printing the corrected text. If a whole sheet was involved the original would probably be destroyed immediately and the new one inserted in its place, but the substitution of a reset leaf or fold would be left to the binder.

Such substitutions are called cancels. The word is loosely used to describe both the original leaf or sheet and the corrected form, but the former is more precisely called the "cancellandum" and the latter the "cancellans". Cancels were due not only to errors on the part of the author or printer, but sometimes to an improved rewriting of a particular passage. Of more general interest are those cancels resulting from an indiscretion of an immoral or libellous nature which it was considered best to amend before publication. When offending passages were published, their effect on the authorities or on a particular individual occasionally forced the publisher to withdraw the book from circulation and to re-issue with a revised text. A cancel, therefore, could produce a new issue of an edition as well as being the cause of a variant state. Dr. Chapman has estimated that in the xviii century one in every three first editions is likely to contain a cancel.[31]

In dealing with a single-leaf cancel the printer would indicate the cancellandum to the binder by defacing it in some way, frequently by cutting it with a knife or pair of scissors. As an added precaution he occasionally added a signature to the cancellans to show the exact position it should occupy in the book. Normally the binder would cut away the cancellandum leaving a stub on which the cancellans was pasted by its inner margin. This particular means of substitution was essential if the sheets had been bound or even sewn but if the cancellation were made earlier the printer could sometimes help the binder to avoid the use of paste. A single-leaf cancellans could be printed with a wider-inner margin so that part of it could be wrapped round the fold and the leaf sewn in position. In the same say, when two conjugate leaves in a sheet were cancelled, a simple fold which could be sewn in place would be the best form of substitution. In fact, it had become normal practice by the xix century to avoid the use of paste by printing a four-page cancel.[32]

It must not be assumed that cancellation was always followed by substitution. There are many examples of simple deletion: blank leaves from different parts of the book; half-titles no longer required in a bound book to protect the title-page; advertisement pages removed on permanent binding, etc. Similarly, when a substitution was made it was not always the same length as the original. A single-leaf cancellandum might have been replaced by a cancellans fold and vice-versa. When a whole sheet had been cancelled the replacement might well have contained a different number of leaves. On collating a book, therefore, one should always suspect the presence of a cancel when a particular gathering contains an irregular number of leaves.

A single-leaf cancellans pasted on to a stub has a certain resistance to opening fully when the leaves are turned. This often provides the first indication that a cancel is present. Suspicion is strengthened if

[31] R. W. Chapman. Cancels. Constable, 1924, p. 10.
[32] Ibid, p. 18.

the stub is visible, but the leaf should be fully examined for additional evidence to clinch the matter. If the cancellation was done sometime after publication the printer may have used a different quality paper; it may also contain a different watermark. The chain-lines may run in the opposite direction from those in other leaves and in a quarto, where the chain-lines are horizontal, those in the suspected leaf may not correspond across the fold with those of the conjugate leaf. In this test, however, the register of the type-pages also has to be checked.[33] Most cancels were, however, printed on the same paper as that used for the book and so the watermark, if present, will be the same. But it may well be found in a position which it could not possibly occupy if the leaf were an integral part of the original gathering. For instance, if in a folio a mark appeared on each of two conjugate leaves, one must be a cancel. Similarly, if in a quarto, where the watermark is usually found cut in half on leaves 1 and 4 or 2 and 3, half is found on the first leaf but its other half is missing from the fourth, then the latter must be a cancel.[34] A similar set of circumstances may be constructed for other formats which inevitably lead to the same conclusion. In tests of this sort, however, allowance has to be made for paper with its watermark off-centre. After 1790, English papers were marked near to the shorter edge of the sheet and Dr. Chapman has shown that in an octavo the watermark will then be missing from half the normal number of leaves.[35]

The printer by signing the cancellans leaf as an indication to the binder of its exact place in the book kindly provided additional evidence for the cancel-hunter. Not all leaves of a gathering were signed: by the xviii century signing was normally restricted to the leaves preceding the sewing. If, therefore, we find a signed leaf which in a corresponding position in other gatherings is unsigned, say the 6th leaf of an octavo, then we should suspect a cancel. Similarly, in a multi-volume work, the first page of each gathering would be marked

[33] McKerrow. Introduction to bibliography, p. 225.

[34] Analysis by watermarks, however, must take into account that they exist as twins. For instance, in establishing that a quarto gathering has not been affected by a suspected cancel one should be able to show that both halves of the watermark appearing across the fold in a pair of conjugate leaves belong to one member of the twin.

[35] Chapman, *op.cit.*, p. 32.

with the volume number in addition to its own signature, e.g. Vol. III C. No purpose was served in adding the volume number to subsequent leaves and when one of these is found so marked a cancel is likely.

Press-numbers can also reveal a cancel. It has been shown that sometimes they appear as often as one to every forme, but no system of accounting would require them to be added more frequently. When two figures are present in the same forme, therefore, we can be sure that one is on a cancellans leaf. Moreover, when a regular pattern of press-numbering has been established throughout a book, any single irregularity is a possible indication of a cancel.

If the cancellans leaf was set and printed some time after the printing of the whole book was finished, even perhaps after publication, there was always the likelihood that some of the original type-pieces would no longer be available. The use of different type, particularly in the less plentiful larger sizes used for running-titles, may, therefore, indicate a resetting. In this connection the evidence of an altered headline has already been considered in a previous section. In addition to the type itself, the manner of its setting may also reveal a cancel. If a leaf has been reset by a different compositor, the measure of the lines may vary from the rest of the book owing to slight differences in stick length. Perhaps more frequently the revised text would not be exactly the same length as the original and may have necessitated an increase or decrease to the number of lines to the page or a crowding-in or spacing-out of the lines towards the foot of the new page.

Much of the evidence considered above is not strong enough to stand on its own but when taken in conjunction may well remove all doubt about the presence of a cancel. Two excellent object lessons on determining the existence of a cancel are provided by Miss Irene Mann in her paper "A Political cancel in the Coblers Prophesie",[36] and by Mr. W. R. Parker in his "A Cancel in an early Milton tract".[37] In the first example, Miss Mann noted various typographical peculiarities in a particular gathering and by checking the headlines, measuring the size of the type-page and searching for abnormal spellings she was

[36] The Library, 4th series. Vol. xxiii, (1942–3), pp. 94–100.
[37] *Ibid.* Vol. xv, (1935), pp. 243–6.

able to offer a reconstruction of the complete resetting of the gathering by a different compositor. Mr. Parker suspected a cancel from the collation of the Milton tract which revealed that all gatherings were of four leaves except the first, last, and gathering G which were of two leaves each. The first and last were readily accounted for, but a further examination of G revealed that the catchword on G2^v was different from the first word of H1. This together with an omission in the pagination at this point indicated some abnormality in the printing. From a further study of the text, Mr. Parker concluded that G had originally consisted of four leaves but was deleted and replaced by a revised text occupying only two leaves.

CHAPTER 12

Bibliographical Description (1)

As the work of identification, dating and analysis proceeds, the bibliographer will record his findings in note-form which may be used subsequently as a basis for a descriptive bibliography. For this purpose the notes would need to be transcribed into a form intelligible to others and the bibliographer will follow a pattern of description which has been evolved to provide as clear a picture as possible of the original book short of actual reproduction. Each description, it will be remembered, is of an ideal copy of an edition and not of any particular copy. Only by this means can it act as a standard of reference against which other copies of the same edition may be compared. But the bibliographer should have a wider purpose than merely to publish a series of isolated descriptions. To be of value to the textual or literary student he should endeavour to show by his analysis and arrangement the relationships that exist between the various editions of a work and between the issues and variant copies within each edition. He should also remember that much of his investigation has been concerned with the materials and methods of printing and his notes may well contain information of value to students of historical bibliography and to other analytical bibliographers. The aim of a descriptive bibliography, therefore, should be to reconstruct the whole printing and publishing history of the books it records. This is not to say that each entry will require the same depth of treatment for some material may be less important to the central purpose of the compilation than the rest. For example, in an author bibliography, one would expect the author's own works to be described and annotated in full, but a less detailed treatment would be acceptable for biographical and critical works about the author.

A comparison of published bibliographies soon reveals that there is no universal formula for the description of books, even when the fullest treatment is demanded. Nevertheless, over the years a pattern has emerged comprising certain fundamentals which no description aiming at more than mere identification should omit. These are:

(1) transcripts of title-page, colophon, head-title, running-title, etc.

(2) technical description including collation and contents.

(3) notes.

It is in the manner by which each of these parts is treated that differences are found between various recommended methods. The most comprehensive work on the subject is Professor Bowers' *Principles of Bibliographical Description*, (1949), in which he surveys the problems in great detail and co-ordinates in his recommendations many of the solutions evolved in past years by practising bibliographers. Some have considered his methods too detailed and exacting for general acceptance, but developments in analytical bibliography in recent years have often proved the importance of aiming at as complete a description as possible for those entries which are to form the major part of any descriptive bibliography. For example, Sir Walter Greg, who spent a lifetime compiling his exhaustive *Bibliography of the English Printed Drama to the Restoration*, recorded any irregularities he discovered in the running-titles some years before their study became an important aspect of analytical bibliography, and his work is now all the more useful because of such foresight. Any bibliographer working in recent years cannot ignore the example of Bowers and Greg in bibliographical description and much of what follows here is based on their recommendations.

SCOPE

Before embarking on the task of locating and analysing the editions to be included in a bibliography, the scope of the work will need to be determined otherwise much time and energy will be wasted on the examination of unnecessary titles. A decision has to be taken on the type of material to be investigated and what limitations, if any, are to be imposed by date. In an author bibliography, for example, in addition to works written by and about the author, the compiler must decide whether or not to include non-bibliographical material. In Mrs. Norma Russell's *A Bibliography of William Cowper to 1837* we find a section headed "Cowperiana" recording the existence and location of personal effects still extant, and under "Iconography" she gives a list of the contemporary portraits of Cowper that have survived. More importantly, the exact delineation of the main subject of the bibliography itself may be hard to determine. One of the most difficult decisions Sir Walter Greg had to make in the bibliography mentioned above was to define what he meant by printed drama. When does dialogue become drama? Did some of the pageants written for the City of London, for example, develop dramatic characteristics? Another problem he had to face was whether descriptions should be included only for works which were extant, or for works known solely from references by previous bibliographers and others.

When one is deciding on inclusive dates, the relative importance of later publications to the study of an author might well be an influencing factor. In the Cowper bibliography, Mrs. Russell included everything written by or about Cowper published during his lifetime and the 37 years following his death in 1800. By this time the texts of his works had become so stabilized that there would have been little additional value in including full descriptions of later editions. Miss J. E. Norton in her *Bibliography of the Works of Edward Gibbon*, (1940), confined her investigation mainly to editions published before 1838 when the first collected edition of Gibbon's Works was published. Editions published before 1800 and a few important ones after that date are treated in full, but for those published subsequently only condensed descriptions are provided. Even a precise limitation by date is not always easy to achieve. Normally the bibliographer will rely on the date of printing and not of literary composition since the latter is often incapable of precise definition. But Greg in his *Bibliography of Printed Drama* found some difficulty in selecting his final date because the closure of the theatres in 1642 put a stop to normal play production and publication during the years of the Civil War and Commonwealth. Wishing to include everything relevant to his chosen period he decided to list all plays known to have been written before the end of 1642 and printed before the end of 1700, together with those written after 1642 but printed before the beginning of 1660. It will be seen from these examples that the scope of a descriptive bibliography is determined partly by the purpose of the bibliography and partly by the nature of the material to be investigated.

ARRANGEMENT

Once the scope of the bibliography has been decided upon the next step to be resolved is the method of arrangement. This, too, must be related to the purpose of the bibliography. If we were to compile a bibliography of a science, say, geology, then we would be wise to consider grouping the books on geology under the natural divisions of the subject. We would need to devise a classification that broke the whole field down into its component parts and each part into its subdivisions until all the ramifications of geology are shown in their exact relationship to each other and to the whole. The bibliographical discipline with which we are concerned in this book, however, has no regard for the subject content of books and this logical or natural order is of little value to our particular study. The nearest approach to it we have seen is the "natural history method" of Henry Bradshaw and "Proctor order" by which xv century books on the evidence of their types are listed under country, town, press and date of publication, each division being arranged in chronological order. The great value of this method was that it enabled comparisons to be made of the materials and methods of early printing which, in turn, made it possible for unsigned and undated books to be attributed to their presses, or at least, their towns of origin. But for the bibliographical study of later periods of hand-printing which, as we have seen, has been primarily concerned with the purity of text, the natural history method would have little value. The choice of arrangement open to the descriptive bibliographer, therefore, lies between an alphabetical and a chronological sequence.

An alphabetical arrangement either by authors or titles is a purely arbitrary one. It treats each entry as a self-contained unit and fails to indicate relationships with other entries or to develop a connecting pattern. It has, however, the advantage of being easily understood and probably affords the readiest means of obtaining the information presented. Bibliographies arranged in author order are common: many of those of xv century books where the entries are generally consulted for their own sake, are in this form. Author order is more significant than title order as it does at least bring an author's publications together, whereas no relationship at all can be achieved if works are listed under titles. Moreover, many works frequently appeared or were known by more than one title, and many of the books of the xvi and xvii centuries bore such lengthy titles that if used as a basis of arrangement would doubtless cause confusion not only in their listing but in their finding.

Since one of the major purposes of a critical bibliography is to show the relationships that exist between the various editions of a text, and since printed editions usually derived from the first in a single line of descent, some form of chronological arrangement by date of publication is usually the most valuable. J. D. Cowley in his *Bibliographical Description and Cataloguing*, (1939), strongly advocated the use of the "annalistic" method in which all entries are arranged in a single chronological sequence. This arrangement would seem to be an obvious one to adopt for a bibliography describing the output of a particular press or publisher, but Cowley recommended its use for author bibliographies. With a single sequence of entries by date of publication, the history of the author's writings is readily revealed, and with events in the author's life, reviews and criticisms of his work also included in the same sequence, a close connection between his life and his literary production as well as its reception by his contemporaries is established. The great disadvantage, certainly to textual and literary students, is that the various editions of a work, and even the issues comprising an edition are separated from each other and, as a consequence, their relationship is not easily ascertained.

The form of chronological arrangement which satisfies the need to reveal relationships and, for this reason, the one most frequently adopted for author bibliographies, is the "pseudo-annalistic"[1] method. This groups all subsequent editions of a work under the date of the

[1] A term coined by J. D. Cowley, *op. cit.*, p. 182.

first, an arrangement, however, which A. W. Pollard called "a folly for which no condemnation can be too strong".[2] His grounds for objection were that its deviation from the single chronological sequence obscures the principle of arrangement and that to find a later edition you have to know the date of the first. But providing the bibliography is equipped with an adequate index the disadvantages would seem heavily outweighed by the benefits obtained in bringing together the whole history of a work so that comparisons between editions may readily be made.

A further deviation from a single sequence results from a preliminary division of an author's work into its literary forms: poems, plays, critical works, etc. Whether this is advisable or not can only be determined in the context of the particular author in question, but one method commonly adopted is to separate collected editions from individual works on the grounds of convenience and because in many cases the author himself was not responsible for their collection and arrangement.

Regardless of the method of arrangement the main sequence of entries in any bibliography must be supported by appendices which throw additional light on the subject of the work and by an adequate index to compensate for any obscurity of arrangement and to provide a ready reference to specific items of information. For example, an author bibliography will contain sections on biography and criticism, and may include others on iconography, allusions, controversies, forgeries, etc. Greg's *Bibliography*, in addition to the main chronological sequence of plays, has sections for the dramatic works recorded in the Registers and Court-Books of the Stationers' Company, Latin plays, lost plays and collections; an appendix containing publishers' advertisements, prefaces, a record of the actors as printed in the plays themselves, reprints of early play-catalogues, etc.; reference lists of acting companies and theatres, printers, publishers and booksellers with their signs, addresses and devices, etc. His final volume includes an introduction explaining the methods he adopted for arranging and describing the plays, together with lists of additions, corrections and an index of titles.

---

[2] "The Arrangement of bibliographies". The Library. New [2nd] series. Vol. x, (1909), p. 178.

If the various editions and issues of a work are brought together under the entry for the first edition some means is necessary to indicate clearly the classification into edition and issue and to note the existence of any variant copies. In a bibliography with comparatively few entries the appropriate descriptions can be labelled in full: "First edition", "Second edition", "Third edition, second issue", and so on. But in a bibliography containing many hundreds of entries, for the sake of economy, some shorthand indication is necessary. In Greg's *Bibliography*, for example, every edition and issue is given an entry to itself, the editions being distinguished by the letters (*a*), (*b*), (*c*), etc., added to the left-hand margin opposite the edition in question, (*A*) being used when only one edition of the work is known. Against each issue a small-cap roman numeral is added to its edition letter, e.g. the second issue of the only edition known is noted as (*A*ii), the fourth issue of the second edition as (*b*iv).

Separate entries are not, of course, provided for variant copies, for whereas a copy of a book may be said to belong to an edition or issue, it merely contains a variant, or a number of variants. Variant states are, therefore, indicated where they occur in the description although they may, in fact, require a separate paragraph if they occur in a part of the book that is transcribed, e.g. the title-page. Greg distinguishes them from one another by the use of the arbitrary signs *, †, §, which being non-sequential do not impose an order to their printing, something which it is frequently impossible to establish.

HEADING

Full descriptions of books result in lengthy entries comprising complicated type-settings which tend to obscure the essential features that make for easy recognition. For this reason a heading is usually constructed for each work to provide a key to the following description and to enable the reader to identify the particular entry he requires without difficulty. The heading should ideally consist of author, brief title, place, printer, publisher and date, but any of these may be omitted if it is common to a number of descriptions standing together. The order in which these items appear in the heading will, of course, depend on the basic arrangement of the bibliography, the key item being placed first or given prominence by the use of bold type. For ease of reference the heading is always set in roman or italic with date in arabic numerals no matter how the various features appear in the original book.

THE ENTRIES

We may now consider the composition of the entries themselves when constructed for a full bibliographical description. Each consists of two main sections: transcripts of the more important pages and a technical description which includes an analysis of the contents. The bibliographer is also at liberty to append any relevant notes which either explain more fully some detail of the description or relate to the printing and publishing history of the book.

Transcripts are made of the following, assuming they are all present in the book:

> title-page
>
> special and section titles, e.g. when a book is divided into parts and each part is provided with its own section-title
>
> half-title, printed on a separate leaf preceding the title-page
>
> head-title, found at the head of the first page of text
>
> running-title, which appears in the headline at the top of the text-pages
>
> explicit, or author's colophon, which sometimes incorporates the finis. It should include the title of the work or the name or initials of the author, and may be distinguished from the printer's colophon by the absence of any mention of printing (Greg)
>
> printer's or publisher's colophon
>
> a selection of catchwords, although these are not included in the transcripts section of the description but come later in the technical paragraphs.

The technical description is concerned with the physical make-up of the book and includes:

> format

signature formula, showing the way in which quires are gathered and how they are signed

numbering of the leaves or pages

numbering and positioning of the plates and insets, such as tables and maps

analysis of contents, describing the various parts of the book and indicating the positions they occupy. For most books of the period reference is usually made by the signatures and every leaf in the book, including those left blank, must be accounted for. The analysis usually takes a separate paragraph although in Greg's *Bibliography*, because of the comparatively short nature of most of the plays, it forms part of the collation paragraph and is not credited with a separate heading

transcription of a selection of the catchwords

details of the book's typography, i.e. the number of columns and lines to the page, measurement of a typical type-page and a brief description of the style and size of type.

Title-page

The purpose of the title-page is to advertise and identify the book. Of all the pages in a book it is the most variable in content since its letterpress usually reflects any purposeful alteration to the text, e.g. a new edition, revision by the author, the addition of a new appendix, etc. It also contains the imprint which supplies the bibliographer with details of printing and publishing. A transcript of the title-page is, therefore, an essential feature of any description.

There are various methods by which a title-page and other parts of a book may be transcribed but only one which can be regarded as scientific and satisfying the requirements of a full description. For ease of use (and, one suspects, of compilation) many bibliographies are provided with simplified transcripts that either render the original letterpress in roman type, or, because of the lengthy nature of many early titles, abbreviate the wording to the main essentials. But to establish a standard of reference against which other copies of the same book may be checked for variants, the original has to be described as exactly as possible and this can only be done by employing the "quasi-facsimile" method of transcription. This requires that the three main classes of type—roman, italic and gothic—are transcribed as they stand with no omissions and with the capitalization followed exactly. Even so, because it is set out in paragraph form, the quasi-facsimile transcript remains a compromise for no indication is given of the size of the original type nor of the spacing and lay-out of the page.

It may be argued that a more efficient way to reproduce the appearance of the original would be to make a photographic facsimile, but this too has its disadvantages in the matter of production costs, and, surprisingly enough, in its annoying capacity for reproducing a blemish in such a way that it looks like a punctuation mark or a special form of type, etc. Moreover, the possibility of retouching photographic negatives to eliminate such blemishes and to improve the quality of the reproduction may inadvertently result in the removal or alteration of evidence of bibliographical importance. It should also not be forgotten that the description is of an ideal copy and in the case of a rare book where all existing copies suffer from mutilation the transcript may have to be constructed: this would be impossible by photographic reproduction.

Borders

Many title-pages were printed with ornamental borders surrounding the letterpress, and these have to be identified or described before the transcript is begun. The term "border" is too vague for precise bibliographical definition and it is usually divided into "compartment" and "frame". Compartment is used for a border made in one piece or of a unified design which has been cut into pieces for ease of assembly around the letterpress. If the border has been constructed of individual blocks which show no evidence of having been designed as a unit, then Bowers recommends the term "frame". Greg uses compartment in the above sense, but retains border in place of frame to describe assembled enclosures, qualifying the term as a "border of pieces" or a "border of ornaments", or if the latter are made of small cast blocks fitted into a pattern, i.e. type-ornaments or fleurons, as a "lace-border". For this latter example, Bowers would prefer to say [within a frame of type-ornaments] or [within a lace frame]. Whenever possible it is convenient to refer to the useful monograph by R. B. McKerrow and F. S. Ferguson: *Title-page Borders used in England and Scotland 1485–1640*, (1932), which provides a numbered list of facsimiles, in which case we would say:

[within a compartment: McK. & F. 207]

Further examples were described by Ferguson in *The Library*, 4th series vol. xvii, (1936), pp. 264–311. Similarly, type ornaments have been reproduced by H. R. Plomer in *English Printers' Ornaments*, (1924), and reference may be made:

[within a frame of type ornaments: Plomer 19]

When such references are not possible the border should be briefly described giving the outside and inside measurements (height before width) as for example:

[within a compartment with the sun at top; signs of the zodiac and female figures at sides; moon and stars at foot; 85 × 58 mm. enclosing 63 × 40 mm.]

In the absence of ornamental borders title-pages were frequently enclosed within lines or rules and these too must be noted before the transcript. If a single rule frame surrounds the letterpress, this may be described as:

[within single rules]
[within a rule], or possibly
[within rules]

A double or treble frame would be noted:

[within double rules]
[within triple rules]

and combinations can be expressed as:

[within a rule, triple at sides], etc.

Sometimes the border surrounding the letterpress is itself enclosed by rules or a rule is placed at its outer or inner edge only. This may be described simply as being:

[within a compartment and rules]

or if one wished to be more precise, the position and number of the rules can be stated, working outward from the title, for instance:

[within a rule, within a compartment], or
[within a lace frame, within double rules], etc.

The letterpress

Excepting the size and spacing of the original type, a transcript by the quasi-facsimile method aims to reproduce as faithfully as possible the typography of the page. Since the transcript is made in paragraph form it cannot reflect the layout of the original and unless there is an indication to the contrary in the description, it is normally assumed that the lines of the original were centred on the page. When dealing with intentionally asymetrical lay-outs, it is best to depart from the continuous form of transcript and preserve the visual arrangement of the original. Line-endings are indicated by an upright bar "|" and although a sloping bar "/" is frequently found its use is not recommended, certainly for bibliographies listing early printed books because of the risk of confusion with the virgule, an early form of printed comma. Some bibliographers double the upright bar " || " to indicate a printer's rule across the page, but this is a doubtful alternative to noting it in square brackets " | [rule] | ". No attempt should be made to correct misprints occurring in the original since the aim is to render as faithful a copy as possible. Nor is it good practice to draw attention to them where they occur by the use of "[!]" or "[sic]" since interpolations should be kept to a minimum. They should be repeated at the end of the transcript either within brackets or introduced by *stet or stent*.

Title-pages are sometimes printed partly in black and partly in red. Greg underlines the words in red with a row of dots and adds at the end of the transcript:

[printed in black and red]

Bowers prefers the explanation to precede the transcript:

[in black and red] THE WORKS OF . . .

and for the words in red to be transcribed with a solid underlining. It should be noted that all notes and explanations must be included in "[ ]" for everything that stands outside these is assumed to be present on the original page.

It is practicable to follow only approximately the typographical style of the original by retaining the three main classes of type—roman, italic and gothic: the exact varieties of type are never imitated. Even so some difficulties arise from this compromise. The roman capital letter W was a late comer to the printer's case and, when needed, was frequently made up by employing two VVs. When the Vs appear as distinct letters, they should be reproduced as they stand, but printers endeavoured to construct a more obvious W by filing down one or both of the inner limbs so that the two faces would stand closer together. The problem in transcription is whether to treat filed Vs as separate Vs or as a W. McKerrow prefers to transcribe all cases of filing as Ws since this would reflect the printer's intention, but because of the difficulty of distinguishing filed letters from damaged and badly inked ones, Greg uses VV when both the inner limbs reach the top of the face, and only transcribes as W when either are less than full height. Bowers feels that even this is not foolproof and recommends that a note of explanation should be added after the transcript whenever two V sorts are transcribed as W.

Roman founts contain an alphabet of small caps[3] in addition to full capitals and lower-case letters. When they stand in the same line as capitals, lower-case letters or arabic numerals, they can easily be distinguished because their height extends no further than the x-height of the lower-case (the height of an x), but when capitals exist in a line of their own there is no way of proving whether they are, in fact, small caps or capitals of a smaller fount that is used elsewhere on the title-page. The rules of quasi-facsimile transcript reflect this dilemma, for while small caps are used when they are distinguishable, a line which consists entirely of what appears to be small caps is transcribed as full capitals. This results occasionally in a minor word of the title which happens to stand on its own line being over-emphas-

---

[3] Greg proposed the use of "small-caps" as an acceptable bibliographical term to distinguish from "small capitals" meaning the capitals of a small fount.

ized in the transcript, but if the line is to be treated as a unit for the purpose of transcription, this cannot be avoided. An absurd position is reached, however, when a word containing demonstrably small-caps is continued on the next line where no other alphabets are present to act as distinguishing agents, e.g. when "IMPRINTED AT LON-|DON" appears in the original, it must be transcribed according to the rules as

IMPRINTED AT LON-|DON

McKerrow was for strictly observing the rules, but Greg, supported by Bowers, preferred the more commonsense approach of continuing the second line in small caps:

IMPRINTED AT LON-|DON

Until the 1790s, when John Bell persistently used the short s throughout, the Roman lower-case alphabet contained a long f which was used at the beginning and within a word in addition to the s which was employed at the end. Where there is no possibility of confusion, as with books published before the latter part of the xviii century, many bibliographers transcribe both forms with a short s, it being assumed that the original practice is well understood. But this is a clear departure from the rules of quasi-facsimile transcription and is adopted for the sake of modern convenience. In a full bibliographical description, therefore, the distinction should always be retained.

Italic capitals, except for about six letters of the alphabet, are found in two distinct styles—the ordinary italic resembling a sloping roman and a more ornamental variety known as "swash" letters. The two styles were frequently used indiscriminately and accordingly it might be argued that in transcription both could safely be represented by the simple italic capital. Certainly to transcribe all swash letters with their modern counterparts would exacerbate the already complicated typesetting by quasi-facsimile and would involve an undue amount of checking and proof-reading. Greg feels there is a case, however, for distinguishing in transcript the forms *I* and *J* and *V* and *U*, as they came to be differentiated in use, the *I* and *U* being used to represent vowel sounds and the *J* and *V* the consonants.

One form of letter peculiar to italic lower-case was the tailed variety of *a, e, m, n, t,* which originally seems to have derived from combining the ordinary form with a following full stop. However, because these letters possessed a certain ornamental quality they came to be used in places where a stop was not required. In these instances Greg ignores them and transcribes with an ordinary lower-case italic, but where their position reflects a combination of letter and full stop, he indicates the stop in brackets after using an ordinary letter, e.g. *a*[.]. Bowers offers an alternative method—a single pointed bracket > following the letter, which may be used to advantage in all circumstances uninfluenced by the purpose of its original employment. From the example given on page 162 of his *Principles of Bibliographical Description* he would follow the bracket with a full stop at the end of a sentence.

Although the varieties of Gothic type were legion they are all transcribed by standard black letter: a more precise description of the original type may be given in the notes at the end of the description. Gothic not only has two varieties of s: "ſ" and "s", but also two forms of the letter r, namely "r" and "ꝛ", and if possible the distinction between these two should also be retained in the transcript, although this might depend on the availability to the modern printer of the ꝛ form.

Ligatures or tied letters exist in their several varieties in each of the three main classes of type, in fact, they appeared more frequently in earlier than in modern books, and were particularly prevalent in Gothic founts. Their counterparts are seldom available nowadays and for this, if for no other reason, they are ignored in the transcript, with the exceptions of æ and œ in their lower-case and capital letter forms. Sometimes the printer had no such ligatures and set them as AE or oe in which case the transcript follows suit. But as McKerrow, Greg and Bowers have pointed out a problem arises when the printer, having no ligatured forms, nevertheless tried to indicate a ligature by inserting spaces between the letters of a word other than between the two digraph vowels, e.g. C O M OE D I E. Should this be transcribed as a ligature or not? McKerrow merely poses the problem but offers no solution, Greg removes the spaces on the grounds that they are normally ignored in quasi-facsimile and transcribes as COMOEDIE, but

Bowers feels there is a case here for representing the printer's intention and reproducing his spacing as it stands: C O M OE D I E.

Turned letters, "ı", etc., should be treated as misprints, i.e. transcribed as they stand and repeated at the end of the transcript. But some letters can cause difficulty because they look almost exactly the same upside-down as when correctly set, e.g. "o" and "s". In such cases, to avoid overcrowding the list of misprints, it seems worthwhile to give the original the benefit of the doubt and not to describe them as misprints. On the other hand wrong fount letters, both those set in a wrong variety of type, e.g. italic for roman, and those of a different size, are usually distinguishable and should be included in the list of misprints. Greg, however, follows the rules very strictly, ignoring wrong-sized letters on the grounds that quasi-facsimile is not concerned with size.

The use of a wrong fount can apply not only to letters but also to punctuation marks. The full stop and comma are virtually indistinguishable between roman and italic and although Gothic marks can be determined, bad presswork often casts doubt on their true identity. Greg prefers to transcribe them by using marks that it would be normal to use and not to list any as misprints. Punctuation marks, however, have been known to distinguish issues and editions, so where there is no question that a wrong fount was used, the mark should be transcribed as it stands but may be omitted from the list unless there is some definite need to emphasize its existence. Attention should also be drawn to obvious misprints, for example, the insertion of a full stop in the middle of a sentence, by repeating the error at the end of the transcript.

Contractions should not be expanded but transcribed either as they stand or in a form which approximates to the original. Some modern printers may have difficulty in matching older contractions and for this reason the expansion of the original by using italic type has been advocated. However, the obvious risk of confusing such expansions with wrong fount letters makes this a very doubtful practice.

Reference has been made to the treatment of printers' rules which run across the page dividing the text into sections, as opposed to those which form a frame enclosing the title. The use of [rule] is taken to mean one which reaches fully across the page or almost so; anything else is indicated by [short rule]. Various kinds of rules, e.g. tapered, wavy, and so on, may be described as such, or else may be gathered under the embracing term [ornamental rule]. A rule is treated in the transcript as a separate line and is both preceded and followed by an upright bar: | [double rule] |.

Small cast ornaments such as stars, acorns, leaves, etc., are sometimes used for the same purpose as rules and if available to the modern printer should be reproduced in the transcript. Often a compromise has to be made by using a standardized form to represent the particular variety in the original, and as a last resort one may use

[row of ornaments]

[group of type ornaments]

[three star ornaments], and similar descriptions.

Ornaments, particularly those used on occasion for head and tail-pieces, may also take a more pictorial form such as a garland, mermaid, helmet, etc., printed from woodcuts or engraved metal plates. A number are listed in H. R. Plomer's *English Printers' Ornaments*, (1924), and may be conveniently cited as [orn: Plomer 75]. Failing such a reference ornaments should be described and measured:

[orn: spirals of foliage, squirrel in centre, 101·5 × 13 mm.]

Title-pages are frequently adorned with woodcuts and engravings depicting printers' devices and illustrations. Devices have been described and reproduced in McKerrow's *Printers' and Publishers' Devices in England and Scotland, 1485–1640*, (1913), and reference is usually made to McKerrow's numbering:

[device: McK. 290]

Otherwise the device should be described briefly and its measurements given. In transcription the terms "woodcut" and "engraving" are best used to describe illustrations as opposed to devices but the treatment is the same:

[woodcut: Hodnett 2252]

referring the reader to E. Hodnett's *English woodcuts, 1480–1535*, (1935), or

> [engraving: in a circle a boy king, facing right, a sceptre in his right hand, diam. 39 mm.]

or simply as [woodcut], leaving the description to follow the transcript or for the notes at the end of the entry.

Engraved title-pages are very difficult to describe successfully and whenever possible should be reproduced by a plate in the bibliography; alternatively the reader may be referred to A. F. Johnson, *A Catalogue of Engraved and Etched English Title-pages to 1691*, (1934):

> [engraved title: Johnson: Marshall No. 55]

If a description is unavoidable the text should be transcribed as far as possible by quasi-facsimile but it must be admitted that some engraved letter-forms cannot be translated accurately into type and approximations are sometimes unavoidable. The overall measurement must again accompany the description and should relate to a rectangle drawn to enclose the printed engraved design. Some books are provided with both engraved and printed titles and are transcribed:

> [engraved title: Johnson: Marshall No. 55]
> [printed title] [within a frame of acorn type ornaments] Epigrammata | Thomae Mori | ANGLI, | ...

If a description has to be provided for the engraved title it is better for this to be relegated to the end of the entry so as to give prominence to the text of the printed title:

> [engraved title: see below]
> [printed title] THE | WORKS | OF...

Finally, on a line following the transcript any variant readings of the title should be noted introduced by:

> *variant title*, or if relating only to the imprint:
> *variant imprint*.

The aim should be to indicate the variant as clearly and concisely as possible, reducing its transcription to a minimum, for example, if the only difference from the first transcribed form is a change of date, only the variant date needs to be noted. It is, of course, assumed that such variants are the result of stop-press corrections, for a cancellans title not part of the original book would be noted with the introduction

cancel title

and its transcript given immediately after that of the original title.

The following specimen quasi-facsimile transcript is of the title-page to Alexander Barclay's translation of Sebastian Brandt's *The Ship of Fooles* printed by John Cawood in 1570 and reproduced on page 161.

Stultifera Nauis,| qua omnium mortalium narratur ſtultitia, admo≥|dum vtilis & neceſſaria ab omnibus ad ſuam ſalutem perlegenda,|è Latino ſermone in noſtrum vulgarem verſa, & iam diligenter|impreſſa. An. Do. 1570. |[woodcut]|The Ship of Fooles, wherin is ſhewed the folly|of all States, with diuers other wozkes adioyned vnto the ſame,|very pzofitable and fruitfull foz all men.| ¶Tranſlated out of Latin into Engliſhe by Alexander|Barclay Pzieſt.

Special titles, section titles, half-title

Various subsidiary titles are sometimes found in a book in addition to that found on the main title-page. For instance, in the collected works of an author, each individual item may be provided with its special title-page; plays may be gathered into sections containing comedies, tragedies, etc., each section separately titled; and from the xvii century onwards books were frequently equipped with half-titles printed on a separate leaf immediately preceding the title-page. A transcript of any of these features present in a book is an aid to identification and completeness and may reveal variations from the order in which the several parts have been gathered. It should follow the rules adopted for the title-page, but with the addition of a signature reference to indicate the exact position the subsidiary title occupies in the book:

special title, P1] THE LAST | THOUGHTS | OF...
section title, 2R1] The | *TRAGEDIES* | [tapered rule]
half-title, π1] The Goodly Cleric | [group of type orn.]

Head-title

The head-title is normally found at the head of the first page of the text, although sometimes it strays to the head of a page in the

Stultifera Nauis,

qua omnium mortalium narratur ſtultitia, admo-
dum vtilis & neceſſaria ab omnibus ad ſuam ſalutem perlegenda,
è Latino ſermone in noſtrum vulgarem verſa, & iam diligenter
impreſſa. An. Do. 1 5 7 0.

The Ship of Fooles, wherin is ſhewed the folly

of all States, with diuers other workes adioyned vnto the ſame,
very profitable and fruitfull for all men.

¶ Tranſlated out of Latin into Engliſhe by Alexander
Barclay Prieſt.

preliminaries. It can offer evidence of resetting and may vary from the title-page title being occasionally the author's own version. The head-title should be noted on a separate line introduced by "HT]" and should include a note of any accompanying ornament and rules unless they form part of the general typographical make-up of the book:

HT] *Chrifts victorie over the Dragon* | [row of acorn type orn.]

Running-title

If the whole or a major part of the book carries a constant running-title, this is now transcribed following the abbreviation "RT]." Sometimes a running-title is omitted and a mere description of the work is provided in its place, as "A Difcourfe", in which case it would be more accurate to begin the transcript with:

RT][none: headline] A Difcourfe

Most running-titles are contained in a single headline but lengthy ones frequently extend across both pages of an opening and occupy two headlines. For these it is necessary to indicate that the title is divided between two pages by the use of an upright bar:

The Myfterie | *of Vintners*

The important part that headlines can play in bibliographical analysis has been demonstrated in the previous chapter. Once a particular set of headlines has been identified its transference from forme to forme can be traced through the gatherings of a book. Identification is usually achieved by noting any variation in the typography, capitalization or spelling of the running-titles, and although their transcription seldom indicates the exact sequence of headline sets, nevertheless it provides a starting place for a more detailed investigation as well as offering evidence of cancels and other kinds of resetting. If the bibliographer has determined the sequence of headline sets, the place for his conclusions is not here but in a note at the end of the entry.

There is an important difference between the transcript of running-titles and those of the title-page and various subsidiary titles we have just considered. These transcripts were each made from one original, but a transcript of the running-title has to represent repeated settings at the head of each page, many of which may offer minor variations. One has to select, therefore, the most-used form of running-title to transcribe and to note any variants. If the variants occur regularly throughout the book it is convenient to use the sign "$", meaning "all gatherings", e.g.

> RT] *Chrifts victorie over the Dragon:* | or, *Satans downfall* [*victory* $5^{v}7$^v]

which signifies that "victorie" was spelt with a "y" on the versos of the fifth and seventh leaves of each gathering.

Where variants occur irregularly one may note the number of times each appears in stated gatherings:

> RT] *Chrifts victorie over the Dragon:* | or, *Satans downfall* [*victory* 2$ *or* 1B—F]

where "victorie" with a "y" appears twice in all gatherings and "or" is set in italic once in gatherings B,C,D,E and F.

But unless the transcription becomes too complicated it is better to give the exact position of the variants:

> [*victory* BC2^v, B3^v, CD4^v, FHI5^v, EG6^v, DEFGH7^v, I8^v; *or* B1, CD2, EF5]

Explicit and colophon

In the early xvi century the title-page gradually assumed the function previously performed by the colophon, but many printers continued to include this feature on the last page of a book. Being a statement by the printer himself about the production of the book it often includes information additional to that found in the title-page imprint. It may contain, for example, the printer's name or initials, the date and place of printing, and perhaps an indication where the book could be purchased. Its transcription is, therefore, of importance and recognising this, Bowers places it immediately after the transcript of the title-page, but it may, as considered here, complete the section of the description comprising the transcripts. It is transcribed in full according to the rules specified for the title-page and its exact position is noted by means of a page reference. When the colophon is precisely the same as the imprint (occasionally it was printed from the same setting of type), its transcript may be omitted but its presence in the book should still be noted:

Colophon, N2^v: [as imprint]

Any ornaments and rules following the colophon should also be described but those preceding are only indicated if they are obviously set as part of the colophon and not as part of the general typographical treatment of the text:

Colophon, G7^v: Imprinted at Londō in Paules churcheyarde, at the signe of the Lucrece | by Thomas Purfoote | 1567. | [double row of type orn.]

The explicit, if there is one, should be treated in exactly the same way. This is, in effect, the author's colophon and is a feature of some early books retained from former manuscript practice. It is not concerned with the book's printing, but with the completion of its writing and contains the finis (if present) as well as the author's name or initials, or at least the title of the work.

Explicit, D6: FINIS. | Thus endeth the fifth and laſt Eg⸗ | loge of Alexander Barclay, of the Citi-|zen and the man of the countrey.

Of course the finis itself does not constitute an explicit and it is only usually noted in the contents, although Greg in his *Bibliography* noted it separately. Sometimes the explicit is syntactically joined to the colophon in which case it is best treated as part of the colophon and no attempt at separation should be made:

Colophon, I4^v: ℭ Here endeth a lptell cronicle tranſlated out of frenche| into englpſſhe at the coſt ⁊ charge of Richarde Pynson| by the commaūdement of the right high and mighty|prince, Edwarde duke of Buckyngham, erle of Glou⸗|ceſtre, Staffarde, ⁊ of Northamton. And impzinted by|the ſapd Richarde Pynſon, pzinter bnto the Kinges no ⸗|ble grace. Cum pziuilegio a rege indulto.

CHAPTER 13

Bibliographical Description (2)

The transcript of the colophon concludes the first part of the full description and we turn now to the technical section which describes the physical make-up of the book. It consists of a collation paragraph, the analysis of contents, a transcription of a selection of the catchwords and a description of the book's typography.

Collation Paragraph

Format

The format is a statement of how the sheets of paper were folded to form gatherings. This is ascertained by examining the paper for the position of the watermark and the direction of the chain-lines as referred to on page 65 when the identification of incunabula was considered. The method is fully described in McKerrow[1] and in the majority of cases the format may be noted by using the familiar symbols 2°, 4°, 8°, 12°, &c. for folio, quarto, octavo, duodecimo, and so on. However, one occasionally comes across a book which appears at first glance to be a quarto, i.e. in shape and size and with its leaves gathered in 4s, but which on examination reveals vertical chain-lines and a watermark in the top inner corner of the leaves. According to the rules of evidence such a book is an octavo. A. T. Hazen[2] has shown that during the xviii century the manufacture of a sheet of paper double the normal size was developed of the same shape as two ordinary sheets joined by their longer edges. The chain-lines still ran parallel to the shorter edge of the sheet and the watermark was retained in the centre of one half. This kind of paper is thought by Hazen

[1] Introduction to Bibliography, pp. 164–74.
[2] "Eighteenth-century Quartos with vertical Chain-lines". The Library. 4th series. Vol. xvi, (1935), pp. 337–42.

to have been produced for reasons of economy as it was almost as cheap to manufacture as normal sized sheets. But although, theoretically, it was possible to print on double sheets, it was much easier to keep to normal sizes, consequently we must accept that the sheet would have been cut in two before printing. Double sheets were occasionally made before the xviii century for Greg came across quartos with vertical chain-lines in compiling his *Bibliography of Printed Drama* which includes no books later than 1700. Indeed, in this earlier period the old hand-press probably lacked the power to print a double sheet.

In establishing format, the basis of calculation is always the full sheet so that a cut is reckoned as a fold. In the books mentioned above, which Hazen calls "Quartos with vertical chain-lines", after cutting each resulting half-sheet was divided twice (= 3 folds) producing octavos with correspondingly normal chain-lines and watermarks. But because of their unusual size and shape Bowers recommends the adoption of Greg's description: (4°-form) 8°: A—L^4. Similarly a 4° produced in the same way would be described as: (2°-form) 4°: A—L^2, and so on for other formats.

Signature formulary

With the format established the make-up of the book may now be defined by listing the gatherings by signatures and indicating the number of leaves each contains by means of a superior index number. "A^6", for instance, stands for a gathering signed A with six leaves formed from three regular folds. There are, however, many variations of signing, numerous cases of non-signing, and gatherings which consist of an irregular number of leaves. To indicate all these possibilities the formulary which has been evolved is inevitably complicated.

Signatures were intended as an indication to the binder of how the sheets were to be folded and gathered. When they were first introduced into the printed book it was common practice to sign all the leaves of a gathering, the first simply with a letter, e.g. B, the second B2 or BII, and so on. Generally, however, until the xviii century gatherings were signed up to the sewing and sometimes included the next leaf to show the binder that another fold was not intended in the centre of the gathering. Today, if the book is signed at all, it is normal for just the first leaf of the gathering to bear a signature. Only the 23 letters of the Latin alphabet were used for signing, J, U and W being omitted. Occasionally we find J is substituted for I and U for V, but W is so rare that its use calls for a special note in the formulary. When quoting signatures it is important to retain the distinction between the use of upper- and lower-case letters, but signatures set in gothic and italic are quoted in roman.

Printers also made extensive use of conventional signs, e.g. *, ¶, &, ℂ, etc., particularly for signing the preliminary leaves and they must be copied as they stand or at least with modern equivalents if the early forms are no longer available to the modern printer.

Normal gatherings are always composed of folds forming pairs of conjugate leaves, thus the index numbers should always be even. When taken into consideration with the format, they indicate the number of sheets of paper that were required for the book and how many times each was folded to form a complete gathering. For example, the formula $4°$, A — E^4 represents a straightforward quarto of 5 sheets, each gathering formed of one sheet folded twice to give 4 leaves. $4°$, A — P^8, however, is a quarto of 30 sheets with 15 gatherings each with 8 leaves constructed from 2 sheets folded twice and quired within each other. Yet again, $8°$, A — P^4 would indicate an octavo consisting of $7\frac{1}{2}$ sheets, each sheet being cut in two to form a book of 15 half-sheets which were then folded twice to form 15 gatherings of 4 leaves each.

It will be noted that when the gatherings each contain the same number of leaves, the signatures are not set down individually, but only the first and last are given to simplify the notation, e.g. A — Z^4 represents 23 gatherings each of 4 leaves. If the leaves per gathering are not constant, the irregularities must be indicated separately: $4°$, A^2 B — P^4 Q^2. Sometimes books are found in which gatherings of different sizes follow in a regular sequence, e.g. A^8 B^6 C^8 D^6, or, A^8 B^4 C^4 D^8 E^4 F^4. This is abbreviated to A — D$^{8\cdot6}$ and A — F$^{8\cdot4\cdot4}$.

If the number of gatherings in a book exceeded 23 the printer usually doubled-up on his alphabet of signatures and subsequently trebled it and so on to form a series of alphabets beginning with a, aa, aaa, or A, AA, AAA, or A, Aa, Aaa, etc. Although upper- and lower-case alphabets are normally preserved as such in quotation, the mixed alphabet Aa, Bb, Cc. . . is treated as though it were AA, BB, CC. . . . To set down multiple series of alphabets in full would result in a very lengthy and cumbersome collation, so we write 2a and 3a in place of aa and aaa, and 2A and 3A for AA or Aa and AAA or Aaa. Moreover, providing the alphabets are complete and the number of leaves in each gathering is constant, as in $8°$, $A — Z^8$, $2A — 2Z^8$, $3A — 3P^8$, the formula may be reduced to $8°$, $A — 3P^8$. It will be noted that the prefixed numeral indicating the series always accompanies the signature letter, e.g. $2Z^8$ and $3P^8$, and it would be incorrect to write $2A — Z^8$, $3A — P^8$. Conventional signs are frequently found in multiples, as $*^2**^2***^2$ for which we would write $* — 3*^2$, each sign treated as though it were an alphabet.

Occasionally we come across not multiple but duplicate signings, e.g. $A — T^4$, $A — O^4$ in the same book. This often occurred when a book was divided between a number of printers, each using a similar series of letters. It is essential for the series to be distinguished from each other otherwise it would be impossible to refer to a particular gathering. For instance, in a book with the collation $A — Z^4$, $A — M^4$, $A — D^4$ there are three gatherings signed D. The distinguishing feature is a superior index figure prefixed to the duplicate series, the above collation being written $A — Z^4$, $^2A — M^4$, $^3A — D^4$. The fact that a doubled alphabet might intervene between duplicate signings does not alter the principle, e.g. $A — Z^8$, $Aa — Pp^8$, $A — E^8$ would be recorded as $A — 2P^8$ $^2A — E^8$. The prefixed figure relates to the alphabet as a whole, thus it is not necessary to repeat it against each letter: we write $^2A — E^8$ and not $^2A — ^2E^8$.

We have assumed until now that all gatherings have been signed, but this is not always the case. By an "unsigned" gathering we mean one which does not bear a letter or symbol on *any* of its leaves to distinguish it from other gatherings. If only one leaf carries a signature we consider the gathering to be signed, but it is not sufficient for the leaves merely to bear numbers, e.g. II, III, etc., in the position where a signature is normally found. Numbers alone do not distinguish a particular gathering, which must, accordingly, be regarded as unsigned. Whenever possible the signature of an unsigned gathering should be inferred, that is, we supply the signature the printer would have used had he signed it. Thus in a book which has an initial gathering unsigned, but with the second signed B, the third C, and so on, it is logical to infer that had the printer signed the first gathering he would have used the letter A. Although the appropriate letter or symbol is supplied in the collation, the fact that the gathering was unsigned has to be recorded, and this is done either by enclosing the inferred signature in brackets, or, as signatures are always quoted in roman, by using italic:

$$[\text{A}]^4 \text{ B } - \text{ M}^4, \text{ or, } A^4 \text{ B } - M^4$$

Of course, conventional signs cannot be italicised and have of necessity to be bracketed: $*^4 [2*]^2 \text{ A } - \text{ P}^4$. Unsigned gatherings occur in the body and at the end of a book as well as in the preliminaries and, again, they should be inferred whenever possible:

$$\text{A } - \text{ L}^4 [\text{M}]^4 \text{ N } - \text{ X}^4 \text{ or, A } - \text{ L}^4 M^4 \text{ N } - \text{ X}^4$$
$$\text{A } - \text{ L}^4 [\text{M}]^2 \text{ or, A } - \text{ L}^4 M^2$$

When inference is impossible as in the case of an unsigned first gathering followed by A, or an unsigned gathering found between M and N, it is necessary to provide an arbitrary symbol. McKerrow suggested the Greek letter π to stand for an unsigned gathering in the preliminaries and later Greg proposed the use of χ for one inserted elsewhere in the normal series. Both letters are now standard practice:

$$\pi^2 \text{ A } - \text{ X}^4 \qquad\qquad \text{A } - \text{ M}^4 \; \chi^2 \text{ N } - \text{ P}^4$$
$$\pi^2 \; *^2 \text{ A } - \text{ X}^4$$

If several unsigned gatherings occur in the preliminaries, none of which may be inferred, they are assumed to be multiples and are distinguished by π, 2π, 3π, and so on: for three unsigned preliminary gatherings we would write $\pi - 3\pi^4$ A$-$ P^4. A number of similar gatherings occurring in the body of a book, either together or separated by signed gatherings, are distinguished in like manner by writing χ, 2χ, 3χ, and so on:

$$\text{A } - \text{ E}^4 \; \chi^2 \text{ F } - \text{ G}^4 \; 2\chi^2 \text{ H } - \text{ L}^4 \; 3\chi^4 \text{ M}^4$$

Greg had another use for π and χ. Occasionally books are found in which the first page of text is signed A but with a preliminary gathering also signed A. If the rule for duplicate alphabets is followed, the main series would be relegated to ^{2}A, e.g. A^2, ^{2}A — Y^4, but to avoid this Greg distinguished the first gathering by prefixing a superior $^\pi$, and so we would have $^\pi$A^2, A — Y^4. In the same way where a gathering has been added to the body of a book bearing a signature which duplicates that of another, usually an adjoining, gathering, for instance A B C D D E, Greg would distinguish the insertion (which has, of course, to be identified) by writing ^{x}D.

We can now turn our attention to the methods of recording the actual number of leaves in each gathering. Index numbers are used for this purpose and represent, as we have seen, the number of regular folds in the gathering: they must, therefore, always be even. Many gatherings, however, contain an odd number of leaves, the result of one or more being cancelled or inserted by the printer. We are not concerned with leaves that have been accidently lost from a book because, of course, we are describing an ideal copy. Nor should it be assumed that the modifications made to the original gathering necessarily affect the text, for a common cause of cancellation was the removal of blank leaves resulting from a miscalculation of the length of copy when the text had been divided between a number of compositors. All modifications whether single leaves or folds are noted in parenthesis, using a minus sign for a cancellation and a plus sign for an insertion. For instance, A^4 (— A2) indicates that the second leaf has been cancelled, and B^4 (B2 + 1) denotes an unsigned leaf has been inserted between B2 and B3; and B^4 (B4 + B5) indicates a signed insertion after the last leaf of the gathering.

When a gathering shows a cancellation or insertion of more than one leaf, it is important, in order to reveal the exact construction of the gathering, to differentiate between leaves that are disjunct (single leaves not forming part of the same fold) and those that are conjugate (forming a fold). This is done by placing a comma between disjunct cancellations and inserts; and, when necessary, a full stop between leaves forming a fold:

C^8 (— C7, 8) indicates the cancellation of the two disjunct leaves C7 and C8.

D^4 ($D4 + D5$, $D6$) indicates the insertion of the two disjunct leaves signed $D5$ and $D6$.

D^4 ($D4 + 2$) indicates the insertion of two disjunct unsigned leaves.

E^8 ($- E1.8$) indicates the cancellation of the fold formed by the conjugate leaves $E1$ and $E8$.

$A - C^4$ $D4$ ($D3 + *^2$) $E - F^4$ $G^4(G2 + g2.1)$ $H^4(H1 + x^2)$ indicates a signed fold inserted between $D3$ and $D4$, a fold inserted after $G2$, the first leaf of which is signed $g2$ but the second is unsigned, and an unsigned fold inserted between leaves $H1$ and $H2$.

Insertions are not necessarily confined within gatherings for leaves or folds are frequently found between one gathering and another. Nevertheless, in the case of single leaves, if there is evidence that they are closely associated with a particular gathering, they should be added to that gathering in the formula:

$A^4(A4 + 1)$ relates the inserted leaf to the preceding gathering.

$A^4(A4 + 2)$ similarly records the insertion of two leaves.

A^4 B^4 ($1 + B1$) relates the inserted leaf to the following gathering.

If insertions cannot be associated with a gathering, or it would be unwise to do so, they should be treated independently:

A^4 $x1$ B^4 for a single leaf insertion, and

A^4 $x1, 2$ B^4 for two disjunct leaves.

The examples quoted have assumed the inserts to be unsigned but signed leaves are treated in the same way, although in some cases the signing may duplicate that of an existing leaf and, as a consequence, the signature of the insertion is placed within single quotes:

A^4 $B^4('B1' + B1)$ $C - F^4$ $*G1$ $G - K^4$ $*1,2$ L^4 indicates a leaf signed B has been inserted before the first leaf also signed B of the first gathering, a single leaf signed $*G$ inserted between gatherings F and G and two disjunct leaves signed $*$ inserted between gatherings K and L.

Folds inserted between gatherings are treated as independent items whether they are signed or not:

A^4 *^{2} B — D^4 x^2 E — F^4 ^{x}F^2 G — L^4 $2x^2$ indicates a single fold signed * inserted between gatherings A and B, an unsigned single fold between D and E, a single fold signed F which duplicates the signature of the preceding gathering and has, therefore, to be distinguished by ^{x} and a final single unsigned fold.

We have considered cancellations and insertions separately, but they can occur in the same gathering, when for instance, we might have A^4 $(- A2; A3 + 1)$ although Bowers prefers to note the insertion first: A^4 $(A3 + 1; -A2)$. A special case of this kind is provided by the presence of a cancel, i.e. when a leaf has been cut out of a gathering and another inserted in its place. We record it as, for instance, A^4 $(\pm A2)$, and when a whole gathering forms a cancel, we write T^4 $(\pm)$. No attempt is made to record whether or not the cancellans is signed. The formula becomes more complicated, however, when

(a) the insertion is greater or less than the cancellation

(b) the conjugacy differs

(c) the cancellans leaves are signed in a different manner from the rest of the gathering.

In these cases we should write:

(a) $A^4(- A2 + x1,2)$ for two separate unsigned leaves replacing A2.

$A^4(- A2 + x^2)$ for an unsigned fold replacing A2

$A^4(- A2 + a^2)$ for a fold signed a replacing A2

$A^4(- A2.3 + x1)$ for an unsigned leaf replacing the conjugate leaves A2 and A3

and so on.

(b) $A^4(- A1.4 + A1,4)$ for two disjunct leaves, the first leaf signed, the second unsigned, replacing the fold A1.4

$A^4(- A2, 3 + A2.A3)$ for a fold of two leaves signed A2 and A3 replacing the two disjunct leaves A2 and A3.

(c) $A^4(- A_1 + {}^*A_1)$
$A^4(- A_1 + a_1)$
$A^4(- A_{1.4} + {}^*A_{1.4})$
and so on.

Sometimes it is quite apparent that a cancellans has been printed on a leaf taken from a gathering in another part of the book. For example, when the text of a book has been started on A_1 (or B_1) and ended, say, on M_3, it would be convenient to print the title on the remaining blank leaf (M_4) and either remove it to the front of the book, or fold it round the back. The formula for such a book would be

$$\pi_1 A - L^4 M^4(- M_4) \text{ or, } A_1 B - L^4 M^4(- M_4)$$

and the fact that M^4 had been used to print the title could be explained in a note at the end of the description. However, it is probably more useful to note this in the formula itself, and we would write:

$$\pi_1(= M_4) A - L^4 M^4(- M_4) \text{ or } A_1 (= M_4) B - L^4 M^4(- M_4)$$

Occasionally a printer would make use of a blank leaf in the preliminaries to print a cancellans required elsewhere in the book, and we could record this, for instance, as:

$$*^4(- *_4) A - E^4 F^4(\pm F_2[= *_4]) G^4$$

Finally, special care needs to be taken when recording an abnormal number of leaves in the last gathering of a book. We have just seen how a last blank leaf was often used for printing the title, but one frequently finds the last gathering short of two leaves, as, for instance, when it consists in an octavo of only six leaves. The printer would have printed a full sheet of eight leaves, and only a careful examination of the gathering can determine the method he employed to remove the two leaves and to ensure that the formula reveals the correct make-up of the gathering. We must, of course, make sure that the text is complete and that the leaves have not been lost (even if they were blank), but assuming this to be so, the conjugacy of the leaves must be checked. The printer could have removed either the inner or outer fold of the gathering leaving three conjugate folds, or the last two leaves may have been cancelled when examination will show that the first and second leaves of the gathering are disjunct. In the first instance the correct formula would be, say, K^6 but in the second the formula must read $K^8(- K7, 8)$.

Statement of signing

Immediately following the signature formulary, many bibliographers include a statement of how the gatherings were actually signed. This should appear in a full description for it may point to the existence of cancels and other abnormalities in the make-up of a book and may help to identify a reprint which is a close copy of an earlier edition.

The method of signing altered in the course of time. In the earliest part of our period it was usual to sign each leaf in the first half of the gathering together with the first leaf following the sewing. After about the middle of the xvii century signing was confined to the leaves before the sewing and this remained standard practice (apart from folios in 2s most of which were fully signed) throughout the xviii century. When the books being described conform to the normal practice for their period there is little point in drawing attention to this, but any deviations should be noted. If, on the other hand, the bibliography spans a lengthy period during which the practice changed, it would seem safer to give a full statement of signing. When provided, it is placed in brackets and it is convenient to make use of Bowers' dollar sign $ when reference is being made to all gatherings. For instance, we would write

$4°$, A — L^4 [fully signed] or [$4 signed]

for a quarto in which all four leaves of every gathering are signed. Where only the first leaf is signed we write:

$4°$, A — L^4 [$1 only signed]

or, if only a few gatherings show variations, for instance, in an octavo when two cases of non-signing and two of extra-signing occur:

$8°$, A — L^8 [$4(—B2, L3; + CH5) signed]

Misprints are also recorded in the statement, the information being provided in the form "misprinting B2 as B3", or, "misprinting F4 as G4", as in the full statement:

4°, A — M4 [$3(— B2, C3; + L4) signed; misprinting D3 as F3].

Bowers notes that signatures printed in other than the normal fount may also be listed, but such discrepancies are ignored by Greg on the grounds that signatures are always quoted in roman type regardless of the fount in which they appear in the original.

Foliation and Pagination

The total number of leaves in the book follows separated from the statement of signing by a comma or semi-colon. The total is obtained by an actual count which must include any blank leaves that are an integral part of the gatherings and should agree with the number of leaves recorded in the signature formula:

4°, A — Z4[$2(+L3) signed], 92 leaves
4°, A — K4 L4(—L2) M4 (±M4) x^2 N — P4, 61 leaves

In most bibliographies the statement of foliation or pagination now follows, although occasionally, if the statement is a long one, it is given in a separate paragraph. Foliation refers to the numbering of leaves or folios (ff.) and pagination to the numbering of pages (pp.). If neither the folios nor the pages of a book are numbered, we write (say): "20 leaves unnumbered", otherwise the numbering is given of the first and last numbers of both the preliminaries (if numbered separately by the printer) and of the body of the book:

20 leaves, ff.i–vi, 1–14

which indicates there are 6 leaves foliated with roman numerals forming the preliminaries and 14 leaves foliated with arabic numerals forming the rest of the book. Note that the printer's method of numeration is given but that no distinction is made between roman, gothic and italic type.

Many books contain unnumbered folios or pages in addition to numbered ones, the unnumbered sometimes being counted by the printer, sometimes not. Of those that were counted, the ones occurring within a numbered sequence, such as blanks or section title-leaves, are treated as though numbered. For instance, in a book paged 1–60 where a section-title appears on an unnumbered page between 40 and 42, the pagination is simply written: 30 leaves, pp. 1–60. However, counted but unnumbered folios or pages found at the beginning of a sequence receive varied treatment from bibliographers. Greg, for example, gives the first and last numbers as they actually appear in the book regardless of any unnumbered folios or pages starting or ending a sequence, but he indicates in parentheses a signature-reference to the page on which the first number stands. Thus for a book which has two unnumbered leaves at the beginning, but which are followed by 28 leaves paginated 5–60, he would record:

30 leaves, paged (A3) 5–60

indicating that both A1, presumably the title-leaf, and the following leaf were counted by the printer yet unnumbered. Some prefer to ignore the fact that the pages are unnumbered (as with interior pages) and simply to write: pp. 1–60; others total the unnumbered pages recording the amount in italics within brackets: pp. [*4*] 5–60, and some infer the unnumbered pages: pp. [*1–4*] 5–60.

Unnumbered preliminary folios or pages *not* counted by the printer may either be totalled:

20 leaves, ff. [*4*] 1–16
20 leaves, pp. [*4*] i–vi, 1–30

as may those which appear at the end of the book:

20 leaves, ff. i–v, 1–13 [*2*]

although in this case the numbering can be inferred:

20 leaves, pp. i–x, 1–26 [*27–30*]

When we write: 30 leaves, pp. 1–60, we mean that the pagination runs normally from beginning to end without any omissions or misprints. But the numbering of books during the first two centuries of printing was frequently haphazard and usually some indication of the errors or omissions have to be given in the collation paragraph. Probably the most frequent error is misprinting: the sequences 21 32 23, 42 44 43, and 54 54 55, show obvious examples which we would note as follows:

30 leaves, pp. 1—60 [misprinting 22 as 32, 43–4 as 44–3, repeating 54].

Instead of "misprinting" Bowers prefers "misnumbering", reserving the former term to distinguish such aberrations as ᚼ7:

[misprinting 47 as "ᚼ7"]

When a printer counted but omitted to number a page that would normally have been numbered within a series, the omission may be noted either at the end of the statement:

30 leaves, pp. 1–60 [p. 33 unnumbered]

or in the statement itself simply by enclosing the missing number in brackets:

30 leaves, pp. 1–32 [33] 34–60

Similarly the "misnumberings" quoted above may also be noted by the formulary method:

30 leaves, pp. 1–21 32 23–42 44 43 45–54 54 55–60

Internal unnumbered pages which have *not* been counted by the printer are noted as italicised totals enclosed in brackets:

30 leaves, pp. [*4*] i–x, 1–24 [*2*] 25–46

In cases where the printer through misprintings or omissions ends his numbering with an incorrect total of folios or pages, it is useful to supply the correct figure in brackets. Each total must relate to the sequence of numbering in which the errors occurred and should not include bracketed totals not counted by the printer:

30 leaves, pp. [*2*] i–vi viii–xi [= 10], 1–18 [*2*] 19–30 32–51 [= 50]

Plates and insets

Illustrations, diagrams, tables, etc., which were printed along with the text form an integral part of the gatherings and as such have been included in the signature formula and in the foliation and pagination. But engraved titles, plates, maps, &c., which were separately printed and subsequently inserted in a book have been omitted from the record up till now since they stand outside the make-up of the original gatherings. They are usually the subject of a separate note at the end of the description but it is convenient also to note their presence immediately after the statement of foliation and pagination:

30 leaves, pp. 1–60; engraved title + plates I–IV

following the printer's numbering. If the plates are unnumbered, the total is given in arabic numerals:

30 leaves, pp. 1–60; plates [4]

preferably indicating where they have been inserted in the book:

plates [4] (opp. C2, D4^v, E3, F1^v)

A plate is only regarded as a frontispiece if it is so labelled, is referred to as such in a list of plates, or if it may be so inferred from the numbering of the subsequent plates:

marked: plates, Front., I–V, *or* plates, Front., II–VI
referred to: plates, [Front.], I–V
inferred: plates, *Front.*, I–V

If a book contains insets as well as plates in a single numbered sequence, they are noted together:

plates and insets, Front., II–X (opp. *etc.*)
otherwise they are separated:

plates, Front., II–VI (opp. *etc.*); insets [3] (opp. *etc.*)

Analysis of Contents

The next paragraph in the description lists the literary contents of the book. These may include an engraved title-leaf, frontispiece, printed title, the constituent parts of the preliminaries, the text and its major sections, appendices, tables and indexes. The position each part occupies in the book is indicated by signature references though most of the bibliographies of incunabula refer by foliation and for books of the xviii century reference is sometimes made by the pagination. The listing should account for all the leaves including those left blank by the printer, and should portray an ideal copy as represented in the signature formula.

Within the above framework there is room for a variety of treatment so long as it is consistent with the purpose of the bibliography. The majority of descriptive bibliographies have been produced as an adjunct to literary study and the analyses of contents have, therefore, been set down with the literary student mainly in mind. His major requirement is to know the precise contents of each work, particularly in the case of collected works, volumes of poetry and the like, including such important secondary features as the dedication, author's preface, letters, &c. In its simplest form, therefore, the analysis can be a mere statement of the various literary contents set down in the bibliographer's own words with the appropriate signature references. For example, in analysing the contents of Hayton's *A Little Chronicle*, printed by Richard Pynson, [1525] we should write:

A1, title; A1^v–2^v, introduction and table of contents; A3–G3^v, The Chronicle; G4, blank; H1–13^v, lists of cities and popes, etc.; 14, blank; 14^v, colophon and Pynson's device.

A more detailed treatment is provided by reproducing the headings as printed in the original. Generally this is done by means of the simplified method of transcription, or as Greg calls it, by "quotation". As employed by Greg in his *Bibliography of Printed Drama* the words reproduced are enclosed within quotation marks and rendered in roman lower-case with appropriate initials: line division is disregarded.

Although quotation is regarded as a simplified method of transcription, its application is not so clear-cut as the straightforward copying of the style and capitalization of the original type by the quasi-facsimile method. A difficulty arises from the fact that it uses initial capitals only when they are regarded as necessary: a vague ruling that leads to much inconsistency. One solution is to follow modern practice and confine capitals to proper names and similar words.

7A

This has the merit of near-uniformity but some bibliographers feel that the result is frequently too far removed from the style of early printing. For this reason the alternative is adopted of using capitals in the same way as the original printer would have done if, instead of laying-out a title-page, he had been setting a straightforward text. In this way words set entirely in full capitals are represented in lower-case with initial capitals used only where it is reasonably certain they would have been employed by the printer.

The second difficulty arising from the reduction of capitals to lower-case occurs because of differences between the old and modern use of the capitals I and V. As McKerrow pointed out[3] both the modern letters I and J were represented until the xvii century by the capital I in its roman, *I* or *J* in its italic and 𝕴 in its gothic forms. Similarly U and V were represented by V (roman), *V* or *𝒱* (italic) and 𝕬 (gothic). To take a head-title in the *Heptamerone* printed in Paris in 1559, we read "LA HVICTIESME IOVRNEE DES NOVVELLES DE LA ROYNE DE NAVARRE". In transcribing this title into lower-case letters we must use those which the original printer would have used in a lower-case setting. During this early period j was never used alone, but only in combination with i as in "Q. Horatij flacci", or in numerals as "vj" or "vij", &c., and v was only used at the beginning of a word, u being used in the middle and at the end. A simplified transcript of the head-title would therefore read:

"La huictiesme iournee des nouuelles de la Royne de Nauarre."

No problem arises when copying lower-case letters for in the transcript these are followed exactly. The use of roman only in the simplified method enables any interpolations to be printed in italic rather than between brackets.

The most informative note not only locates the major parts of the book but, by transcribing the headings in quasi-facsimile, permits copies to be checked for evidence of resetting in these areas. The presence of borders, ornaments and initials is also noted.

The first of the two following examples illustrates a contents note

---

3 Introduction to Bibliography, p. 310.

made by the simplified method and the second by quasi-facsimile transcription:

(a) For Edmund Bolton's *Elements of armories*, printed by George Eld, 1610.

π1: *title.* π1ᵛ: *quotation.* π2: *dedication* 'To the Right Honorable, Henrie, Earle of Northampton. . .' *signed* 'E.B.' π2ᵛ: *blank.* π3: 'The Opinions, and Offices of sundry choyce, and quallified Gentlemen, friendes to the Author, touching these his Elements of Armories'. π3ᵛ—A2ᵛ: *letters and poems to author.* A3: 'The Author to the generous, and learned Reader', *ending on* A4ᵛ 'Fare-well'. B1–2D1: *text.* 2D1ᵛ–2E2: 'A short table of some hard words, and phrases, with a few briefe notes'. *At foot* 2E2: 'Erratata.' *sic.* 2E2ᵛ–2E4ᵛ: 'A Table of matters, those principally which are not in the Contents of the Chapters.'

(b) For Girolamo Conestaggio's *The Histories of the Vniting of the Kingdom of Portugall to the Crowne of Castill,* translated by Edward Blount and printed for him by Arn. Hatfield, 1600.

A1: title. A1ᵛ: blank. A2: TO THE MOST NOBLE| and aboundant prefident both of |*Honor and vertue*, HENRY| Earle of Southampton.| [signed] EDW.BLOVNT. A2ᵛ: [ornament]| The Authors Apologie vnto|the Reader. A4ᵛ: THE GENEA-LOGIE OF THE | Kings of Portugall from the beginning of that | *kingdome, vnto the ende of the houfe of Por-|tugall, with the pretendants to | that Crowne.* B1: text [First book]. On D3: THE SECOND BOOKE. On F6: THE THIRDE BOOKE. On K2ᵛ: THE FOVRTH BOOKE. On N3ᵛ: THE FIFTH BOOKE. On R1: THE SIXTH BOOKE. On T3ᵛ: THE SEVENTH BOOKE. Y2ᵛ: THE EIGHT BOOKE. On 2B1ᵛ: THE NINTH BOOKE. 2D3ᵛ: THE TENTH BOOKE. 2F1: A Table of the efpeciall matters contained|*in this Historie.* On 2F4: FINIS. 2F4ᵛ: blank.

Catchwords

A selection of catchwords is included in the full description for this can provide a useful check on the resetting of pages and can help to distinguish an edition which is a close copy of another. It might also enable an imperfect copy of a book to be assigned to a particular edition. It is impractical to list the catchwords in full and the normal procedure is to take about half-a-dozen from the interior rather than the final pages of gatherings. The reason for this is that in following the setting of an earlier edition a compositor would be less concerned to match his composing page for page than he would be to conclude each gathering at the same place in the text. There is more likelihood, therefore, of coming across variant catchwords on the interior pages of a gathering than at the end. Of course, if in the examination of a number of copies, a variation is found, it should be included in the selection to be transcribed.

Catchwords should be transcribed as they stand by the quasi-facsimile method and any accompanying punctuation marks should be included. Their locations are indicated by signature-references and if a catchword is absent from a page on which it should normally appear, the signature-reference is given as usual followed by [none] and the first word of the following page in brackets. Brackets are also used to enclose the first word of the next page when it differs in any way from the catchword, and to enclose the warning *sic* or *stet* after a catchword containing an irregularity when this is repeated on the following page. Where a catchword consists of the end of a word only, the beginning of the word is supplied in parenthesis:

CW] C5^v Like F6^v 'Twould K3 Bu [But] M2^v [none] [Dramatis]
CW] B2^v I Pleb. [I *Pleb.*] D3 feirce [*sic*] F4^v (rabble)ment

Typographical Note

The final paragraph of the description proper is concerned with the book's typography. Some idea of the appearance of the title-page, sectional-titles and other main captions, were provided by the transcript paragraphs but the lay-out and dimensions of a typical page of text together with the style and size of type have now to be described. Such detailed information may be considered superfluous in a bibliography having as its primary aim the study of literature, but a description intended to be as definitive as possible is incomplete without it. Moreover, it should not be overlooked that typographical evidence may help to date a book or bring to light some irregularity of printing which has not been disclosed elsewhere in the description. The page chosen for description and measurement must be filled with type without any spaces between paragraphs or sections of the text, and should be specified in the note by its signature-reference.

We deal firstly with the layout of the type on the page and secondly with the type itself. If the type has been composed in two or more columns this fact is stated at the commencement of the note, otherwise just the number of lines of type to the page precedes the measurement of the type-area. Normally, each full page of text will contain an equal number of lines, but it is advisable to check various pages throughout the book to establish such uniformity. In some instances variations will be found and these should be noted in parentheses after the normal total: 36 (35–38) lines.

Measurements for the type-area are given in millimetres, first for the height of the block of type comprising just the text, and second, for the height of the total type-page which includes the headline at the top and the signature and catchword line at the bottom. The width of the letterpress then follows with the addition of an overall measurement if any marginal notes are present. The note so far may be written as follows:

36 lines + headline and signature & catchword line + marginal notes 148(160) × 86(96) mm. (G2)

or, since the formula is now firmly established, the statement may be abbreviated to:

36ll., 148(160) × 86(96) mm. (G2)

In taking these measurements of the text area the distance recorded is from the top of an ascender in the first line of the page to the bottom of a descender in the last line. The overall height should be similarly measured when the headline and signature and catchword line are included. It should be remembered that variable paper shrinkage can affect the result and pages from different gatherings in the book should be measured to ensure that the figures quoted represent the norm.

Two major problems present themselves in measuring some type-pages: pages of verse, and pages on which the text is enclosed by a rule-frame or ornamental border. With verse, the lines vary in length and none may extend to the full measure of the page. However, either the folio or page number or the catchword will run to the right-hand margin of the type-page, and the distance from the left-hand edge to an imaginary line drawn vertically from the end of the number or the catchword will provide the measurement required. In books without numbering and catchwords, the width can still be determined, providing the register is correct, by holding the leaf to the light and noting the point at which the letterpress begins on the verso.

In dealing with pages of text enclosed within frames and borders it is difficult to devise a formula capable of general application to the varied arrangements that may be encountered. Bowers recommends that such pages should receive individual treatment but this must include a note showing the relation of the rules to the headline and signature and catchword line as well as the overall measurement inclusive of the rules, borders or type in addition to that of the basic text area:

> 36ll., text 148 × 86 mm. Rule-frame encloses text and sig. & cw. line but excludes hdl. From hdl. to rule at foot, 160 mm. Width between rules, 94 mm. (G4^v)

> 48ll., text 154 × 90 mm. Frame of type-ornaments encloses text and hdl. and sig. & cw. line. 172 × 100 mm. enclosing 158 × 96 mm. (G3)

The measurements of the type-page as indicated above will meet the requirements of the majority of readers, but it is sometimes useful to include a note of the printer's measure. For example, when the pages have been set in two or more columns:

> 2 cols., 36ll., 140(150) × 96 mm.; printer's measure: 45 mm.

or, when two measures were used by the compositor, one for prose and one for verse. The prose measure will extend the full width of the type-page, but the verse measure will be shorter and its length can be ascertained by measuring an unfinished line which the printer had to continue on the line below or the one above. Both measures should be given:

> 36ll., 140(150) × 96 mm. Verse measure, 80 mm.; prose measure, 96 mm.

In an earlier chapter (p. 126) it was shown that distinct changes in measure can point to simultaneous setting by two or more compositors. As this may have an important bearing on textual problems, such changes, if discovered, should always be noted.

The second part of the typographical note is concerned with the style and size of the type itself. The style is usually confined to the major classes, roman, italic and gothic, but the last may be subdivided into textura, bastarda, rotunda and lettre de somme. The measurement, following established practice, should be the height of twenty lines set solid, taken from any point in one line to an exactly corresponding point on the twenty-first line above or below. The measuring should be done on the same page that was chosen to describe the type-area. The most intensive bibliographies will also include a similar note for the type used for the running-titles and, perhaps, for the preliminaries, should these differ from that used for the text. A basic typographical note may read as follows:

2 cols., 48ll., 160(168) × 88(96) mm.; text, roman with some italic 86 mm. for 20 ll. (C2^v); preface, italic 98 mm. (A3)

Finally, the presence of woodcut or metalcut initials, type-ornaments, borders, etc., should be mentioned; their positions noted and, if considered of sufficient importance, descriptions given or references made to standard handbooks for identification.

Notes and Annotations

In his *Bibliographical description and cataloguing*[4] Cowley considered that it was the notes at the end of a description which distinguished a bibliography from a mere catalogue. It is to be hoped that his words are not taken too literally for, of course, they deny the very basis on which the whole of the descriptive entry has been built: that of the ideal copy. Nevertheless, much valuable and interesting information may be found in the notes appended to entries in the more intensive bibliographies. The nature of such notes will vary from book to book and will depend a good deal on the primary purpose of the bibliography as well as on financial considerations, for lengthy annotations can increase considerably the bulk of the finished work. For these reasons it is impossible to construct a set of rules for their compilation, yet certain information which must be included is now examined. It should be noted, however, that in recent years, some of the material which previously had appeared as notes or annotations, is often extracted to form the introduction to a series of related entries, as for example,

4 p. 130.

those describing a work of major literary interest, or, as in the case of some author bibliographies, the material may be woven into a general narrative linking the entries with events in the life and work of the author.[5]

Whatever notes are provided should relate to the edition or issue being described and not to an individual copy of the work unless one is found, on examination, to contain manuscript notes or corrections likely to have a bearing on the text. Normally in this paragraph we expect to find additional information on the printing and publishing history of the book; explanations of any peculiarities in the composition and printing which may be of textual significance, and an elaboration of those matters purposely left in the description for fuller treatment. Information of a literary or historical nature is equally legitimate providing it is not of the kind found in booksellers' catalogues which indicates the price, condition, provenance, binding, &c., of particular copies.

Naturally, the reader will wish to know where he may see and handle copies of the editions described, so a list of libraries and collections in which they will be found forms an essential part of the notes. The bibliographer should distinguish copies he has personally examined from any others listed and should indicate against each copy any of its imperfections, otherwise it is assumed that they all correspond with the description of an ideal copy. It is usual, of course, to use initials as abbreviations for the holding libraries and an explanatory list of these should be provided in a convenient position in the bibliography. If one so desires, references may be made to entries in other bibliographies and, in conclusion, it is useful to give the numbered entry for the book in the STC., Wing, or other standard authority.

Specimen Description

The following specimen description is of *Two Discourses* by Walter Charleton, (1669), which also contains *Some Observations concerning the ordering of wines* by Dr. Merret:

5 A good example is J. E. Norton. A Bibliography of the Works of Edward Gibbon, (1940), in which an account of the writing and publication of Gibbon's works is considered, to some extent, an account of Gibbon himself.

[within double rules] TWO | DISCOURSES. | I. Concerning the Different | WITS of MEN: | II. OF THE | MYSTERIE OF | VINTNERS. | [rule] | [square of acorn type-orn.] | [rule] | *LONDON,* | Printed by *R.W.* for *William Whitwood* at | the Sign of the *Golden-Lion* in *Duck-* | *Lane,* near *Smithfield,* 1669

Special title, A3: [within double rules] A Brief | DISCOURSE | Concerning the | Different | WITS of MEN: | Written | At the Requeſt of a Gentleman, | Eminent in Virtue, Learn- | ing, Fortune. | In the Year 1664. | [rule] | and now Publiſhed with Con- | ſent of the Author. | [rule] | [square of acorn type-orn.] | [rule] | [Imprint as main title]

HT] [row of acorn type-orn.] | OF THE | DIFFERENT WITS | OF | MEN. | [rule]

RT] [within rules] *Of the Different Wits* | *Of MEN.* [swash *E* in *MEN* BCHIK5, DEFGH6]

Special title, K6: [within double rules] THE MYSTERIE | OF VINTNERS. | OR | A Brief Diſcourſe concern- | ing the various *Sickneſſes* of | WINES, and their reſpective | *Remedies,* at this Day com- | monly uſed. | [rule] | Delivered to the | ROYAL SOCIETY, | Aſſembled in *Greſham-Colledge* on | the 26 of *November,* | *Anno Dom.* 1662. | [rule] | [Imprint as main title except *R.W.* omitted.]

HT:K6] [double row of acorn type-orn.] THE | MYSTERIE | OF | VINTNERS. | [rule]

RT] [within rules] *The Myſterie* | *ofVintners.* [*Of*M2 M6]

HT: O5] [double row of acorn type-orn.] | SOME | OBSERVATIONS | Con- cerning the | ORDERING OF WINES. | [rule] | By Dr. Merret. | [rule]

Coll: 8°: A — P⁸ Q⁴ [$4 (−Q3, 4) signed], 124 leaves, pp. [*16*] 1–142 142 144–230 [*2*]

Contents: A1: blank. A2: title. A2ᵛ: blank. A3: title of first discourse. A3ᵛ: blank. A4: [double row of type-orn.] | THE | CONTENTS. | [rule]. B1: HT with text (init. I4) headed SECT. I. | ARTICLE I. On K5: *THE END.* K5ᵛ: blank. K6: title of second discourse. K6ᵛ: blank. K7: HT with text (init. E4). On O4ᵛ: *THE END.* O5: HT with text (init. T4). On Q3ᵛ: *THE END.* Q4: blank.

CW] A7 *VVit* C⁸ com- [comprehended] E⁸ ate; [ate,] G4ᵛ *Languages* L5 wines, [Wines,] N2ᵛ veſſel. [veſſel;]

Typ: 22 lines, 126(140) × 68 mm.

Wing 3694

Notes: . . .

CHAPTER 14

Eighteenth Century Books

In considering the differences between xvii century and modern printing methods, Greg expressed the opinion that the one which has had the greatest effect on bibliography was "probably the fact that in early times type was not as a rule kept standing". We can see the first evidence of change by examining books of the xviii century which, although still produced by hand methods and thus subject to the same criteria of analysis and description outlined in the preceding chapters, show distinct trends towards modern production practice. As a consequence, they present new problems to the bibliographer which now have to be examined.

By the beginning of the xviii century the control over the trade formerly exercised by the state and its agent, the Stationers' Company, had greatly diminished. The expiration of the Licensing Act in 1693 had left both authors and publishers without any protection and, despite the efforts of the Company to maintain past customs by passing byelaws to prevent the printing of other printers' copies, piracy, for a time, was rife. Even the first Copyright Act of 1709, which gave authors and publishers the protection they sought did not prevent the piracy of copies by their less tractable colleagues. Of more importance, however, was the effect on the trade of the loss of control by the Stationers' Company. The former restrictions imposed on the size of editions and the use and re-use of type were no longer enforced, with the result that books were frequently reprinted, sometimes from new settings of type, but now, for the first time on a large scale, from type which had been kept standing.

New "impressions" in place of new editions were made increasingly possible by the great change that occurred during the century in the type-founding industry. Composition and printing methods of earlier times were largely influenced by the fact that printers owned only limited quantities of type. In England, the number of typefounders had been restricted by law and the cost of importing type from Holland and N.W. Germany forced printers to manage with the minimum of founts. In the latter half of the xvii century there had been only three foundries in London of any consequence and Cambridge University Press itself was short of type as late as 1750: the Rev. William Ludlam was upset with the University printers who, he complained, had spoilt the appearance of his early tracts by using daggers turned sideways as they had no plus signs.[1] But apart from such occasional lapses, printers by this time were able to purchase all the type they could afford as the type-founding industry was now in a position to supply home printers with their requirements and, stimulated by the work of William Caslon, even to export type to the Continent.

With the much greater availability of type, reprints could be undertaken with ease, and as a result, publishers tended to order only a sufficient number of copies of a book to satisfy immediate demands. Certainly, with the more ephemeral works—pamphlets, plays, political tracts, etc.—a cautious publisher would prefer to keep his editions small because, if popularity so warranted, he could always rely on a further printing without much delay. A second order to the printer could be met with the traditional new edition from a fresh setting of type or else from a re-impression from standing type, for the publisher, to save setting costs, now often asked his printer to keep the type intact. The multiple editions and impressions of xviii century books that resulted from these practices now present the bibliographer with a most difficult problem of identification and ordering.

Complications arise over the common practice of publishing editions and impressions which were not labelled as such, and even when a so-called second edition, for instance, was published, it may well have been preceded by one or more unannounced editions printed to meet a continuing demand for copies. In fact, the labelling of editions was often used as a device to promote flagging sales, copies being

---

[1] Marjorie Plant. The English book trade. 2nd ed. (1965), p. 176. A London printer could, however, have sent round to Caslon's foundry and bought enough plus signs on the spot.

labelled "Fourth" or "Fifth edition" to delude the public as to the book's popularity. On the other hand, books of major importance were frequently printed from new settings of type, but not labelled as new editions, to trick the purchaser into thinking he was obtaining a copy of the first printing.[2]

New editions, however, usually contain some evidence in their setting, typography or paper, which enables their ordering to be determined, though sometimes not without difficulty. But with the multiplicity of impressions of many xviii century books, some produced with hardly any interval between them, the problem is very much greater. The usual evidential criteria frequently fail to distinguish one from another and examination by a Hinman collating machine may prove the only solution. David Foxon[3] distinguishes four categories of re-impressions but points out that quite often different sheets in a book will fall into different categories:

1. Reimpressions, often made within a day or two, where the type has been locked up in the chases.
2. Reimpressions where the type pages have been tied-up, sometimes with the headlines and direction-lines removed, and then reimposed.
3. Reimpressions with textual revisions.
4. Partial reimpressions with part of the text reset.

He goes on to show how each of these categories may be detected by the Hinman collating machine. The first is the most elusive since, theoretically, there should be no movement of the type between printings and it is only when a shift occurs because the quoins were re-tightened before the second impression that it may be distinguished. The second involves a reconstruction of the skeletons, and the use of different furniture would cause the lines of type to move relative to each other. The third contains corrections in the wording or punctuation of the text, and, consequently, has in the past often been mistaken for a completely new setting of type. But the machine readily identifies two printings from the same setting because the arrangement and spacing of type where no changes were made presents the same pattern.

[2] William B. Todd. "Bibliography and the editorial problem in the eighteenth century". Studies in Bibliography. Vol. IV, (1951–2), p. 44.
[3] "Modern aids to bibliographical research". Library Trends. Vol. 7, (April 1959), pp. 574–81.

Finally, the superimposition of images from pages of books belonging to the fourth category distinguishes between those printed from the same setting and those from a different one.

Even without assistance from a Hinman collating machine, the bibliographer has two tools at his disposal for the identification and ordering of multiple impressions. The first of these—press-numbers—has already been discussed on page 134. Although their original purpose is still open to question, there is no denying their value to bibliographers of xviii century books. Not only can they identify resetting or reimpressions in whole or in part, point to interruptions or abnormal sequences in printing and indicate variant states and cancellations, but they can also provide evidence that the printing of a book was divided between two or more shops, and even whether each press was operated by one or two men.[4] Their importance is such that they form an essential part of the bibliographical description for the books in which they appear, but as their significance has only been widely appreciated for the past twenty years, no single method of recording their presence has been universally accepted. The simplest and, perhaps, most frequently used method is that adopted by Professor Todd who uses either page numbers or signature references followed by the press figure. They can either be added to the statement of signing or given in a separate paragraph:

Figures: 8 — 1 15 — 3 21 — 5 31 — 6, *or*
Figures: B1^v — 2 C2 — 3 D3^v — 1, *etc.*

The second alternative provides more information since the number is located by sheet and forme. But even this falls short of some requirements, e.g. in recording variant figures, and more elaborate methods of recording are sometimes advocated. The most useful are by means of tables which show a list of figures in their order of appearance in the book and which summarize certain information such as the number of inner and outer formes containing figures and the number of times each figure appears in each location.[5]

---

[4] Todd, *op. cit.*, p. 47.

[5] Thomas Tanselle. "The Recording of press figures". The Library. 5th series. Vol. 21, (1966), pp. 318–25.

The second tool available to the bibliographer, and one which has been used with considerable success by Professor Todd, is the literary review. Contemporary journals, such as *The Gentleman's Magazine*, *The London Magazine*, &c., often printed reviews of new books shortly after publication with lengthy extracts of the text by way of illustration. By collating the text as printed in the journal with those of indeterminate editions, it will, of course, only agree with the one from which it was copied, and so may establish the priority of that edition in the sequence.[6]

The value of the contemporary printed extract may be seen in its use by Professor Todd in determining the order of the four settings of Volume One of Smollett's *Humphry Clinker*, which for many years had confounded every attempt at analysis. Of two editions bearing the same date, 1771, one (either A or B) was first issued on 18th June and the second completed approximately on 1st September. Between these two dates a total of 74 pages from the novel was reprinted in four reviewing journals. Todd discovered that the reprinted pages contained 138 readings all differing from those in B, but all agreeing with those in A. He concluded that A was unmistakably the first of the two editions. With this established, the sequence of the other settings was easily determined.

It should be obvious by now that the three bibliographical groups —edition, issue and state—on which the description of books printed in earlier centuries is built, are no longer adequate to portray the full-life-histories of books printed in the xviii century. The bibliographer has to introduce the term impression, relate each impression to its parent edition, and to admit a further application of issue and state.

Edition relates to a single setting of type and, regardless of the publisher's designation on the title-page, *new edition* results from a different setting of the book. Particularly in the xviii century, however, we frequently meet the hybrid book printed partly from standing, and partly from reset, type. Bowers's contention that this must be treated as a new edition if produced lawfully (page 110) still stands, but, as a rule of thumb, it might prove convenient to accept Todd's suggestion[7]

[6] Todd, *op. cit.*, p. 49.

[7] "Recurrent printing". Studies in Bibliography. Vol. XII, (1959), p. 191.

that *new edition* should be used to designate any book reset in two or more consecutive gatherings. Acceptance of this would reflect the original intention of the printer to distribute his type and his subsequent need to reset before he had finished in order to meet a pressing demand for further copies. An *impression* is a complete run of sheets through the press and *new impression* refers to a second printing from substantially the same setting of type (as we have seen, re-impressions may contain corrections). A *new issue* relates to changes that have taken place after printing apart from minor alterations made to create an ideal copy, and *state* refers to changes made before publication. Both issue and state can, therefore, be applied equally as well to impression as to edition, for just as some copies of an edition differ from others by belonging to a particular issue or exhibiting a variant state, so too do some copies differ from others of the same impression.

The use of the term "impression" implies a separate printing for which evidence exists in the form of different sets of press numbers or other points of difference. But many xviii century impressions followed one another with bewildering rapidity and without the use of a Hinman collating machine (and at times, one suspects, with it), it becomes impossible to distinguish separate from continuous printing. Some copies, it is true, have the impression number printed on their title-page, and whilst this may be accepted by the bibliographer as a true indication of a separate printing in whole or in part (though not necessarily of its correct numbering), it is still his duty to distinguish points of difference from earlier impressions. The difficulties encountered sometimes make impossible the ordering of impressions with any certainty, and to admit of this dilemma in a descriptive bibliography, Professor Todd has suggested[8] the use of the term *recurrent impression*. He applies this to books which exhibit a different title-page and at least one other point of difference. For even more intractable copies where only the title is changed, he recommends the use of *recurrent impression (assumed)*.

It is only in recent years that the complex nature of xviii century printing and publishing has been realised. Similarly, it is only lately that the tools most suited to the investigation of xviii century books

[8] *Ibid.*

have become available to bibliographers—the Hinman collating machine and the knowledge of how to apply the evidence afforded by press numbers. Recently, too, there has been a growing appreciation of the need for a more scientific approach to field techniques. The use of a control copy, either an original or microfilm copy against which other copies of the same edition or impression can be compared, and an acceptance of the need to cast one's net as wide as is humanly and economically possible so as to examine numerous copies of the same recension, has deepened our understanding of the period. As a consequence, many of the standard bibliographies of xviii century authors compiled in former years do not reflect current knowledge and are sadly inadequate and confusing in the way in which they attempt to chart the sequence of editions and impressions of the many works they describe.[9]

The form of bibliographical description applied to xviii century books should follow, with certain modifications, that adopted for the works of the preceding two centuries. The modifications that are acceptable stem from the greater regularization of printing methods during the century, which, combined with the use of standing type, resulted in less typographical change between separate printings than in earlier times. There is little point in transcribing in full the title-pages of a succession of editions and impressions if they exhibit only partial revision and the reader's patience may be better preserved by referring him to the original transcript of the title and by noting in their appropriate places only the changes that have occurred. Similarly, books published in many volumes should have their separate titles recorded with the minimum of repetition. On the other hand, there is a greater availability of collateral evidence relative to printing and publishing which may be culled from contemporary literary reviews, booksellers' advertisements or from the preserved letters of authors and publishers. Such evidence forms a natural addition to the notes at the end of a descriptive entry or in a narrative introduction to the work. For a more detailed discussion of the description of xviii century books the reader is referred to Chapter 8 of the *Principles of Bibliographical Description*.

9 William B. Todd. "Bibliography and the editorial problem in the eighteenth century". Studies in Bibliography. Vol. IV, (1951–2), p. 46.

PART IV

NINETEENTH AND TWENTIETH CENTURIES

CHAPTER 15

Bibliographical Study

It was only at the beginning of this century that the "New Bibliography" was born. It is hardly surprising, therefore, that it has been applied almost entirely to hand-printed books which, because of their comparative individuality, offer such a rich field for investigation. But during the last twenty-five years or so, a younger generation of bibliographers mostly in America has been concerned with the machine-printed books of the xix and xx centuries. Their work is bringing a growing realization that although the problems presented by these books may be different, they are none the less as real and numerous as those posed by the products of earlier centuries.

The general attitude to modern books (as we shall call them) at the beginning of this century may be seen in the treatment of their description proposed by Falconer Madan in his paper on "Degressive bibliography" (see page 19). His designation of four kinds of bibliographical description included "Form C: a short description such as befits modern literature", and he gave as his example:

> C—Godley, Alfred Denis. OXFORD IN THE EIGHTEENTH CENTURY. By A. D. GODLEY... WITH SIXTEEN ILLUSTRATIONS.
>
> London (pr. at Edinb., for) Methuen & Co.: (1908): 8°: pp. ix+[1]+291+[1] +40, and 16 illustrations. Contents:— p. iii, title: i–ii, v–vii, ix–x, prefatory matters: 1–280, the work in 9 chapters: 281–6, appendix: 287–291, [1], index, etc.: 1–40, catalogue of Methuen's publications.
>
> Remarks ...

This is a far cry from the full standard description outlined earlier and the value of Madan's description to a historical, textual or literary student is negligible. That this casual approach to modern books continued with little change until the last war may be attributed to three main causes: the nature of scholarship itself, the physical characteristics of the modern book, and a disinclination on the part of bibliographers to venture into a field of study which had been polluted by pseudo-bibliographical work serving the commercial interests of dealers rather than advancing our knowledge of important literary texts.

In the first chapter the course of bibliographical study was traced in brief outline from its purely enumerative beginnings to the detailed descriptions now considered essential. With the majority of incunabula neatly documented away and with the exciting prospects of analysis opening up before them, it was natural that the first generation of the "New Bibliography" should first apply their newly found skills to an intense study of the texts of Shakespeare. Gradually the net was widened to include other writers of the Elizabethan period and, judging from the papers printed in bibliographical journals, it is clear that this study is by no means exhausted. Later, books of the xvii and xviii centuries became legitimate objects for investigation but the resistance to anything more than a casual appraisal of modern texts has remained strong. For one thing it is not in the nature of scholarship to concern itself with contemporary matters when so much of the past still demands attention. Scholarship is most content when dealing with well established and fully documented source material[1] and would have a natural aversion to treading the shifting sands of xix and xx century literary studies. The closer one approaches the present the less definitive must be the result of one's investigations. Moreover, bibliographical study of the earlier centuries concentrated on the book itself[2], on the materials of which it was made and the methods employed in its manufacture. But with modern books, because of the apparent standardization of their production, the search for collateral evidence in the form of authorial, printing and publishing records becomes more desirable. This extension to strict analytical bibliography has not proved amenable to all bibliographers, but in Sadleir's view it is this emphasis on publishing history that distinguishes today's practice in bibliography from that of yesterday.

[1] Bowers, Principles of Bibliographical description, p. 357.

[2] M. Sadleir, "The Development during the last fifty years of bibliographical study of the books of the XIXth century". The Bibliographical Society 1892–1942: studies in retrospect, (1945), p. 146.

From its printing and make-up, the xix century book does not appear, at first sight, such an interesting quarry as its hand-made predecessor. The attitude to the xx century book in general remains even more resigned. Contemporary printing is held to be so mechanically perfect and regularized that a full description of its products based on a careful analysis of make-up can have little value for the textual or literary critic. Moreover, present day printing methods are so complex that they require a practising printer rather than a bibliographer to comprehend them.[3] However, the brave souls who have ventured into this waste-land have revealed that all is not so well with modern texts as had been supposed. Textual variants have been discovered in copies of impressions printed from the same or duplicate sets of plates made from a single original setting of the type. Even more unexpected is the news that copies within an impression can vary. To trace the causes for such differences demands an understanding of modern printing processes just as a study of earlier practices has explained many of the reasons for variants found in hand-printed books. Unfortunately, we have no Moxon or McKerrow as guides.

Bowers also attributed the reluctance on the part of bibliographers to concern themselves with modern books to the excessive importance placed by dealers and collectors on the minor points of variance which have given inflated values to certain copies of xix century books.[4] The differentiation of copies belonging to the first edition to establish (sometimes by dubious methods) an absolute priority of publishing gave rise to compilations which signposted commercially valuable "points". T. J. Wise was the greatest exponent of this kind of bibliography in which the finished product was everything and there was no attempt to investigate the circumstances of the book's publication or the nature of its production. The resulting "bibliographies" were purely enumerative in conception and were being published just at the same time as the "New Bibliography" was extending the scope of the discipline into a field which promised rich rewards to literary scholarship. It is not to be wondered that the advance guard wanted little to do with a

3 M. J. Bruccoli, "Twentieth-century books". Library Trends. Vol. 7, (April 1959), pp. 566–73.

4 Bowers, *op. cit.*, p. 359.

pitch that had already been queered by this pseudo-bibliography. The later knowledge that such studies had been tainted with forgery and that Wise himself had been involved in the manufacture of bogus first editions was a further barrier to a serious investigation of modern books.

The forward progress of bibliographical studies was, however, not to be denied: the barrier was breached and gradually selected isolated peaks of xix century literature were explored. That bibliographers turned to the peaks and not to the general terrain was necessitated by the impossibility of dealing with the overwhelming mass of literature now being produced by the continued speeding-up of machine-printing. No longer is it possible for a single bibliographer to survey a whole period as Wing did for the latter half of the xvii century, or even a particular form of literature, as Greg investigated pre-Restoration printed drama (Sadleir's *Nineteenth-century fiction* was compiled primarily for the collector). He needs must confine himself to the work of an individual author. But, whereas in one sense a restriction, nevertheless such studies have extended the scope of descriptive bibliographies to include information about the author himself so that his life and writing is integrated with the printing and publishing history of his books. In fact, such a bibliography not only contains a life-history of the author's work, but by an examination of his works can reveal much about the author's life and the way his writings were received by his contemporaries. As E. T. Cook wrote: "Bibliography is, in short, the historical material of criticism."[5]

The other change noted from bibliographical studies of the books of previous centuries is the greater use of collateral evidence to offset some of the difficulties in analysing the books themselves. Not only do contemporary reviews serve their purpose as in the xviii century,[6] but the records of publishing houses can form an important source of information concerning the size of edition, the changes that may have been ordered in the course of publication, etc. An example of new

[5] Introduction to the Bibliography of Ruskin. Vol. 38 of the Library Edition of his Works, (1912), p. xx.
[6] For a xx century application *see* William L. Phillip's account of his investigation of the first printing of Sherwood Anderson's *Winesburg, Ohio* (1919), publd. in Studies in Bibliography. Vol. IV, (1951–2), pp. 211–3.

bibliographical material coming to light from an investigation of a publisher's records is afforded by Franklin P. Batdorf's report of his findings on the reprints of the works of George Crabbe published by John Murray after the poet's death.[7] It is necessary, however, to treat this kind of information with a certain amount of reserve, using it as a means of checking direct bibliographical evidence rather than accepting it without question. Bibliographers do not always meet with ready co-operation from publishers who sometimes cannot be bothered with, or even resent, enquiries for information of their former practices. The histories that exist of publishing houses are unfortunately of little value. They have been likened to "a poor compromise between a pedigree and an advertisement, often having been issued for an anniversary celebration".[8] Even the unpublished records, when accessible, are frequently disappointing by their failure to reveal information concerning the printing of books. The division in the trade between publishing and printing by the xix century may account for the publisher himself not knowing the details of production. Nevertheless, the recent decision of the firm of Macmillan to present their earlier papers to the British Museum and Reading University, where they will be available for bibliographical research, is an action to be applauded.[9]

Bowers in his admirable summary of xix and xx century bibliography[10] states the requirements that need to be met in an intensive bibliography of modern books:

(1) Full description of the book as a material object which is the product of a printing press.

[7] Studies in Bibliography, *ibid*, pp. 192–9.

[8] Rollo G. Silver, "Problems in nineteenth century American bibliography". P.B.S.A. Vol. 35(1), (1941), p. 45.

[9] It is perhaps a little surprising that apart from D. F. McKenzie's recent study *The Cambridge University Press, 1696–1712*, 2 vols., (1966), and *A Ledger of Charles Ackers printer of The London Magazine*, edited by D. F. McKenzie and J. C. Ross, O.U.P., for the Oxford Bibliographical Society, (1968), the surviving records of prominent printing firms remain largely unworked. Such studies are valuable for the way in which they complement Moxon by showing the actual methods employed in specific printing houses, and surveys of other firms can only add to our still limited knowledge of earlier printing and publishing practices. There are signs, however, that this gap in bibliographical studies will soon be filled, for possible future studies include publications on the Bowyer and Strahan families of the xviii century as well as an examination of the Chiswick Press papers in the British Museum.

[10] Bowers, *op. cit.*, Chapter 10.

(2) Full description of the contents of the book as a work of literature. It is no part of the duty of a bibliographer to evaluate the contents by literary criticism, but students of a book have a right to know its complete contents both from the description and from indices.

(3) Full study of the transmission of text through a detailed history of impressions, issues and editions.

(4) Linked with the above, a study of the history of the book as a material object, its varying form, dress, and contents after first publication; the circumstances of its first and subsequent appearances including price, distribution, and size of sale; when necessary, a study of these matters in relation to publishing practice of the time. With (3) above, this constitutes the life history of the author's work.

(5) Full study of the relations of the author to the book both as a man of business and as a man of letters.

The first three requirements form the basis of bibliographical study of the earlier centuries; the last two feature in some descriptive bibliographies of xviii century material, for it is from this period that records of authorship and publishing, with a few notable earlier exceptions, have survived. Michael Sadleir has re-inforced the importance in a bibliography of modern books of an account of the publishing history of the items described. It should include:

every incident, mishap or change of policy which may occur in the life of a book from the moment when a contract is made for its publication to the moment (maybe many years later) when it goes finally and irrevocably off the market, even the last copy of a remainder issue having been sold. The bibliographer may, therefore, be called upon to show knowledge and understanding of the relationship between author and publisher; the type of contract usual at any period. . .; the fashion for part issue merging into that for magazine serial; the processes of book manufacture—paper, typography, illustration, binding and end-papers—in vogue at different times; the machinery of sale by the publisher to wholesaler, retailer and circulating library, involving trade terms and other technicalities; the sequence of "secondary" and of cheaper editions and their physical qualities; the publisher-jobber who sold other firms' sheets over his own imprint; the gradual development of the remainder as we understand today.[11]

[11] Sadleir, *op. cit.*, p. 154.

CHAPTER 16

Problems and Solutions

In their endeavour to meet the requirements of a full descriptive bibliography, bibliographers of modern books are faced with a different set of problems from those which confront their colleagues examining the products of the hand press. Early books, because of the anonymity with which they were produced, have often proved difficult to identify, assign and date, but the relatively unsophisticated manner of their production and the ease with which corrections and emendations could be made, has enabled bibliographers to trace in great detail the history of important texts. On the other hand, modern books, although presenting few problems of identification and dating, have been printed on presses of ever-increasing complexity. To understand the processes involved now requires more than an elementary knowledge of the principles of composition and presswork and many bibliographers do not feel inclined to make the necessary effort. They feel, too, that as printing has been so perfected and regularized, the detailed analysis of a modern book wastes so much time and effort that could be put to better use on the more rewarding and worthwhile material still awaiting investigation from earlier times. Moreover, what is the point of such analysis when modern texts must be well-nigh perfect representations of the author's original words?

The examination in recent years of xix and xx century material mostly by American bibliographers has, however, made it clear that no matter how efficient modern book production may be, it is still by no means perfect. Carelessness still results in mistakes, corrections are still necessary, and current editions of modern texts frequently contain variations from the original manuscript. In fact, classifying and ordering editions, impressions and issues, and revealing their discrepancies is just as vital for editors of modern texts as for those of Elizabethan.

When T. S. Eliot was confronted with a list of variants in the text of his poem "Gerontius" as printed in seven separate editions, it was found that not one conformed exactly with his original intentions.[1] Between the first edition of *The Great Gatsby* by F. Scott Fitzgerald in April, 1925, and its appearance in *Three Novels* in the Modern Standard Authors Series in 1953, there were seventy-five changes in the text, thirty-eight with Fitzgerald's sanction and thirty-seven without.[2] Analytical bibliography still has a role to play in furnishing the editor with incontrovertible evidence of variants, cancels, differences between impressions, &c., even in a world of mass production and seeming uniformity.

Nevertheless, it remains true that in analysing copies of modern texts the bibliographer is faced with considerable problems. These emanate partly from the uniformity of modern printing and partly from the complexity of modern publishing arrangements. Since many books are now published simultaneously, or within a few weeks of each other, in more than one country, the bibliographer cannot be satisfied, when constructing a family tree of editions and impressions, with tracing just one line of descent but has to take into account the possibility of collateral lineage. There may well be more than one parent edition, for example the first American and first English editions printed from two different settings of the text which may exhibit minor variations in their composition. It might be supposed, however, that within each line of descent, the identification of various impressions would be an easy matter since modern publishers are usually very liberal with such announcements. But the details supplied by publishers should not always be accepted without question: on the one hand, concealed impressions, i.e. those which have not been numbered or otherwise designated by the publisher, are quite common, and on the other hand, the announcement of "the second [third or fourth] printing before publication" may not always pass without a sneaking suspicion that the publisher is out to boost the sale of his book by pretending that he has an overwhelming demand to meet.

[1] William H. Marshall, "The Text of T. S. Eliot's 'Gerontius'". Studies in Bibliography. Vol. IV, (1951–2), pp. 213–7.

[2] Bruce Harkness, "Bibliography and the novelistic fallacy". Studies in Bibliography. Vol. XII, (1959), p. 70.

Edition, impression, issue and state

Before we can deal with what evidence there is for identifying editions, impressions, issues and states of modern books, definitions have first to be constructed which permit the inclusion of all acceptable alternatives yet which are mutually exclusive. Up to date the only attempt to deal fully with this problem may be found in Chapter 11 of *Principles of Bibliographical Description* by Professor Bowers and neither the student nor the practising bibliographer can afford to omit it from his studies. Much of what follows here owes its origin to this source.

The concept of *edition* and *impression* as applied to modern books remains the same as that discussed in the preceding pages. An *edition*, as before, is considered to consist of all the copies of a book printed from the one setting of type. A *new edition* can only be created by a completely fresh setting and nowadays, of course, is undertaken more often than not to publish a revised text, although there is no bibliographical reason why the text of a new edition should not be exactly the same as that of the previous edition. An edition does not necessarily appear at one time but may be published over many years, for as long, in fact, as the original setting of the type is used to print more copies. Each printing is called an *impression* which refers to the number of copies of a book printed at any one time from the same setting of the type without removing the type or plates from the press. An impression is, therefore, part of an edition.

These definitions are no different from those applied to hand-printed books but they are insufficient on their own to cater for the complex nature of modern publishing. For this reason it is convenient to subdivide the parent edition not only into its different impressions but into "subsidiary editions" each of which in turn may have its own series of impressions. The basis of subdivision may be geographical e.g. *American, English* and *Colonial editions* printed from the same set of plates or from a different set made from the same type; or, by form, e.g. *revised editions* which contain alterations which are more than just a correction of errors and yet are insufficient to warrant a complete resetting of the text, or *enlarged editions* where additional material has been added to the original text of sufficient importance for the publisher to order a new title-page to draw attention to it. These and other kinds of subsidiary editions are noted by Bowers (pages 383-4).

Although it is more a matter of convenience than an act of pure bibliography to designate subsidiary editions as a means of arranging material in a bibliography, nevertheless the relationships between the subdivisions must be recorded whenever possible. The literary or textual critic will want to know, for example, whether there are any differences between the American and English editions of a book. Were they printed from the same set of plates?—if so, was any revision carried out between the one printing and the other?—or, were both editions printed from a duplicate set of plates?—and so on. It is only by the proper use of the terms impression, issue and state that the bibliographer can answer these questions with any clarity, and we now have to consider these terms in their modern setting.

Impressions are printed from the edition setting and may remain unaltered from one printing to another except, perhaps, for the publisher's announcement "new impression", "2nd impression", etc., on the title-leaf. But the opportunity is frequently taken between printings to correct obvious errors, replace broken or turned types, and possibly to make minor corrections to the text. Sometimes, too, the date on the title-page will be altered or the whole page reset. But in no instance are the alterations sufficiently extensive to necessitate resetting to the extent of creating either a new parent or subsidiary edition.

Both *issue* and *state* are included within *impression* and in general they conform to the definitions advanced for their use in connection with hand-printed books. Basically, *issue* should be regarded as an act of intent by the publisher to effect some change in the yet unbound copies of an impression after the publication of some copies has taken place. As with hand-printed books, these alterations may include the addition of more textual matter or the deletion of material followed sometimes by substitution. One common form of re-issue is still the cancellans title-leaf bearing a new date or changes in the publisher's imprint. Whatever the alteration, it must come as the result of an intention on the part of the publisher to alter or improve the contents of his book and not merely to make good a publication which has fallen short of his expectations. *State* is distinguished from issue because the alterations are found in only some sheets of either a whole impression or of an issue of an impression. These alterations are made during printing, a common example being the correction or repair of type or plates. Sometimes the alterations can be made after publication to the unbound sheets providing they are of a nature that repair certain defects in the finished product, an act which may legitimately be considered to be an attempt on the part of the publisher or printer to construct ideal copies of the book. Instances of this kind of alteration are the occasional errata and other pasted-in notices found in modern books.

In the all-embracing definitions of issue and state given by Bowers in Chapter 11 of *Principles of Bibliographical Description*, reference is made to binding variants, an aspect of book production with which the bibliographer working on hand-printed books is not concerned. Since the mid-1820s, however, following the introduction of cloth binding, whole or parts of editions have been bound in the same way and for this reason a description of a book's binding forms a legitimate part of the bibliographical treatment of an ideal copy. But although binding descriptions can be of value as a means of identification, particularly with regard to Victorian fiction which changed their cloth with almost every new impression and re-issue, they throw no light on the development of the text. Their inclusion in a bibliography is, therefore, of more value to the student of historical bibliography than to the editor or textual critic. At best they can only corroborate a suspected re-issue, etc., but it would be very rash indeed to suppose that a change in binding is sufficient to demonstrate the existence of a new impression or a re-issue. Yet the act of binding can affect the make-up of a book. The first and last gatherings may in some copies have a different number of leaves than in others due to the variable treatment on the part of the binder in suppressing blank leaves. Furthermore, the contents of a book may sometimes appear in a different order than in other copies because of a wrong collation of the gatherings. The results of both these actions should be considered as variant states.

Until the 1920s it was common practice for a publisher to include in a book lists advertising his other publications. The lists found in some copies of an edition differ occasionally from those in other copies usually because they were brought up to date before being marketed. When the lists were printed separately from the rest of the book and bound-in, they have no relevance to the text sheets and should never be used as as sole evidence for the ordering and dating of impressions and issues. Even when used in support of other evidence their admissibility is doubtful. Sometimes, however, advertisements were printed on leaves which form an integral part of the text sheets and thus they have a close relationship with the printing of the book. But because their up-dating was only occasioned by, and was not the reason for, the printing of further copies, Bowers is of the opinion that such alterations must be considered as variant states rather than re-issues.

This rather brief explanation of the terms impression, issue and state, in relation to the description of modern books has only been concerned with the essential differences which help to separate and identify them. But there are many border-line cases which present the bibliographer with difficult problems in deciding their correct classification. For information on these and for examples of modern books which reflect the various nuances with which the bibliographer is often confronted, the student should make a thorough study of Chapter 11 of *Principles of Bibliographical Description*.

Distinguishing evidence

We are now in a position to consider the evidence by which editions, impressions, issues and states may be distinguished. Editions seldom offer many problems because the publisher will have made certain that all new editions are labelled as such because of their obvious sales value. Although a new edition can be a word-for-word copy of its predecessor, we tend, nowadays, to assume that when one is announced, a thorough revision has taken place on the grounds that no publisher would normally go to the expense of ordering a resetting unless there is need to bring the text up to date. But in compiling a bibliography, we must always test a publisher's conception of a new edition with the accepted bibliographical definition. From an examination of many so-called "new editions" it will be obvious that a complete revision of the text has not taken place but that only isolated parts of the book have undergone changes. We should regard these instances as subsidiary revised editions and not new parent ones. In the same way, "enlarged editions" can be found masquerading under the label of "new edition".

A recent innovation likely to bring revolutionary changes in the printing industry is the process known as "filmsetting" which dispenses with metal type altogether. Text is composed by exposing negative characters on to film or sensitized paper which is then transferred to plates for printing. This new process will bring its own problems to future bibliographers who will have none of the usual evidence associated with moveable type to aid their investigations. However, Mr. James Moran suggests[3] that it may be possible to determine filmsetting from the letter design. The process enables different sized founts to be obtained by simple photographic enlargement and reduction, but the design of the characters may well, in such cases, differ from those printed in metal type of the same sized fount. He has also drawn attention to the ease with which simultaneous publication may be achieved because it is a cheap and simple matter to dispatch batches of film negatives made from the same setting to different printing centres. As a result, bibliographers may find it very difficult, if not impossible, to determine a single parent edition and may have to settle for a number of first subsidiary editions.

Concealed impressions present greater difficulties to the bibliographer than editions or subsidiary editions, because when the text of a book has been altered between impressions, the changes are inevitably restricted and demand a close examination of the text. Even more difficult is the re-impression in which no changes have taken place, for then one is forced to look for wear or damage to type or for evidence of re-imposition. This kind of minute examination without mechanical aid is very arduous and time-consuming and one that is conducive to error especially when a lengthy text is being collated. Fortunately for those with access to one, the Hinman collating machine relieves the bibliographer of much eye-strain and enables even bulky novels to be examined with equanimity. Two copies of an edition can be examined at the rate of 40 pages an hour after practice, although for

---

[3] "Filmsetting—bibliographical implications". The Library. 5th series. Vol. xv, No. 4, Dec. 1960.

identification purposes it is not usually necessary for a whole text to be collated. A sample investigation of 50 or so pages will usually suffice.[4]

With the high-speed machines in use today stop-press correction is very rare, so that when textual emendations are discovered it is more than likely that two or more impressions were printed. Re-impressions may be taken from standing-type, from metal or plastic plates, from re-casting a Monotype spool, or by photographing the pages of the first impression and reprinting by photolithography. Printing from standing-type is being superseded by the other methods mentioned, but smaller provincial printers lacking the wider facilities of city firms do still make use of it. On occasion even leading publishers will order type to be kept intact, for, as Robert L. Beare has revealed[5], the type for the English editions of T. S. Eliot's works was set in Monotype and kept standing. There is, of course, more chance that accidents will happen to the type between impressions with this practice than if plates are made. Beare has shown, for example, that in the line from one of the later impressions of *Murder in the Cathedral*, "Not in this or guise, for my present purpose", the "or" had dropped out and been replaced in the wrong position. However, standing-type does allow the author to make small alterations in the text with the minimum of expense, and examples of where T. S. Eliot took advantage of this are given by Beare.

The common practice in modern times is, however, to re-impress from stereo or electro plates, or in recent years from plates made of rubber or plastic. Although the process of emendation is not so straightforward as that for standing-type, metal plates can have offending words or letters chiselled out and new type soldered in. With rubber and plastic plates replating is necessary from a new page setting of type, although recent advances with plastics have enabled single types to be moulded ready for insertion in plates that require correction or alteration. These textual emendations are generally only brought to light

---

[4] Matthew J. Bruccoli, "Twentieth-century books". Library Trends. Vol. 7, (April 1959), pp. 566–73.

[5] "Notes on the text of T. S. Eliot: variants from Russell Square". Studies in Bibliography, vol. IX, (1957), p. 25. footnote.

by careful collation although a quick check may be obtained by noting any words or lines which appear to have been printed more sharply than the surrounding type, for the new type will not have been subject to the wear that the original plate will have received. This effect can be seen en masse on those pages of the *Encyclopaedia Britannica* which have been revised since the last annual printing. For another example of plate emendation between impressions the reader is referred to John Cook Wyllie's account[6] of the changes that occurred in the text of Hervey Allen's novel *Anthony Adverse*, (1933).

Theoretically, it is possible for a Monotype spool to re-run through the caster to produce not a new, but a duplicate setting of type, though the practice would seem to be rare, at least, in this country. The position occupied by the holes punched in the spool determines which characters are cast and the precision of the machinery is such that a re-run should produce a second setting which is the exact replica of the first. However, Bruccoli has recorded[7] the experience of an American press which suffered an error factor of sufficient magnitude to require a second proof-reading. I can find no evidence of a similar discrepancy elsewhere, but what would prove a source of textual variation is the failure on the re-run to correct those compositor's errors which had been rectified by hand before the first printing.

A practice which is becoming increasingly common is reprinting by offset-litho. The leaves of an earlier impression are printed down on to a litho plate by photographic means for re-impression. Even with this method corrections can be made before reprinting by the simple, if somewhat tedious method of pasting printed corrections over the offending passages or by blocking out minor errors in white before the leaves are photographed. The re-publication in 1958 of F. Scott Fitzgerald's *The Beautiful and the damned* thirty-six years after it had gone out of print affords an example of this. Bruccoli has discovered[8] as many as 78 corrections which were made to the text by the methods just described. He has also drawn attention to two other

---

[6] "The forms of twentieth-century cancels". P.B.S.A. Vol. 47(2), (1953), p. 102.

[7] "A Mirror for bibliographers: duplicate plates in modern printing". P.B.S.A. Vol. 54(2), (1960), pp. 87–8.

[8] "Bibliographical notes on 1958 printing of F. Scott Fitzgerald's The Beautiful and the damned, 1922". Studies in bibliography. Vol. XIII, (1960), p. 260.

disturbing possibilities which can arise from photo-offset impressions: the first is that for the sake of sharpness an early impression is often used as copy for a later impression, which would therefore revert to an early form of text; and since in photo-copying it is easier to use the pages from two copies of the work than from one, if these were not of the same printing, the resulting re-impression could be a hybrid one made up of revised and unrevised leaves.[9]

In addition to receiving intentional textual emendations, plates, over the course of time, frequently have to be altered and repaired because of batter or damage. Metal plates are particularly susceptible to "batters" through mishandling during storage and make-ready, or else to distortion and breakage through the stresses they receive during actual printing. In the vast majority of cases plates have to be removed from the press for repair so that evidence of emendation is almost always an indication of re-impression.[10] Even if free from damage both plates and standing-type are subject to wear over successive printings and the degree of deterioration may help to determine the sequence of impressions.

To avoid printing too often from worn plates, some publishers order a duplicate set to be made at the outset for works which are likely to have a long-standing popularity. The plates used for the initial impressions may during their lifetime receive intentional textual emendations, but there is always the possibility that when these plates are discarded in favour of the duplicate set, the latter will be machined without the corresponding alterations being made. So we have another example of the anomaly that later impressions can revert to an earlier and less correct version of the text. This was demonstrated by Mr. Bruccoli in his investigations into the text of Sinclair Lewis's *Babbitt*. The first four printings in 1922 show progressive plate correction, but later impressions printed for The Modern Library and Harbrace Modern Classics revert to the second state of the first printing (there was a rare case of stop-press correction in the first impression affecting both sets). Reference to the records of Harcourt, Brace and Co., showed that a duplicate set of plates was manufactured in 1922

---

9 "A Mirror for bibliographers", p. 86.
10 "Twentieth-century books". *Op. cit.*, pp. 566–73.

but not used until the set from which the original impressions were printed was melted down in 1941.[11]

Duplicate sets of plates can also give rise to two variant forms of text when a book has been selected by a book club for printing and distribution to its members. The normal practice, at least in America, appears to be for the publisher to sell or lease one set to the club for this purpose, and with two organizations now involved it is not difficult to imagine that corrections made to one set would not necessarily be made to the other. A very interesting investigation concerning duplicate sets used in this way was made by Bruccoli into the printing of Edith Wharton's *The Children*, (1928).[12]

Similar variations of text can arise from yet a further possible example of duplicate printing when one impression is machined from standing-type and the other from plates made from that type. This may happen when a publisher decides to produce a limited printing in *de luxe* format in addition to the normal trade publication. It may well be difficult to ascertain the priority of impression. On the one hand, it is possible that the type would be used for the *de luxe* printing before being subjected to the plate-making process so as to achieve an impression of the highest quality, but Bruccoli suggests that the usual practice is to make the plates first to minimize the possibility of type batter.[13]

Evidence of re-imposition may provide a final way of recognizing re-impression for the one inevitably follows from the other. A change in the manner in which the gatherings were quired indicates re-imposition and for an example of the use of this kind of evidence we may turn again to the work of M. J. Bruccoli. He distinguished two impressions of F. Scott Fitzgerald's *The Beautiful and the damned*, (1922), from the fact that two forms of the novel were gathered differently, one in 8s and the other in 16s.[14] He has also pointed out that a significant variation in gutter measurement—more than 2 mm.—at the

[11] "Textual variants in Sinclair Lewis's *Babbitt*". Studies in Bibliography. Vol. XI, (1958), pp. 263–7.
[12] "Hidden printings in Edith Wharton's *The Children*". Studies in Bibliography. Vol. XV (1964), pp. 269–73.
[13] "A Mirror for bibliographers". P.B.S.A. Vol. 54 (2), (1960), p. 86.
[14] *Op. cit.*, p. 258.

centre of gatherings is another indication of re-imposition, and therefore, of re-impression.[15] We move now to the evidence for recognizing the existence of issues and states in modern books. Both form parts of an impression, and as we have seen, after the initial publication of some copies a new issue is occasioned by changes made which are sufficiently important to warrant a new title-page, and a variant state is produced by alterations made during the course of printing and by post-publication attempts to create ideal copies. But a re-issue is sometimes formed by alterations to the text of a book which go beyond those that form an attempt to create ideal copies, and yet which are not necessarily referred to by means of a new title-page. The classic example of a modern re-issue with internal changes of this kind is Somerset Maugham's novel *Painted veil*, (1925), the circumstances of which are cited by Bowers (p. 419). The decision to change the setting of the novel from Hong Kong to Tching Yen necessitated the ordering of cancellans to be prepared of 15 single leaves and 2 complete gatherings for the bound copies awaiting distribution, and complete cancellans gatherings for all affected parts of the text in the unbound sheets. The cancellans leaves are detectable by evidence of pasting-in and their presence led to the discovery of the two complete cancellans gatherings. The pasting-in of single leaves is, of course, an expensive operation in modern book production and preference would always be given to the substitution of complete gatherings. These are very difficult to detect and unless their presence is already suspected, the only practical means of identification is by mechanized collation.

Stop press corrections creating variant states of an impression or issue are extremely rare nowadays with high speed presses, and most corrections, e.g. of misprints, are usually made between impressions. However, Bruccoli has discovered at least two examples which appear to have been made during the course of printing. One is in the first impression of *Babbitt*,[16] the other in the initial printings of *The Children*.[17] As mentioned above, the latter book was printed from duplicate sets

[15] "Twentieth-century books", *op. cit.*, pp. 566–73.
[16] *Op. cit.*
[17] *Op. cit.*

of plates, but in the machining of one set, pages 122 and 135 were damaged and had to be re-plated. In re-setting the type for this the compositor misspelt "motors" as "moters". Because of the indiscriminate gathering of the sheets, four states of the book were created from the two printings.

The detection of variant states in the text of modern books is most unlikely without the aid of a Hinman collating machine. There is, however, a section of some books in which alterations are more easily discernable although they have no textual significance and do not come within the category of stop-press corrections. They are changes to the advertisement pages forming an integral part of the sheets. Bowers considers such changes to form variant states since they have only an incidental connection with the publication of the book itself and for this reason should not be considered, as they so often are, a sufficient reason for calling the resulting copies a re-issue.[18]

Evidence of imposition

We have seen that for a hand-printed book an analysis of its format and the structure of each gathering was essential for an understanding of the way in which the book had been printed. It also helped to determine whether the book was complete with all its leaves intact, and whether its original printed form had subsequently been altered by the addition or deletion of leaves or gatherings. The format can usually be determined by noting the position of the watermark and the direction of the chain-lines in the paper. With this established, a count of the regularly folded leaves in the gatherings will determine their structure, i.e. whether each was formed from a single sheet of paper, a number of sheets, or only half a sheet. Odd leaved gatherings will be examined carefully for evidence of additions or deletions. The position the type-pages occupied in the inner and outer formes can now be specified and from the evidence afforded by type, headlines, press-numbers, etc., the order of printing the formes may frequently be established. Further examination of the chain lines for the indentations they leave in the paper, of signatures added to stray leaves, of watermarks appearing unexpectedly, and so on, will verify suspected cancels and reveal an

[18] *Principles of bibliographical description*, p. 422.

alteration to the original construction of the book. But with modern books many of these old familiar criteria have gone.

Following the advent of the Fourdrinier machine at the beginning of the xix century, paper was no longer made in individual sheets from pairs of moulds but in a continuous web which was cut into sheet form, or, later, was left wound up in reels for use on the rotary press. With machine-made paper, the watermark, if present, is impressed on the surface by the dandy-roll, but with the much larger sheet sizes available from the machine, one can no longer rely on finding it in the centre of one half of the cut sheet. Moreover, most machine-made paper is "wove" with an almost imperceptible pattern of wire-lines offering no evidence in a leaf of how the parent sheet was folded and cut. The dandy-roll can also be used to impart imitation chain-lines to the paper, but here again, the evidence is of little value unless the size of the original sheet is known.

Books are now printed mostly on flat-bed cylinder presses, but the hand-press continued in use by many firms throughout the xix century. Its traditional wooden construction was superseded in 1800 by the iron-press of Earl Stanhope with its greater rigidity and strength. This not only enabled the size of the platen to be increased but by a system of levers eliminated the necessity of pulling the bar twice to print a whole forme.[19] Stanhope's press was followed by other iron presses, the best known being the American "Columbian" and the English "Albion", the latter being used by William Morris in the 1890s at his Kelmscott Press. When standard sized sheets of laid paper were used on these presses, the classic criteria for establishing the formats of books and the imposition schemes used in their printing may still be applied. But when wove paper was used and, as was sometimes the case, signatures were dispensed with, the problem is much more difficult. Occasionally, the point-holes left by the pins holding the sheet on the tympan may be found in uncut or lightly trimmed copies. When present, they are usually seen on the shorter axis of

---

[19] Stanhope was not the first to eliminate printing two pulls to the forme. A number of French press makers of the late xviii century had experimented with various methods of constructing a *presse à un seul coup*, but Stanhope's was perhaps the first to be widely used. *See* J. Mosley's edition of *Charles Earl Stanhope and the Oxford University Press* by Horace Hart. Printing Historical Society, (1966), pp. xx–xxi.

the sheet and their appearance through certain leaves will determine the position of the corresponding type-pages in the forme and from this, in turn, the format may be deduced.

The effect of much larger sheet sizes on modern imposition schemes brings us to one of the darkest areas yet to be penetrated by the analytical bibliographer. With hardly any limit to the size of paper, the cylinder press was able to increase the area of its bed until we now have presses accommodating 128 pages to the forme. This, in turn, has brought about methods of folding, cutting and gathering which were unknown in the period of hand-printing. Most books today are printed on quad sheets (i.e. four times the area of standard single sheets) containing 64 octavo pages quired in gatherings of 16 pages, so that 4 gatherings are printed on the single sheet, But depending on the size of the press, the methods of imposition have been legion since the first cylinder press was introduced by Frederick Koenig in 1812.

The problem is made more complicated by the fact that the arrangement of type-pages in the forme depends on whether printing is by sheet or half-sheet work. Sheet work refers to printing the first side of the sheet from one forme and the second side from another forme. Thus, on a quad press printing an octavo book with 64 pages to the sheet, 32 pages would be imposed in one forme and a further 32 in the second so that when perfected the sheet would contain 64 pages. With half-sheet work, or "work and turn", the matter for both sides of a sheet is set in one forme using paper double the size of the sheet required. For example, the octavo book referred to above could be printed on a double-quad press with 64 pages composed in a single forme. The paper is first printed on one side and then turned over, end for end, and perfected from the same forme. After cutting in two the result is as before except that two identical gatherings of 64 pages have been produced with the same amount of machining.

It is only within the last few years that any attempt has been made to determine the method of imposition in modern books from the evidence presented by the books themselves. A pioneer in this field is the American bibliographer, Oliver L. Steele, who, from an examination of the first American impressions of two novels by James Branch Cabell, has determined the significant physical characteristics that are required to satisfy two common modern imposition schemes.[20] The evidence is afforded by the nature of the edges of leaves in separate gatherings of partially unopened and uncut books. By noting the incidence in gatherings of leaves with smooth machine-cut edges or with rough uneven edges and leaves which were once joined in folds at the fore-edge (these show indentations along the edge of one leaf which corresponds exactly with the projections of the other, and *vice versa*), Steele demonstrated that the imposition for the first American impression of *Jurgen*, (1919), was a half-sheet scheme in formes of 32 pages quired in gatherings of 8 leaves. Similarly, from an analysis of the first American impression of Cabell's *Gallantry*, (1907), he could point to half-sheet imposition in 64-page formes with gatherings of 8 leaves.

Steele has also investigated[21] the problem of imposition by means of the evidence obtainable from plate damage, i.e. damage to stereotype and electrotype plates used in modern printing. He has pointed out that the operation of the cylinder press imposes more damage on the type-pages around the edge of the forme than on the inner ones. The leading edge of the forme which takes the first impact of the cylinder is the most vulnerable and the opposite following edge receives more stress than the side edges. It follows, therefore, that the incidence of observed plate damage may indicate how the type-pages were imposed in the forme. But Steele warns that the damage must be present in both inner and outer formes of gatherings and that one's investigations must cover a large enough sample of copies of an impression to reflect a ratio of damaged states which is statistically sound. This last condition is often difficult to determine for in many instances the size of the impression will not be known. But from an analysis of plate damage in 150 copies of the first impression of Ellen Glasgow's *The Wheel of Fire*, (1906), Steele was able to establish that the type-pages were imposed by placing the inner and outer 8-page formes of two gatherings together in one chase and printing by work-and-turn.

[20] "Half-sheet imposition of eight-leaf quires in formes of thirty-two and sixty-four pages". Studies in Bibliography. Vol. xv, (1962), pp. 274–8.

[21] "Evidence of plate damage as applied to the first impressions of Ellen Glasgow's *The Wheel of Life* (1906)". Studies in bibliography. Vol. XVI, (1963), pp. 223–31.

Binding variants

Bibliographers of modern books, especially those of the xix century, who wish to treat in full the publication history of the books they examine, are faced with the task of distinguishing and describing the varieties of binding in which copies of many editions are to be found. This problem is absent from the bibliographical study of preceding centuries because binding was not a part of publication. Apart from a few isolated cases when, for instance, John Bell established a "house binding" in the 1780s by issuing his books in calf with a uniform treatment of the lettering and tooling, publishers sold their books in quires or in some purely temporary binding so that their customers could have them subsequently bound to their own taste. But with the greater purchase of books at the beginning of the xix century not everyone necessarily wished to incur the expense of an individually styled binding, and gradually the temporary protection offered by a plain paper wrapper gave way to paper boards with title labels. They were poor substitutes for calf or morocco bindings but at least they gave semi-permanent protection. The need for a binding of this sort was affirmed by the many book societies and circulating libraries which sprang up in the first thirty years of the century for whom an unlabelled paper wrapper was useless. But the innate conservatism of the trade had left publishers unable themselves to handle the technical problems created by the increased demand for books to be bound before publication and so the door was open to a class of middlemen known as "novel-distributors" who bought books from publishers in sheet form, had them boarded and labelled, and rushed them at great haste to awaiting libraries. As each distributor selected his own style of binding, we have, for the first time, copies from the same impression of a book appearing in boards of different colours with variously designed and printed labels.

The publication of books all bound in a uniform style had to wait the introduction of cloth as a covering material in the mid 1820s. It is one of the puzzles of xix century publishing that the appearance of this new style was so little heralded and that its subsequent adoption by the mass of publishers was comparatively slow. Undoubtedly, the original glazed "calico" of the first cloth bindings presented a very

8

drab appearance and even the grained cloths devised to simulate morocco were no substitute for the leather bindings found in every gentleman's library. But the discovery of a process for treating the surface of cloth to receive lettering and ornamentation blocked in gold ensured its ultimate acceptance as a binding material. By 1840 the use of labels had disappeared and each new book now had its title resplendently impressed on the cover in gold. Within a few years, however, both lettering and decoration were being blocked in ink and this cheap substitute for gold paved the way for the flood of cheap editions which poured from the presses at the end of the 1840s.

Of the many types of books published in Victorian times, the novel withstood the change from boards to cloth longer than any other. In fact, it was not until about 1860 that cloth became the standard material for binding fiction, with the result that a novel published before this time may be expected to be found in at least two varieties of original binding.[22] Until the end of the 'forties, a publisher would offer his books in quires or else bound in boards, cloth or half-cloth. We have already seen that many of the former would be purchased by the novel-distributor who was responsible for a different style of binding. In the later 'thirties, he was superseded by the wholesaler who purchased at a discount in quires before publication and had them bound in time to appear on publication day in a style different from that of the publisher. There may be something to be said for collectors preferring a book in the binding ordered by its publisher, but the fact remains that before 1840 such a binding can claim no priority of appearance over a copy wearing a different guise. In the 'fifties the binding of novels became more standardized in cloth or half-cloth and, with the wider range of material then available, a larger number of copies were bound by the publisher before publication. Eventually wholesalers purchased their discount copies in this form.

In addition to the variant forms of original binding that are found, the bibliographer is also faced with the changes that occurred during the life of a book to form what are known as "secondary" bindings. The variants we have discussed till now are generally found on books that were popular or for which there was, at least, a good

[22] John Carter. Binding variants in English publishing, 1820–1900, (1932), pp. 32–3.

chance at the time of their publication of an assured success. But many books, of course, disappointed their publishers and languished in quires unsold. It is interesting to reflect that not all the blame for this lack of success should be levied on the author himself or on the popularity of his subject, but at times must be attributed to the high prices demanded by the publisher. The three-decker novel usually sold at 31s. 6d. which was beyond the reach of the ordinary purchaser and, apart from a few wealthy customers, was acceptable only to the circulating libraries which, because they took a substantial part of any new edition, were allowed a good discount. Publishers were apparently not prepared to risk large editions and offer them to a wide reading public at a cheap price, but, on the contrary, were willing to accept a limited profit from selling the bulk of their editions, not many of which exceeded 500 copies,[23] to the circulating libraries. Naturally, however, none was averse to improving his profits by the disposal of unsold copies and during the board and label period these were sold to firms of jobbing publishers who inserted their own cancel titles and offered them for sale at a price of 15/- or less.[24] This practice resulted in some copies of a novel appearing in the binding of the first issue but under a different imprint and usually with a later date. When cloth became firmly established, the publisher himself would remainder his unsold copies by issuing them in a cheaper grade material than the initial binding, with lettering in gold from ordinary type instead of from specially cut dies, and even, perhaps, using ink instead of gold. As a further economy, the three-decker novel was often cut down in size to appear in a cheaper format as a single volume.

From this brief survey of xix century publishing practice it should be apparent that the Victorian book could appear dressed in a number of different fashions, and from the importance given in sale catalogues to binding priorities one could be forgiven for thinking that a change in cloth must have a great bibliographical significance. But although, at times, a particular binding may be linked to a new impression or a new issue, it is very dangerous to assume, without corroborative

[23] According to Gladstone in 1852. Cited by Richard D. Altick in "English publishing and the mass audience in 1852". Studies in bibliography. Vol. VI, (1954), p. 17.
[24] Michael Sadleir. Trollope: a bibliography, (1928), p. xiv.

evidence, that the connection is anything other than completely fortuitous. The binding of a book can have no relation to the printing of the sheets and a variant should never be used to differentiate impressions or to determine issues and states. In general, it should be accepted for what it is and not regarded as a means of solving textual problems. But because binding variants help to tell the life story of the books they cover, it is the bibliographer's job to explain the circumstances behind their appearance. For this reason and for the sake of collectors who seek after books in their original condition he will also endeavour to place variant bindings in their order of priority.

What tell-tale clues does he look for? The answer is seldom as clear cut as when a three-decker novel suddenly appears as a single volume, but is usually an aggregate of small pieces of evidence obtained from the cover or inside of the book with, occasionally, corroboration from external sources. Often the correct solution is reached only after a long acquaintanceship with Victorian publications with the eye trained to recognize the significance of the many forms in which binding variants are found. But some points of recognition have been revealed by Michael Sadleir[25] and John Carter[26] in their authoritative studies in this field. The cloth itself can be of assistance in dating especially when a particular variety enjoyed a brief but wide popularity. Carter has traced the development of styles from the early smooth glazed versions of the 'twenties by way of the grainings carried out by the ribbon-embossers and the brief vogue of flowered cloths of the 'thirties, through a succession of different grainings, to return full circle in the 'seventies to the smooth but more sophisticated versions of glazed cloth. Providing the style was not too long lasting, as with ribbed and sand-grain designs, a cloth may be dated to within 10 or 15 years with some practice.[27] With a similar approach to the study of lettering and ornamentation this span of years may be considerably reduced. But with lettering we are not on such safe ground as when dating by material, and a fair degree of accuracy can only be achieved if the style of lettering is known to have had a brief but popular exist-

[25] The Evolution of publishers' binding styles, 1770–1900. Constable, (1930).
[26] Binding variants in English publishing, 1820–1900. Constable, (1932).
[27] Carter, *op. cit.*, p. 58.

ence. Some idea of priority can be obtained from the cut of the letter, for the majority of primary bindings were blocked from specially cut binding dies, whereas, to save expenses, secondary bindings were frequently lettered by ordinary type.[28] The difficulty for the non-expert is, of course, in distinguishing between the two. Secondary bindings in two or three volume novels may also be suspected if their spines lack a publisher's imprint at their foot for it was common (but not universal) practice for primary bindings to sport one.[29] Of course, a *different* imprint leaves no doubt about the secondary nature of the binding.

Inside the cover a clue to the problem of binding priority is sometimes afforded by the endpapers. Generally the elaborate and relatively expensive endpapers of a primary binding would be replaced in a secondary by a plain and cheaper alternative, although as Carter warns,[30] this evidence is insufficient on which to stipulate priority without corroboration from other sources. Endpapers seldom bear dated watermarks and because of the varying time-lag between their manufacture and use in binding, all one can be sure of is that a book could not have been bound before the date of its endpaper. For this reason, as Carter explains, "watermarks are more useful in detecting secondaries than in establishing primaries".

A book may have inscribed on its endpaper the name of the owner and the date of acquisition. If this happened to be contemporaneous with the date of initial publication, it provides a very good indication that the book is a primary. A manuscript date some years later than the date of publication does not, of course, in itself denote a secondary binding but, as Carter points out, if from a number of copies of the same book in two styles of binding, those in one style bear dates of ownership all earlier than those of the second style, the chances are that the first style is the earlier of the two.[31]

Endpapers were often used to carry publisher's advertisements. These would be printed quite independently from the text of the book and sent to the binder with instructions to insert them between the

28 & 29 Sadleir, *op. cit.*, p. 90.
30 Carter, *op. cit.*, p. 48.
31 Carter, *op. cit.*, p. 46.

covers of, perhaps, a number of specified books. Such lists would be kept up to date and were, consequently, subject to more frequent change than styles of binding. It is quite conceivable that in binding up a particular edition, the binder might well exhaust one batch of endpapers and, to complete the job, start on a second batch containing entries of more recently published books than the first. In these circumstances there can be no foundation to a claim which seeks to prove that the appearance of the later list in a particular copy demonstrates either a new issue of the book or a secondary binding. But in cases where the endpaper advertisements bear a different imprint than the one on the title-page, or if the imprints are the same but the title-page is obviously a cancellans, it is most likely that the book has been sold from one publisher to another and is, therefore, a secondary.[32]

Sometimes the state of the edges of a book can suggest whether it is likely to be in a secondary binding or not, although such evidence should not be relied upon without further proof. In secondary bindings the edges will often be cut or trimmed whereas in a primary they appear uncut, i.e. with the margins full-size, and as a general rule the trimming or fore- or top-edges may be taken as evidence of a secondary binding.[33] The condition of the tail-edge of a book is of no significance in this investigation.

Apart from these pieces of internal evidence, support for the belief that a particular binding may be a secondary can occasionally be found in the records that have survived in publishers' offices. If an order to a binder can be traced instructing him to change the style of binding and copies of the book survive which reflect this change, then we have the best available means of distinguishing a primary from a secondary binding and of dating the change. Unfortunately, such information is not easy to come by and the records of xix century binding firms are even more scarce. In contradistinction to this kind of proof, information in publishers' catalogues of the day may well indicate that two styles of binding were available simultaneously. A book may be advertised in boards or in cloth, thus absolving the bibliographer from any further investigation into priorities.

[32] Sadleir, *op. cit.*, p. 93.
[33] Carter, *op. cit.*, p. 78.

Binding variants which prove extremely difficult, if not impossible, to place in order of appearance often result from the binding of books issued in parts. A subscriber could, of course, have them bound to his own specification by a local binder, or he could return them to his bookseller for binding. The bookseller, in turn, would either send them back to the publisher for binding in the "official" style, or, alternatively, would put them out to a binder with whom he had some business connection. So we can have different styles of binding none of which may be dated earlier than the others. Furthermore, the publisher would frequently reserve some sheets of an edition for binding in volume form when publication in parts had finished, and the implications of this state of affairs for the collector concerned with "original condition" is examined by Carter who says he must take his choice between "earlier-sheets-in-later-binding and later-sheets-in-earlier-binding".[34]

Finally, it must be reiterated that the order of binding does not necessarily relate to the order of publication. The fact that we have two copies of a book in different bindings is *ipso facto* no indication that we are dealing with two distinct editions or even two issues of the book. The decision to re-issue a book is a conscious act on the part of the publisher, but, as we have seen, he cannot be held responsible for many of the binding variants that are found on modern books.

[34] Carter, *op. cit.*, p. 76.

CHAPTER 17

Bibliographical Description

A glance through a number of published bibliographies of modern books will reveal that various methods have been adopted in compiling the descriptive entries for the books examined. This state of affairs results from a wide-spread feeling that exact transcriptions serve little purpose because the uniformity of modern printing practices has reduced the number of recognition factors giving evidence of resetting, re-imposition, etc. Furthermore, full collational information is, in many instances, no longer ascertainable. Nevertheless, Professor Bowers, whose *Principles of Bibliographical Description* contains the only examination in depth of methods for compiling full descriptions of modern books, recommends that they should be based on the principles established for hand-printed books because a disregard of the basic rules will often obscure what bibliographical evidence the book has to offer. For this reason he recommends a continued use of quasi-facsimile transcription and an adherence to the treatment previously outlined for other paragraphs of the description, modified only where necessary to meet the circumstances of modern printing practices.

Transcripts

Quasi-facsimile transcripts require that the style of the original type should be followed and a strict observance made of the use of capital and lower-case letters. The size and weight of the original letter is ignored, although some bibliographers attempt to approximate the comparative values of the original title-page by using larger and smaller founts, or by reserving small caps for lines of lesser importance. (See, for example, Geoffrey Keynes. A Bibliography of Rupert Brooke, 1954.) This practice, however, ignores the basic rule that each line of the original should be treated as a separate unit and this, although it does not necessarily convey a very accurate impression, is at least consistent and admits of no confusing approximations. Some special treatment, however, is necessary to indicate the presence of ornamental types. Bowers recommends the use of [fancy] immediately after each word or line composed in these types, or when possible an initial general statement such as [title, less imprint, in fancy type] before commencing the transcript. In the same way [sans serif] could be used to indicate a particular style of type which has been popular in both classical and grotesque forms throughout the xix and xx centuries.

The treatment of borders, printers' flowers and publishers' devices should not differ in any marked way from their descriptions compiled for hand-printed books. Unfortunately there are no authoritative works with facsimiles of modern designs to which reference may be made. Consequently some brief description is usually necessary, although in the case of fleurons, similar specimens are probably available to most printers and carefully chosen examples could be used as generalized substitutions.

Transcripts of any special titles present in the book may be given immediately following the main title, or alternatively, as in the case of the half-title, left to the contents note. This is also the place for a transcription of the printer's imprint.

Technical description

A wide variety of treatment will be found of the items comprising the technical part of the entry. The differences are not only in the method of presentation but also in the sequence the items are dealt with, and it must be admitted that few technical descriptions are as complete as a full bibliographical description properly demands.

It is normal to begin with the format and the signature formulary, but we are immediately faced with a problem for, as we have seen, it is virtually impossible to discover the format of a modern book. The fact that a book is constructed of gatherings each of 8 leaves does not necessarily make it an octavo, because the type-pages could have been imposed for a sheet four or even eight times the basic size and both sheet and half-sheet imposition could have been used. Again, the printing of the sheets often bears no relation to their subsequent folding. Certainly in the xix century, printing was often in 12s, i.e. 12 leaves to the sheet, but after cutting the folding was in 8s; alternatively, the sheet may have been printed in 8s but the gatherings constructed (by using an inserted fold) in 12s. If the format can be ascertained, for example, by plate damage or from the nature of the leaf-edges (see page 218), then, of course, it should be stated because it remains the only real indication of how the book was constructed. If it is not known, however, it should be omitted.

Whilst in no way acting as a satisfactory substitute for an unknown format, a statement of the size of a typical leaf will give the reader some idea of the shape and dimensions of the book. Height is given before width and it would seem a matter for personal choice whether they are expressed in inches or centimetres. Bowers prefers inches since they are related to the point measurement of type and are more easily visualized by both American and British readers. But the metric system is the method traditionally used in bibliography for earlier books and precise measurements are more easily handled in millimetres than in fractions of an inch. If the latter is chosen, Bowers recommends measuring to an accuracy of a 32nd of an inch, although with the tight bindings of many books this may prove impossible. In view of its impending adoption in this country it is likely that the metric system will gain more favour amongst bibliographers in the future. Whichever method is used, it should be noted whether the paper is cut or uncut: "uncut 20·2 × 13·4 cm." unless this information is provided separately in a note on the paper.

Few entirely new problems are encountered when compiling the collation formulae of modern books and the rules outlined earlier for older books should be applied. Signatures, whether in the form of letters or numbers, still retain some usefulness to the binder and comparatively few English books are completely unsigned even though the outside fold of each gathering may be marked on the back by a series of steps printed by quads to provide a quick check that the gatherings have been assembled in the correct sequence. On the other hand, most contemporary American books are unsigned and for these signatures have to be inferred by using numbers within brackets or in italics:

[$1 - 24^8 \ 25^4$], 196 leaves; or, $1 - 24^8 \ 25^4$, 196 leaves.

In either case, if thought desirable, the statement may be prefixed by the word "unsigned".

One often finds in present day books a very abbreviated form of title printed in small type at the foot of the first page of each gathering. This must not be regarded as an additional or alternative form of signature even when the book is otherwise unsigned for it gives no indication of the order of gatherings. It is provided solely to avoid the possibility of gatherings going astray when a large bindery is dealing simultaneously with a number of books in sheet form. Its presence in a book is disregarded in the description.

Another contemporary practice is to construct gatherings from cut sheets inserted one within the other, the inserts being identified by individual signature marks. For instance, in a book gathered in 16s each signed gathering may have the 5th leaf separately signed: in $A - G^{16}$, say, A5 is signed A^* or A^2, B5 is signed B^* or B^2, etc. Bowers recommends that the signings of regularly quired inserts should be ignored in the formula, the collation being written simply as $A - G^{16}$, but that the presence of the two signings per gathering should be noted in the statement of signing, e.g. [\$1,5 signed; \$5 with added asterisk], or, [\$1,5 signed; \$5 with added superior 2]. But it is possible to indicate the precise signing in the formulary by indicating that each gathering (in the above example) is composed of two signed sets of 8 leaves: $A/A^* - G/G^{*8/8}$. This signifies that in the first gathering the letter A is signed on the first page and that A^* is signed on the 9th page ($= A^*1$) and so on throughout the book. This method was adopted by Professor Fred H. Higginson in his *A Bibliography of the works of Robert Graves*, (1966).

A few xix century books have gatherings regularly constructed of an odd number of leaves and Jacob Blanck in his *Bibliography of American Literature* departs from the rule that index numbers to signatures should always be even by stating the actual number of leaves found in these books. Thus, in *The Coronal* by Lydia Maria Child,

Boston, 1832, he gives the collation as "$[-]^4$, $[1] - 15^9$, 17^8". Bowers condones this practice providing that it represents the normal construction of the gatherings and that the odd leaf is inserted in the centre of the quire.

As with hand-printed books, the collation formula is only concerned with the actual sheets of the book and should not include an analysis of extraneous leaves forming binder's endpapers, fly-leaves, or inserts of advertisements and catalogues which are not an integral part of the first or last gathering. Of course, a whole final gathering of the same paper as the rest of the book may have been used for a publisher's catalogue and may have been printed at the same time as the text, although in practice this is unlikely. One way of noting the presence of such a gathering is that adopted by Jacob Blanck in the bibliography mentioned above. He adds the gathering to the end of the formula preceded by the word "plus": $1 - 12^8$, plus $[13]^8$, but only when the gathering is printed on book stock and is not part of the text nor conjugate with any of the fly-leaves or endpapers.

It may be noted here that the reference to a leaf which is part of a gathering signed by a figure is confusing if written in the normal way. For example, we can write A5 when we wish to indicate the fifth leaf of gathering A, but we can hardly write 15 when referring to the same leaf in gathering 1. The problem may be overcome, however, by using an inferior figure for the leaf number and writing 1_5.

At the end of the collation formula, whether or not a statement of signing is included, the total number of leaves in the book should be given. This must, of course, coincide with the number of leaves indicated in the formula.

A statement of the pagination follows next, normally on the same line, but if a very full treatment is considered necessary as a separate paragraph. The principles outlined for hand-printed books should be followed and the statement should always check with the signature formula. It is not, therefore, concerned with endpapers, fly-leaves or publishers' inserts even if these are numbered, although if the last have been included in the signature formula following the word "plus", it would be consistent to indicate their pagination in the same manner.

The aim should be to produce as simple a statement of pagination as is consistent with clarity. The only real difficulty is dealing with unnumbered pages for sometimes they will have been counted by the printer in paging the book and sometimes not. Treatment depends on whether the unnumbered pages fall at the beginning or end of a sequence or somewhere within a sequence.

Counted but unnumbered pages at the beginning or end are best inferred since if the need should arise to refer to one of these pages, the inferred number may be used:

[i — iv]   v — xii,   [1 — 3]   4 — 376   [377 — 380]
or,   i — iv   v — xii,   1 — 3   4 — 376   377 — 380

but where they have been neither numbered nor counted then inference at the beginning of a sequence is impossible and in this case the total number of unnumbered pages is given in italicized arabic figures within brackets:

[4] i — xii,   [3] 1 — 376

Internal unnumbered pages which have been counted by the printer are not normally listed separately. For example, *Principles of Bibliographical Description* has the following unnumbered pages: i–vii, xii–xiii, xviii, 1–3, 35–7, 124, 135, 193, 255, 269, 312, 322, 352–355, 371, 427, 454–457, 463, but since they have been counted in the paging we would write:

[i — vii]   viii — xvii   [xviii],   [1 — 3]   4 — 505   [506]
or,   i — vii   viii — xvii   xviii,   1 — 3   4 — 505   506

Note that the unnumbered blank page at the end of the book is given an inferred number. Preliminary and final blank leaves providing they are integral with the first and last gatherings must be included in the statement of pagination even if pasted down on the cover, because they would have been included in the signature formula and both statements must check.

Finally, unnumbered and uncounted internal pages should be inferred where possible, but otherwise given as bracketed totals:

[i — iii]   iv — viii   [2]   [ix]   x — xviii,   1 — 23   [4]   24 — 28   [29]
30 — 36

To avoid possible confusion between bracketed totals and inferred pagination, the latter could be given in italics:

i — iii iv — viii [*2*] *ix* x — xviii, 1 — 23 [*4*] 24 — 28 *29* 30 — 36

Where a very full note on pagination is thought desirable, in addition to the statement all unnumbered pages are listed whether counted in the paging or not and information is given concerning the position of the numeral on the page, the presence of broken figures, the use of brackets to enclose numerals, etc.

Contents note

An analysis of contents can be of value to readers in a number of different ways providing it is prepared in sufficient detail. A straightforward list of the major parts of the book may reveal a variation in the order in which these appear in some copies and a check with the collation formula will show if the book has suffered some alteration in its make-up as a consequence. The list will also provide a literary student with a detailed account of the text's contents which may be particularly revealing when the book is a collection of poems, essays and the like. The textual student, however, will require the titling and caption headings to be transcribed in quasi-facsimile as an added check on possible resetting. For the student of historical bibliography, the contents note should contain the printer's imprint, a statement of edition and impression, a note on copyright, etc. To meet the requirements of as many readers as possible a detailed quasi-facsimile transcript of the major parts of the book is essential but whatever the method treatment chosen, it should be followed consistently throughout the published bibliography for changes in compilation from one entry to another would only confuse the user.

The same procedure is followed in compiling the note as that outlined for hand-printed books except that reference is made from the page number instead of the signature. It is better to give the page first followed by its contents rather than the other way round. Reference to unnumbered pages counted by the printer is made by inferred numbers in brackets or in italics: all blank pages are noted. An example of a reasonably full contents note is given below for W. W. Greg's

Collected papers, (1966), edited by J. C. Maxwell, and the student's attention is also drawn to the various examples provided by Bowers in chapter 12 of his book.

Contents: pp. [*1–2*] blank. p. [i] half-title 'W.W. GREG|COLLECTED PAPERS'. p. [ii] blank. p. [iii] title. p. [iv] publisher's imprint, copyright and printing notice. p. [v] preface. p. [xi] contents. p. [xiii] list of plates. p. [xiv] blank. p. [1] text, headed '1. Webster's *White Devil* | An Essay in Formal Criticism'. p. [29] '2. Fairfax's Eighth Eclogue'. p. [44] '3. Theatrical Repertories of 1662'. p. [48] '4. The Bakings of Betsy'. p. [75] '5. What is Bibliography?'. p. [89] '6. John of Basing's "Greek" Numerals'. p. [95] '7. An Elizabethan Printer and his copy'. p. [110] '8. Massinger's Autograph Corrections'. p. [149] '10. *The Spanish Tragedy* —a Leading Case?'. p. [156] '11. *The Escapes of Jupiter*'. p. [184] '12. The Riddle of Johnson's Chronology'. p. [192] '13. Shakespeare's Hand Once More'. p. [201] '14. A question of Plus or Minus'. p. [207] '15. The Present Position of Bibliography'. p. [226] '16. Three Manuscript Notes by | Sir George Buc'. p. [239] '17. Bibliography—an Apologia'. p. [266] '18. The Function of Bibliography in Literary | Criticism Illustrated in a Study of the | Text of *King Lear*'. p. [298] '19. A Formulary of Collation'. p. [314] '20. Was There a 1612 Quarto of *Epicene*?'. p. [322] '21. Time, Place, and Politics in *King Lear*'. p. [341] '22. Entrance in the Stationers' Register: | Some Statistics'. p. [349] '23. The Damnation of Faustus'. p. [366] '24. Old Style—New Style'. p. [374] '25. The Rationale of Copy-Text'. p. [392] '26. The Printing of Shakespeare's | *Troilus and Cressida* in the First Folio'. p. [402] '27. Was the First Edition of *Pierce Penniless* | a Piracy?'. p. [406] '28. *Ad Imprimendum Solum*'. p. [413] '29. Richard Robinson and the Stationers' | Register'. p. [424] '30. Samuel Harsnett and Hayward's | *Henry IV*'. p. [437] index. p. [450] printer's imprint. pp. [451–2] blank.

Running-titles

In a full description running-titles may be transcribed here in quasi-facsimile or, as is more frequently the case, included in the note on typography.

Typography and paper

It is quite a common practice amongst bibliographers of modern books to include in their descriptions a note about paper, but frequently no mention is made of the type. It is difficult to see how this omission can be justified when the object should be to provide as complete a picture as possible of the book. Moreover, the investigations of Carter and Pollard into the activities of T. J. Wise have shown that typographical evidence still retains its value in tracing the existence of false editions. Wherever possible, therefore, some information on type and paper should be included and bibliographers have reason to be grateful for the increasing tendency amongst contemporary publishers to provide a note in their books on these two aspects of production. The method of composition should also be stated, if ascertainable, since textual variants between copies or impressions may, as we have seen in the previous chapter, be related to the composition of type, whether by hand, Linotype, Monotype or filmsetting. Admittedly, it may prove very difficult or even impossible to track down some of these facts and time and the economies of publication may impose their restrictions, but one never knows what item of bibliographical evidence will be of value. To tailor one's descriptions to the known needs of the moment is, in the long run, to be of disservice to some future investigator.

The typography of the book is described by stating the number of lines on a typical page of text, the dimensions of the type-page, the size and style of the type, and whether the lines are leaded or not. A full note would read:

43ll. $7\frac{3}{16}$ $(7\frac{7}{16})$ × $4\frac{1}{8}$; Monotype Van Dijck, 12 pt., solid.

Measurement of the type area is given both for the block of text and separately in parentheses for the overall dimensions which in height include the headline and signature line, and in width any marginal notes that are present. If possible, the type-face should be identified and a statement given of the size of the particular fount used. The description is not complete without a note on the setting—whether the lines of type have been set solid or leaded. This can be ascertained by noting whether there is a gap between the descenders of one line and the ascenders of the line next below. If there is no discernable gap then the page has been set solid, otherwise the lines have either been leaded or, as is more frequent with machine composition, the printer has used a type cast on a larger body than normal, e.g. a 12-point fount cast on a 13-point body gives the effect of 1-point leading between the lines. There is no visual evidence that will decide between leading and using a larger bodied type and in many instances the bibliographer can only record that the type has been "leaded" as an indication that it has not been set solid. In addition to the description of the text-type, a note should be given of the type used for chapter-headings, running-titles and footnotes, stating briefly the type-face used if different from the text and the size in each case.

The note on the paper used for a book is often combined with a description of the binding. It is, however, always preferable to deal with the sheets of the book separately from the endpapers, fly-leaves, treatment of edges, and coverings which are all the product of the binder. Paper lends itself more easily to description than does typography since most of the information can be ascertained visually: its colour; whether it is of the laid or wove variety; the distance between the chain-lines in laid paper (for a full description), and the design and position of the watermark. This last item should be included as a possible clue to the identification of unsuspected impressions, and for the same reason, the thickness or bulk of the sheets should be measured with a pair of calipers. Occasionally this measurement is found combined with one which includes the thickness of the binding as well, e.g. $1\frac{1}{4}/1\frac{5}{8}$ in. would indicate that the sheets bulk $1\frac{1}{4}$ in. and that with the binding included, the overall measurement is $1\frac{5}{8}$ in. Of course, the second figure has no value unless the book is still in its original binding. A note on paper might therefore read:

> Paper: cream laid unwatermarked, vertical chain-lines $1\frac{1}{8}$ in. apart. Sheets bulk $1\frac{1}{4}$ in.

Plates

All plates and frontispieces should now be described by noting their location and whether they have been tipped or bound in the book. The method of printing and the colour of the inks used should be stated and a transcript made of any letterpress captions on the plates or on any protective tissue guards. A note might read:

> Fifteen coloured illustrations by Barnett Freedman, all versos blank, tipped-in facing pages 4, 10, 24, 44, 62, 82, 116, 140, 160, 176, 202, 218, 232, 258 and 286. Printed by auto-lithography in blue, yellow, brick-red and black. All signed bottom right-hand corner "*B.F.*"

Binding

The description up to this point has been concerned with the printed text and any conjugate blank or printed leaves integral with the sheets, but in this section the rest of the book, all of which results from the activities of the binder, should be described. Firstly, the colour and form of the binding itself is stated, i.e. whether it is of leather, vellum, cloth, paper-wrapper or boards. Paper-wrappers were used before paper-covered boards at the beginning of the xix century and consisted of a single piece of paper which served as a temporary protection for the book. Wrappers were often plain, but some were printed or are found bearing a printed label. "Boards" is a term used in bibliography to indicate paper-covered boards although it was also employed in xix century publishers' catalogues for cloth-covered boards, which we would describe simply as "cloth".

In the last chapter we saw that binders' cloth was dyed various colours and passed through engraved rollers which imparted an embossed grain to its surface. The main manufacturers of book cloths, e.g. Winterbottom, used letters of the alphabet to designate their various patterns and these are frequently adopted in bibliographies along with brief descriptive terms. Some guidance in the correct designation of binders' cloths may be found in John Carter's *Binding variants in English publishing 1820–1900*, (1932), which provides a table of manufacturers' letters with their relevant descriptions (e.g. H — diaper pattern, C — sand grain, T — ribbed, etc.), and both Michael Sadleir's *XIX century fiction*, (1951), and Jacob Blanck's *Bibliography of American literature*, (1955-), have many illustrations of cloth bindings, the former labelled with descriptive names and the latter identified by letters. More recently, G. Thomas Tanselle has put forward a plea not only for a standardized method for use in bibliographical description to specify the texture or grain of book cloths,[1] but also for a system of colour identification. He has pointed out that bibliographers in the past when describing the same book have often come up with two different colours for the cloth — yellow being confused with pale cream and even light brown, etc. After reviewing the three colour systems generally in use today, he recommends[2] the adoption of the

[1] "The Specification of binding cloth". The Library. 5th series. Vol. 21, (1966), p. 246–7.
[2] "A System of color identification for bibliographical description". Studies in Bibliography. Vol. xx, (1967), p. 203–34.

American ISCC-NBS (Inter-Society Colour Council—National Bureau of Standards) method which may be found in N.B.S. Circular 553 (1955), *The ISCC-NBS Method of designating colors and a dictionary of color names*.

The description continues with a transcript of the lettering and ornamentation found on the front cover, spine and back cover, e.g.

Bound in black cloth; front and back blank; spine blocked in gold: [rule] | AN | INTRODUCTION | TO | BIBLIOGRAPHY | McKERROW | [publisher's device] | OXFORD | [rule]

The state of the edges is now recorded by indicating whether they have been cut, trimmed, or left uncut or unopened:

Cut should be used when the three edges of the book have been cut smooth by a plough or guillotine.

Uncut refers to leaves which have not been cut by the binder or, when related to hand-made paper, that the original deckle is still present.

Unopened should not be confused with uncut. It relates to the bolts (i.e. the folds) of the leaves and signifies that they are intact. To read an unopened book it is necessary to slit the bolts with a paper knife, after which operation the book is said to be "opened".

Trimmed properly refers to a book having a cut top-edge but with the leaves at the tail and fore-edge only lightly trimmed so as to remove the largest projections but leaving a generally rough and uneven appearance.

Unfortunately, not only the compilers of sales catalogues but even bibliographers disagree over the appropriate use of these terms and sometimes to avoid the confusion which exists in many minds between uncut and unopened, they evade the use of cut and uncut completely. For instance, in the *Bibliography of American literature*, untrimmed is used to mean uncut and rough-trimmed is used in place of trimmed. The decoration of the edges by the binder should also be mentioned here—whether they have been gilt, stained or sprinkled. The omission of such a note implies that the edges were left plain.

The binding note is also concerned with the other elements of the book with which the binder has been involved: the endpapers, fly-leaves and inserts of advertisements and notices. Their full description would include the kind of paper used, whether wove or laid, its colour and the presence of watermarks. Endpapers should be distinguished from fly-leaves. They are double leaves used at the front and back of a book to attach the sheets to the covers, one leaf being pasted down on the inner side of the cover, the other sewn or tipped to the first (or last) leaf of the first (or last) gathering. Endpapers are frequently found either tinted or decorated, but normally only on one side of the paper, the other (nearest the sheets) being left white. A note should be included in the description of any such treatment, it being understood that unless otherwise specified the tinting or decoration is confined to one side only. Fly-leaves are blank inserts added by the binder between the free endpaper and the first and last gatherings and are more common in American than in British books. They are seldom tinted or decorated being usually of the same quality paper as that used for the sheets.

The presence of inserted catalogues and advertisements should be noted for whereas they have no relevance to the printing of the book they may sometimes indicate the time of binding. Such inserts were frequently subject to alteration and copies should be checked for variants either in the number or titles of the books listed. Sometimes they have their own imprint and if this differs from the one found on the title-page it would indicate the disposal of unsold sheets from the original publisher to a second.

Finally, if the book has a dust-jacket, this should also be described if only by transcribing the letterpress on the front cover and spine which relates to author, title and publisher.

The existence of binding variants should be noted, for the description, of course, should relate to the whole edition or impression, and the following binding note taken from Michael Sadleir's *Trollope: a bibliography* shows how this may be tackled:

(The note is part of the entry for *The Three Clerks*. R. Bentley, 1858.)

Binding: (i) Brown paper boards, quarter grey cloth. Paper labels, lettered in black: THE | THREE CLERKS. | BY | A. TROLLOPE. | *rule* | IN THREE VOLUMES. | *rule* | VOL. I. *II. III.* White end-papers.

(ii) Dark grey-purple watered cloth, blocked on front and back with decorative frame in blind; also blind-blocked on spine and gold-lettered: THE | THREE | CLERKS | *rule* | VOL. I. *II. III.* | LONDON | BENTLEY. Yellow end-papers.

(iii) Cloth and end-papers as (ii) but with paper labels as (i). I have only seen one copy thus bound, which may have been a hybrid and therefore of no bibliographical significance.

(i) and (ii) were probably of simultaneous issue.

All edges uncut.

Notes and annotations

As with the description of hand-printed books the bibliographer should include a note of any evidence pointing to the existence of different impressions, issues and variant states of the book. The final paragraph should also include as much relevant detail as possible concerning its publication history: dates of the first publication and of separate impressions; the number of copies printed on each occasion; the published price, and any other information which adds to an understanding of the book's progress in the world. In the more intensive bibliographies different impressions may receive individual treatment especially if they have some particular significance. Some information may prove impossible to trace, in which case it has to be omitted from the description, but Professor Fred H. Higginson in his *Bibliography of the Works of Robert Graves* has a novel treatment for this situation. Where it has not been possible to determine the number of copies, he uses:

"Unknown" to mean that the publisher no longer knows,

"Undisclosed" when he has not revealed the number, and

"Undetermined" when the publisher no longer exists or has not responded to letters.

From the same source[3] comes the description printed on page 241 which gives an example of a reasonably full treatment for a modern

---

[3] *A Bibliography of the Works of Robert Graves* by F. H. Higginson © Copyright 1966 Fred H. Higginson published by Nicholas Vane (Publishers) Ltd. by permission of Kaye & Ward Ltd.

book. Professor Higginson's descriptions are admirably constructed with full collations as are those found in Timothy d'Arch Smith's *A Bibliography of the Works of Montague Summers* (1964), also published by Nicholas Vane Ltd. The student is also referred to the Soho Bibliographies, a series published by Rupert Hart-Davis Ltd. These volumes are all produced to a general pattern but each exhibits its own strengths and weaknesses. Some examples are: *A Bibliography of James Joyce* (1953), by J. J. Slocum and H. Cahoon, with full descriptions of first editions and quasi-facsimile transcripts of title-pages and binding lettering; *A Bibliography of Ronald Firbank* (1963), by M. J. Benkovitz which, although omitting the gatherings, gives full treatment to the description of bindings and very detailed publication notes showing the relationship between the author and his publishers concerning the production of his books; and *A Bibliography of E. M. Forster*, 2nd rev. imp. (1968), by B. J. Kirkpatrick, which again lacks a list of gatherings but uses quasi-facsimile transcription and gives full contents and binding notes and very useful information on the sizes of editions and impressions.

A43 CLAUDIUS THE GOD 1934

a. First edition:

ROBERT GRAVES | [*heavy rule*] | [*light rule*] | CLAUDIUS | THE GOD | *and his wife* | MESSALINA | *The troublesome reign of Tiberius Claudius* | *Caesar, Emperor of the Romans (born* | *B.C. 10, died A.D. 54), as described by* | *himself; also his murder at the hands* | *of the notorious Agrippina (mother of* | *the Emperor Nero) and his subsequent* | *deification, as described by others* | [*publisher's emblem*] | 1934 | [*light rule*] | [*heavy rule*] | ARTHUR BARKER: LONDON

Collation: [A]⁸ B–Z⁸ 2A–2N⁸, 288 leaves.

p. [1] CLAUDIUS THE GOD | *and his wife* | MESSALINA; p. [2] *By the same Author* | I, CLAUDIUS; p. [3] title-page; p. [4] printer's, publisher's and edition notices; pp. 5–6 AUTHOR'S NOTE; p. [7] CLAUDIUS THE GOD; p. [8] blank; pp. 9–76 text; [genealogical table of the Herods pasted to p. 77]; pp. 77–302 text; p. 303 map; pp. 304–353 text; pp. 554–559 THREE ACCOUNTS OF CLAUDIUS'S DEATH; pp. 560–575 THE PUMPKINIFICATION OF CLAUDIUS; p. [576] blank; [genealogical table of the Roman Imperial Family tipped to p. [576]].

21·4 × 13·8 cm. Bulk: 3·7/4·3 cm. White laid paper; top and fore-edges trimmed. White wove endpapers. Bound in black cloth; front and back blank; spine stamped in gold: ROBERT GRAVES | [*double rule*] | CLAUDIUS | THE GOD | *and his wife* | MESSALINA | BARKER

Price: 10s. 6d. Number of copies unknown. Published in November 1934 in white dust-jacket printed in light and dark blue, pink and red-brown.

Notes: Impressions: 2nd, November 1934; 3rd, December 1934; 4th, January 1935; 5th, December 1935; 6th, May 1936 ('cheap' edition). Translated into Danish, Finnish, German, Greek, Hebrew, Italian, Magyar, Norwegian, Polish, Portuguese, Russian, Slovenian and Swedish.

There are two combined issues of A42 and A43. The first is bound in red morocco, top edges gilt, sheets of A42*a* and A43*a*, issued in December 1935 at 25s. the set. The second is bound in three-quarter green leather, top edges gilt, sheets of A42*c* and the cheap issue of A43*a*, boxed, issued in November 1936 at 21s. the set; mottled pink and grey endpapers, inside which, front and back, is a heavy binder's sheet of two leaves; spines stamped in gold: [*heavy rule*] | [*light rule*] | I, CLAUDIUS | ROBERT GRAVES | [*light rule*] | [*heavy rule*] and [*heavy rule*] | [*light rule*] | CLAUDIUS | THE GOD | ROBERT GRAVES | [*light rule*] | [*heavy rule*].

In August 1939 the Barker rights were taken over by Methuen, who received 1,100 copies; of their impression in 1940 (3,000 copies), 1,500 copies were destroyed by enemy action.

INDEX

abbreviations in mss. and incunabula, 37

Ackers, C. (printer), 201*n*

advertisements, relation to issue, state, 207–8, 215; relation to binding, 224; signature formulary, 230; binding note, 238

Albion press, 216

Aldus, *see* Manutius

Alexander Grammaticus, *Doctrinale*, 56

Alexandrian library, catalogues, 1

Allde, E. (printer), 95

Allen, H., *Anthony Adverse*, plate emendations, 211

almanacks, used in bindings, 56

Altick, R., 221*n*

analytical bibliography, definition and purpose, 13–14, 16–17; relation to literary studies, 10–12; methods (*hand printing*), 108–41, (*xviii cent.*), 190–4, (*modern*), 203–25

Anderson, S., *Winesburg, Ohio*, 200*n*

annalistic arrangement, 146

annotations, bibl. desc. (*hand-printed*), 185–6, (*modern*), 239

Apocalypse, date of block-book, 50

appendices in bibliographies, 147

Ariosto, L., *Orlando furioso*, 96–7

arrangement of bibliographies, 145–8

Ars Moriendi, date of block-book, 50

author bibliographies, 200

authors, form of names in incunabula, 64; illegible copy, 92–3; spelling, 97

Bald, F. C., 104, 120

Barber, G., 111

Batdorf, F., 201

'batters', 212

Baumgartner, P., 45

Beale, J. (printer), 107

Beare, R., 210

Beaumont & Fletcher, text of 1647 Folio assigned to different compositors, 129

Bell, J., use of short s, 155; 'housebinding', 219

Benkovitz, M., *Firbank* bibliography, 240

Bennett, H., 92–3

Besterman, T., 2*n*, 3*n*

β-radiography, detecting watermarks, 49

Biblia pauperum, date of block-book, 50

bibliographical catalogues, 29

bibliographical description, aims and purposes, 17–18, 20–1; treatment, 18–20; (*hand-printing*), 142–87; (*xviii cent.*), 194; (*modern*), 197, 226–41.

bibliographical study (*incunabula*), 27–9; (*xvi–xviii cents.*), 87–90; (*modern*), 197–202

bibliographies, vs. catalogues, 2, 17, 185; of incunabula, 72–83; scope of, 143–5; arrangement of, 145–8

bibliography, an independent study, 19–20; and literary studies, 19–20, 87–8

Bibliography of American literature, 229–30, 236, 237

binding (*incunabula*), 43, 46–8; value of evidence, 55–6; identification, 56; (*modern*), 219–21; relation to issue, state, 221–2; evidence for priority, 222–5; bibl. desc., 207, 238–9

Blades, W., 7

Blanck, J., *American literature* bibliography, 229–30, 236, 237

blank leaves, importance in collating, 66

Bond, W., 99, 132–3

book-hands, 36–7

Borde, A., *Pryncyples of Astronomye*, nature of copy, 93

borders, in incunabula, 40, 54; on titlepages, description, 151–3, 227; on text pages, description, 184–5

Boston, J., his catalogue, 1–2

Bowers, F., 12, 18–20, 66–8, 100, 103, 109, 127, 130, 132, 201–2; *Principles of Bibliographical Description*, 18, 20*n*, 22*n*, 60, 70, 111, 117, 121, 143, 151 *et seq.*, 194, 198, 199*n*, 200–1, 205 *et seq.*, 215*n*, 226 *et seq.*

Bowyer family (printers), 201*n*

brackets, square, in bibl. desc., 154

Bradshaw, H., natural history method, 6–7

Gesamtkatalog der Wiegendrucke, 6, 69, 70, 76–8
Gesner, C., *Bibliotheca universalis*, 2–3, 13
Glasgow, E., *Wheel of fire*, imposition of, 218
Godscalci Preceptorium, 56
Goes, H., use of Caxton's types, 38
Goff, F., *Incunabula in American libraries*, 78–9
gold tooling, introduction of, 43
Goldschmidt, E., 39, 41, 55
gothic type, 36–7; transcription of, 156
Gouge, W., *Whole armor of God*, errors in text, 106
Greg, Sir W., 8n, 10, 11, 91, 95, 96–7, 98; *Bibliography of drama*, 13, 143, 144–5, 147, 148, 150 *et seq.*; *Collected papers*, 232–3; *Formulary of collation*, 66; *Shakespeare First Folio*, 98
Griffi, F., type-cutter, 37
Gutenburg, J. (printer), 39; *Gutenberg Bible*, see *Forty-two line Bible*

Haebler, K., 69, 70; *Study of incunabula*, 4n, 32n, 35n, 38n, 41n, 51n, 56n, 61n, 80n; *Typenrepertorium*, 52–3, 64
Hain, L., *Repertorium bibliographicum*, 6, 72–3
half-sheet imposition (*hand-printed*), 101–2, determined by headlines, 132; (*modern*), 217
half-titles, transcription of, 160
hand-press, use in xix cent., 216
hand-printed books, bibliographical study of, 87–90
handwriting, manuscript hands, 36–7; author's poor, 92–3
Harington, Sir J., MS. of his *Orlando Furioso*, 96–7
Harkness, B., 204n
Hazen, A., 165–6
headings, bibl. desc., 148–9
headlines, composition, 100; sets indicative of edition size, 104; evidence from, 129–32; transcription of, 160, 162
Higginson, F., *Graves bibliography*, 229, 239, specimen entry from, 241
Hind, A., *History of woodcut*, 55
Hinman, C., 120n, 121–2, 127, 130–1, 133; *Prentice Hand*, 98; *Printing and proofreading of First Folio*, 121

Hinman collating machine, 121–2, 190, 209–10, 215
Hirsch, R., 36, 37
historical bibliography, 14
Holtrop, J., 7
Hunte, T. (printer), 56
hyphens, evidence of order of editions from, 114

I and J (i and j), transcription of, 180
ideal copy, definition, 18; of incunabula, 28; bibl. desc., 142
illustrations, (*incunabula*), 41–3, origin and dating, 55; (*hand-printed*) on title-pages, bibl. desc., 158–9, as plates, bibl. desc., 178; (*modern*), as plates, bibl. desc., 235
imposition, (*hand-printing*), 99–102; (*modern*), evidence of, 215–8
impression, definition, 21–2; new impressions distinguished by press-numbers, 136; multiple impressions in xviii century, 188–90, 193; (*modern*), alterations between, 206; concealed impressions, 209; evidence of re-impression from re-imposition, 213–4
incipit, 36, 64
incunabula, natural history method of arranging, 6–7; bibliographical study, 27–9; ideal copies, 28; physical characteristics of, 30–44; dating from evidence of materials, 45–8; identification of, 63–70; bibliographies of, 72–83
index figures, even vs. odd, 67–8; collational formula, 167
initials, 40; value of evidence for dating books, 54–5; bibl. desc., 185
ink, drying qualities of, 104–5
inking by ink-balls, 103; type drawn out by, 119
insertions, collational formula, 67–8, 170–3; (*modern*), signed, 229
insets, bibl. desc., 177–8
Inter-Society Colour Council–National Bureau of Standards (ISCC-NBS), 237
Isaac, F., 52n
issue (*hand-printing*), definition, 22–3, 193; evidence for re-issue, 116–18; separate issues, 117; bibl. desc., 148; (*modern*), 206; evidence for re-issue, 214
italic types, the first, 37; italic capitals, evidence for distinguishing editions, 115